Building Character in Schools

Building Character in Schools

Practical Ways to Bring Moral Instruction to Life

Kevin Ryan

Karen E. Bohlin

Foreword by Sanford N. McDonnell

JOSSEY-BASS
A Wiley Imprint
www.josseybass.com

Published by Jossey-Bass
A Wiley Imprint
989 Market Street, San Francisco, CA 94103-1741   www.josseybass.com

Chapter Three excerpt from "New Life, Far from the Bright Lights" by D. Gonzalez, 1/25/98 copyright © 1998 by The New York Times Company. Reprinted by permission.

Chapter Three poem "Yes and No" from *I'm a Stranger Here Myself* by Ogden Nash. Copyright 1936 by Ogden Nash. Used by permission of Little, Brown, and Company and by permission of Andre Deutsch Ltd.

Chapter Four excerpt from CROW AND WEASEL by Barry Lopez, with illustrations by Tom Pohrt. Text copyright © 1990 by Barry Holstun Lopez. Illustration copyright © 1990 by Tom Pohrt. Reprinted by permission of North Point Press a division of Farrar, Straus & Giroux, Inc.

Appendix K poem "Good-Bye, Six—Hello, Seven" reprinted with the permission of Atheneum Books for Young Readers, an imprint of Simon & Schuster Children's Publishing Division from IF I WERE IN CHARGE OF THE WORLD AND OTHER WORRIES by Judith Viorst. Text copyright © 1981 Judith Viorst.

Appendix L excerpts from *Sadako and the Thousand Paper Cranes* by Eleanor Coerr, New York: Bantam, 1977, reprinted with permission.

Appendix M excerpts from THE LITTLE PRINCE by Antoine de Saint-Exupéry, copyright 1943 and renewed 1971 by Harcourt Brace & Company, reprinted by permission of the publisher.

Jossey-Bass books and products are available through most bookstores. To contact Jossey-Bass directly call our Customer Care Department within the U.S. at (800) 956-7739, outside the U.S. at (317) 572-3986 or fax (317) 572-4002.

Jossey-Bass also publishes its books in a variety of electronic formats. Some content that appears in print may not be available in electronic books.

Library of Congress Cataloging-in-Publication Data

Ryan, Kevin.
    Building character in schools : practical ways to bring moral
instruction to life / Kevin A. Ryan, Karen E. Bohlin ; foreword by
Sanford N. McDonnell. — 1st ed.
      p. cm.
    Includes bibliographical references.
    ISBN 0-7879-4344-4 (cloth : acid-free and chlorine-free paper)
    ISBN 0-7879-6244-9 (paperback)
    1. Moral education—United States. 2. Character—Study and
teaching—United States. I. Bohlin, Karen E. II. Title.
LC311 .R93 1999
370.11'4—ddc21   98–25497

FIRST EDITION
HB Printing 10 9 8 7 6 5 4
PB Printing 10 9 8 7 6 5 4 3

Contents

Appendixes Part Three: Curriculum

Foreword

In 1748, Baron Charles de Montesquieu published his magnum opus, *The Spirit of Laws,* a work that had a profound effect on our nation's founders. In it, Montesquieu developed the concept of separation of powers, which formed the basis of our Constitution over two hundred years ago. Montesquieu also explored the relationship that must exist between a people and their government, without which no form of government can survive. For example, a dictatorship depends on fear, and when fear disappears the dictatorship is overthrown. A monarchy depends on the loyalty of the people and dies when loyalty dies. The most desirable form of government is a free republic, obviously; but it is also the most fragile form of government, because it depends on having a virtuous people.

Virtuous people, people of character, live by high ethical standards. But what do we mean by "ethics"? One of the best definitions I have come across was given by Dr. Albert Schweitzer: "In a general sense, ethics is the name that we give to our concern for good behavior. We feel an obligation to consider not only our own personal well-being but also that of others and of human society as a whole." Therefore, in a free republic the leaders and a majority of the people are committed to doing what's best for the nation as a whole. When that commitment breaks down, when the people consider only their own personal well-being, they can no longer be depended on to behave in the best interests of their nation. The result is laws, regulations, red tape, and controls—things designed to force people to consider others. But these are the instruments of bondage, not of freedom.

Benjamin Franklin underlined this concept of Montesquieu's when he said, "Only a virtuous people are capable of freedom." Throughout most of our history, certain basic, ethical values were considered fundamental to the character of the nation and to the people who made up the nation. These values were passed on from generation to generation in the home, the school, and religious institutions—each one undergirding and reinforcing the others. We had a consensus not only on values but also on the importance of those values; and from that consensus, we knew who we were as a people and where we were going as a nation.

In 1831, Alexis de Tocqueville came to this country to find out what it was that made this upstart nation so progressive and prosperous. He traveled all over the country and talked to people from all walks of life. He then went back to France and in 1835 published his classic *Democracy in America*. Incidentally, de Tocqueville hated slavery and considered the true America to be the northern, free states. In that context he wrote, "America is great because she is good, but if America ever ceases to be good America will cease to be great."

Today in America we have far too many twelve-year-olds pushing drugs, fourteen-year-olds having babies, sixteen-year-olds killing each other, and kids of all ages admitting to lying, cheating, and stealing. We have crime and violence everywhere and unethical behavior in business, the professions, and government. In other words, we have a crisis of character all across America that is threatening to destroy the goodness that, as de Tocqueville put it, is the very foundation of our greatness. That is the bad news, but the good news is that we know what to do about it: get back to the core values of our American heritage in our homes, our schools, our businesses, our government, and indeed in each of our daily lives.

In other words, we need to dramatically uplift the character of the nation. How can this be accomplished? First of all, we need to understand what we mean by character—*good* character. Kevin Ryan has a very succinct definition: "knowing the good, loving the good, and doing the good." So when you build character, you must address the cognitive, the emotional, and the behavioral—the head, the heart, and the hand.

Traditionally, character was built primarily in the home, but today far too many of our homes have fallen down on that responsibility. In the past, the church and synagogue played a major role in building character in our young, but their influence on our children seems to have waned considerably. The business and professional worlds have in recent years begun to put more emphasis on ethical behavior, but they have a long way to go before they are the role models we need for our children. The media, especially television, are having perhaps the most powerful impact on the character of old and young alike; but it has been a more negative than positive influence. Unethical behavior in our government, at the state and national levels, is rampant. Our national leaders are often poor role models.

When our country was founded, building character was considered just as important as imparting intellectual knowledge by our educational system, from the first grade through college. However, for many reasons formal character education has been largely absent from our public schools over the last thirty to forty years. Nevertheless, our educational system is the most logical and potentially effective place to begin the rebuilding of our national character.

Today's students are tomorrow's leaders and citizens. If the schools educate them to be young people of high character, our country will eventually become a nation of high character. Also, one of the many benefits of character education in the schools is that academic performance goes up with good behavior. It is obvious that if teachers spend all their time maintaining discipline in the classroom, there can be no effective learning. It is not as obvious, but equally true, that if you create a moral and caring community in the classroom, not only can the teacher teach, but the students will feel better about themselves and work harder. The unmistakable conclusion: character education should be an integral part of the country's formal education system, from kindergarten through graduate school.

Indeed, character education has come back into vogue, but there is far too little understanding of what it is really all about and even less knowledge of how to implement it. The danger is that too many schools, in their ignorance, will implement what they consider to be a character education program but what in actuality is a woefully inadequate substitute. And when their programs do not live up to their expectations, they might reject the entire character education movement as ineffective. In this book, Ryan and Bohlin provide the information needed to counter that potential problem. *Building Character in Schools* is a tremendous resource for anyone wanting to understand, design, and implement an effective, comprehensive character-building program in their school.

It won't bring us back to the goodness of de Tocqueville if we graduate young people from our schools who are brilliant but dishonest, who have great intellectual knowledge but don't care about others, or who have highly creative minds but are irresponsible. It will bring us back to the goodness and greatness of de Tocqueville if we teach our young to "know the good, love the good, and do the good." That is character education, and that is what Ryan and Bohlin are all about.

August 1998   Sanford N. McDonnell
                                 Chairman Emeritus, McDonnell Douglas
                                 Chairman of the Board,
                                 The Character Education Partnership

Preface

In recent years, efforts in our public schools to foster good character in students have generated enormous interest. Although it is difficult to determine just what the impetus for this renewed interest in character has been, it appears to have come from outside the educational community. Politicians on both the left and the right, spurred on by a rising drumbeat of frightening statistics about youth homicides and suicides and by soaring numbers of teenage pregnancies, began calling teachers and administrators back to what is now being called character education. In earlier decades, the call would have been for "moral education" or, more recently, "values education." But even though concern for the moral domain and the teaching of moral values never disappeared from our schools, until very recently moral education was noticeably on the professional educator's back burner.

One of the most positive changes in American culture in recent years has been what Stephen Covey has called a paradigm shift away from a "personality ethic" and toward a "character ethic." This change has been marked by a departure among Americans from an individual moral compass driven by a desire for personal popularity or power and the emergence of a moral compass directed by a desire to become a good person, a person of character. This concern for character represents a search for personal qualities that are more stable and enduring than merely projecting a positive attitude or learning to be more open with one's feelings. The "how to win friends and influence people" mentality, with its focus on external behavior and social skills, has dominated much of our popular psychology and culture. It is still very much with us today, but Covey and others suggest that it is slowly being replaced. The focus has gradually returned to something deeper and more fundamentally human: the centrality of character in a worthy life. Nevertheless, as other parts of American society began talking about the importance of good character, our schools were still functioning in the "personality mode," heavily influenced by the idea that the schools should be a place for personality adjustment and emotional therapy. It was only a matter of time, though, before the need for genuine character development caught up with the schools. And thankfully, it has.

By 1998, there had been six White House–congressional conferences on character education in this decade. The term *character education,* coupled with appeals for schools to reengage this mission, has become prominent in the president's annual State of the Union address to the nation. Educators, who have become accustomed to harsh criticism about students' low test scores, are now also being blamed for the moral failings of their students and urged to "do something."

Over recent decades, as elementary and secondary schooling have taken up more and more of the time, attention, and energy of young people and as we have come to perceive a person's education as the key factor in his or her economic success, pressure has been building on educators. They have become accustomed to harsh criticism and agile at moving in on perceived problems and shortcomings. They are typically supported in their responses to problems—both real and trumped-up ones—by an army of commercial curriculum developers and consultants and by myriad special interest advocacy groups and professional associations. Such has also been the case with this recent call for character education.

Since few teachers hear about character education in their teacher education programs or, for that matter, their postgraduate training, these efforts would appear to be especially necessary. In fact, many teachers and administrators fear being sued for dealing with even the most benign moral issues, such as citizens' patriotic duty to their country. They report being warned in education courses and elsewhere "to stay away from all that values and moral stuff." They have been cautioned to leave these topics to parents or religious leaders or someone else. Now, however, things have turned around sharply, and both conservatives and liberals (with varying degrees of sympathy) are entreating teachers to become "character educators." Many teachers welcome this, because it speaks to their deepest motivations for becoming a teacher in the first place. Some are ambivalent and surprised because they did not experience character or moral education in their own schooling during the 1970s, 1980s, or 1990s. And some are put off by what they see as yet another job being foisted on them that should be performed by someone else. Overwhelmingly, though, educators acknowledge that they need help in responding to this call to build good character in our students and schools.

As elementary and secondary school educators have asked for help in this matter, they have been met by the usual array of advice, admonitions, and curricular materials. Several dozen books, ranging from highly practical to overly theoretical, have been published about character education. At least four large national organizations have come into being to provide guidance to the field. A dozen or more centers related to character education have been established on college and university campuses. Materials of widely varying quality for classroom and schoolwide use have been made available. Education conferences have devoted keynote addresses and "special strands" to character education. Education magazines have begun hawking T-shirts, ballpoint pens, and coffee cups with kitschy character education slogans. What was once a modest movement has become a thriving industry. But although educators of good will are taking these messages seriously and attempting to transform their educational programs accordingly, there is one large stumbling block: "character education" has dozens of meanings, some quite contrary to others.

The impetus for this book is to provide a blueprint for educators who seriously wish to help children forge good character. Two years ago, with our colleague Judy Thayer, we wrote and circulated a one-page document entitled "The Character Education Manifesto" (see Appendix A). Our purpose was to offer seven guidelines to educators who were considering taking a more conscious and active role in this area. A number of leading scholars and education leaders, including Diane Ravitch, Robert Coles, William Bennett, and Diane Berreth, liked what we had written and became signatories. So, too, did eight sitting governors. Since that time we have gone on to other character-related activities, but we kept getting inquiries about the manifesto, from school board members and administrators and teachers trying to infuse their classes with character education. Often it was clear that the inquirers wanted more specifics, not just our guidelines. They agreed with the principles, but they wanted more. They wanted a fuller understanding of what "character" actually is. And they wanted to know what specific steps they needed to take to translate a personal commitment to character education into a schoolwide vision and effort. This book is our response.

Chapter One, "Character Education: What Is It and Why Is It Important?" is the foundation. One important reason we wrote this book is because all sorts of ideas and materials are being embraced under the name of character education that have little or nothing to do with character. Our vision is person-centered. We are interested in helping educators engage the heads, hearts, and hands of their students so that students may come to *know* the good, *love* the good, and *do* the good. Coming to grips with who our students are and who we want them to become—persons of good character and integrity—is the foundation to everything else. Whatever a school does should rest on the bedrock of a strong understanding of this core goal.

Chapter Two, "Views, Values, or Virtues?" discusses how some educators are building flimsy, substandard character education programs. The chapter's main theme, however, is that the keystone of good character is virtue. Without a keystone firmly in place, even the grandest building can quickly become a pile of rocks and rubble. Therefore the focus of energy and support in any character education initiative or program must be virtue.

Chapter Three, "Building a Community of Virtue," is about framing the building, putting up the structural elements that support the various components of character education. Although some authors and consultants suggest that a school's character education efforts can and ought to rest on a single element (for instance, a schoolwide word-for-the-week program), we believe character education is a good deal more demanding. The frame is all about *who we are* and *what we stand for.* All the elements of school life, from the sports field to the cafeteria, from the faculty room to the school bus, contribute to or detract from this framework for character education.

Chapter Four, "Cultivating Character Through the Curriculum," takes us to the raw materials of character building. A good builder has an intimate knowledge of the materials he or she uses—the bricks, the wood beams, the foundation stones, the paints and plasters—and knows how to use them well. The content students learn, the books they read, the skills they master—all have a great deal to do with their developing good character. We argue in this chapter that a school's curriculum is more than knowledge to be learned; it is also the means by which students gain good character.

Chapter Five, "Engaging Parents in Character Education," takes up the crucial connection between parents and teachers in the work of character education. Our theme here is that parents are (or should be) teachers' principal partners in this building enterprise. In this chapter we discuss not only the need to keep parents informed about teachers' character education efforts but also the need to involve them in those efforts, to make them understand their responsibility in helping their children develop strong character.

Chapter Six, "The Teacher's Work: Nurturing Character," is concerned with the mortar that keeps the bricks in place. The commitment of the total school staff to the goal of student character formation is the glue that keeps all the elements of a character education effort focused and working together. In this chapter we address how to engage all of the professionals in our schools in this mission and make it a central part of their work together.

Chapter Seven, "Helping Students Take Command," brings us to the core of the book, the transformation of students. We see students both as works under construction and as apprentice builders in their own right, both as "the craft" and as "craftsmen." Students are neither totally in charge of their character formation nor merely passive recipients of character training. Accordingly, this chapter emphasizes teachers' role as mentors in their students' character education.

Every good set of blueprints includes some specialized sheets detailing the heating plant, the electrical system, and any particularly tricky aspects of the design. Likewise, we have included a number of appendixes for those who want to apply our design to their own situation. Among them are "The Character Education Manifesto," mentioned previously, "Pitfalls to Avoid in Character Education," our list of "One Hundred Ways to Bring Character Education to Life," and many others.

Everyone who puts pen to paper or fingertips to keyboard has debts. When we write, we stand on the shoulders of others, hoping to see just a littler bit farther, a little bit more clearly. Certainly that is our hope. Whether we have achieved it we leave to you, the reader, to decide. Nevertheless, we need to acknowledge a number of people whose shoulders bear the imprint of our boots. Among them are our colleague Steven Tigner, whose eye for detail, thoughtful feedback, and commitment to character education have been a source of inspiration to us. Additionally, we are grateful to our colleagues William Russell, Judy Thayer, Edwin Delattre, Emma Adler, Carol Ingall, Cathy Stutz, Sue Tauer, Esther Schaeffer,

Ellen Cavanagh, Charles Glenn, Stephan Ellenwood, John Yeager, Charles Griswold, Ed Wynne, F. Washington Jarvis, James Stenson, Jacques Benninga, Marie Oates, Tom Lickona, Joseph Delaney, Carol Jenkins, Peter Greer, Peg Murphy, Phil Tate, Rosemary Jordano, Brian Jorgensen, David Roochnik, Michael Foley, Phil Vincent, Ana Paula Tostado, Michael Aeschliman, Lee Gaudreau, and Danny Pacious. None of these kind souls and good minds should be held responsible for the manner in which we have wrenched and rendered their ideas. We would like to thank all of those who have pioneered in building schools of character, especially the faculty and staff of the Montrose School, the Montclair Kimberly Academy, the Benjamin Franklin Classical Charter School, and the Hyde School. We would especially like to thank Deborah Farmer, whose unwavering commitment to this project has been invaluable. From fact-finding to manuscript formatting, from moral support to substantive contributions and lesson plans, she has left her imprint on this book and on our hearts. We are also indebted to our students, past and present, who have taught us what it means to take our own character building seriously. We thank the dedicated educators we've worked with in teachers' academies and all those teachers and parents who every day go unacknowledged in their quiet but loyal effort to help children develop good character. There are also those who believed in the importance of this book. First and foremost we would like to thank Lesley Iura, senior editor at Jossey-Bass. We are also enormously grateful to a number of friends and associates. Among those at the Center for the Advancement of Ethics and Character are Danielle Tymann, Maren Gibb, Melissa French, Emily Nielsen Jones, Rachel O'Boyle, Ruth Bell, and Kelly Bortlik. We would like to thank our friends at Bayridge. Last but not least, we wish to thank all of our family and friends who supported us, especially Marilyn Ryan and Theodore J. Bohlin.

Boston   Kevin Ryan
August 1998   Karen E. Bohlin

The Authors

KEVIN RYAN is the director of the Center for the Advancement of Ethics and Character at Boston University. A former high school English teacher, Ryan has taught on the faculties of Stanford University, the University of Chicago, Harvard University, the Ohio State University, and the University of Lisbon. He has written and edited eighteen books, among them *Moral Education: It Comes with the Territory; Reclaiming Our Schools: A Handbook for Teaching Character, Academics, and Discipline* (with Ed Wynne); and *Those Who Can, Teach* (with James Cooper). He received the University of Pennsylvania National Educator of the Year Award and the Paideia Award for excellence in educational leadership. Ryan is the current president of the Character Education Partnership.

KAREN E. BOHLIN is the assistant director of the Center for the Advancement of Ethics and Character at Boston University and is completing her dissertation on moral motivation. She has taught middle and high school English and directed several student drama productions. For more than ten years, she has led student educational and service programs, including trips to England, Italy, and Lithuania. Her experience includes curriculum development in literature, language arts, and character education. She has served as a trustee of the Benjamin Franklin Classical Charter School in Franklin, Massachusetts, and is currently on the board of the Montrose School in Natick, Massachusetts. She has also worked as a consultant to corporations in education. Bohlin is a member of the Association of Teacher Educators (ATE) National Commission on Character Education and assists with special programs at Bayridge, a center for university and professional women in Boston.

Building Character in Schools

Chapter One

Character Education: What Is It and Why Is It Important?

The same week in 1997 that the world mourned the deaths of Princess Diana and Mother Teresa, a lesser-known individual quietly died in his sleep. Viktor Frankl, the author of *Man's Search for Meaning* and thirty-one other books, was ninety-three when he died. *Man's Search for Meaning*, which was translated into twenty-six languages and sold over two million copies, was one of the most influential books of the last half of the twentieth century. It is a personal account of one of humanity's darkest moments, when the Nazi death camps of World War II metastasized across Europe.

Frankl was a young, rising Austrian academic when the Nazis gained power. His novel insights had brought him to the attention of Sigmund Freud and other leading psychiatrists of the day. When the war broke out, he was just completing an important manuscript. Being Jewish, and concerned about the Nazis' takeover of Austria, he obtained a visa to America, where he planned to take his young bride until things settled down in Europe. However, concerned about his parents' safety, he hesitated too long, and when the Germans gained control of Austria, Frankl, his young wife, and his parents were swept up and sent to the dreaded Auschwitz. Early on, he was separated from his wife and parents. It was not until after the war that he discovered that they, too, had been murdered, along with millions of his fellow Jews.

His book is an unforgettable account of man's inhumanity to man, but it also portrays the human spirit's dignity and capacity to endure. We travel with Frankl in the packed railway cars filled with desperate, confused people. We feel their panic when they discover they are pulling into Auschwitz. We drudge along with him as he approaches the SS officer who, with a flick of his index finger, assigns each man, woman, and child his or her bitter fate, either the gas chamber or—for most merely a longer death—the work camp. After a long glance at Frankl, the officer waved him to the work camp line.

The Nazis took his manuscript, which he had been hiding on his person. They unceremoniously stripped him and his fellow prisoners and shaved them from head to toe, all in a systematic effort to dehumanize them. Without their family, friends, or possessions, the prisoners were left degraded and lonely. Viktor Frankl, promising scholar, beloved son and husband, became Number 119,104, a number he wore on his arm to his death. They did not strip him of his character, however.

His book describes his struggle to survive—first physically and then spiritually. Early he came to understand that his captors could maim, torture, or destroy him at their whim. But they could not control his mind. Even in the midst of such great suffering, his mind and spirit could take him away, out of Auschwitz. Frankl tells how at the darkest moments he fought off despair by focusing his mind on his beloved wife. They had already taken her life, but his image of her nevertheless sustained him. Eventually, Frankl returned to civilized life and used the strength he had gained from his experiences to counsel patients, showing them how to find meaning in their lives through loving another person, through their work, through their suffering, and by serving God.

Frankl's response to the extraordinary cruelty he endured reveals the remarkable strength of the human spirit. His example and work are truly a moral inheritance—a powerful lesson in character. Frankl's own words poignantly illustrate what it means to respond well to the challenges of life: "We must never forget that we may also find meaning in life even when confronted with a hopeless situation, when facing a fate that cannot be changed. For what then matters is to bear witness to the uniquely human potential at its best, which is to transform a personal tragedy into a triumph, to turn one's predicament into a human achievement. When we are no longer able to change a situation—just think of an incurable disease such as inoperable cancer—we are challenged to change ourselves."[1]

Another true story that illustrates the power of character is that of Osceola McCarty, a recently retired laundress. McCarty became rather famous in 1995, at the age of eighty-seven, when someone at the University of Southern Mississippi at Hattiesburg told her secret. This aged and poor black woman had given the university her life's savings, some $150,000, to support scholarships for local African American students. She had saved the nickels and dimes from a lifetime of washing and drying clothes for the local gentry, and she wanted to help the young people of her community. She told the university officials, "I'm giving my savings to the young generation. . . . I want them to have an education."[2]

McCarty did not have much of an education—not much of a formal education, that is. When an aunt became ill, she left the sixth grade to care for her. She also helped her mother and grandmother with their backyard laundry business. When her aunt was back on her feet, Osceola was convinced that too much time had gone by for her to return to school. She would be much bigger than the rest of her class. So she became a full-time helper in the business, getting up with the sun and washing, drying, starching, and ironing until the sun went down. Her world was her three tubs, her scrub board, and her Bible.

Never having married, without children of her own, and crippled with arthritis, Osceola decided to let the young have what she couldn't have. "I had to work hard all my life," she said. "They can have the chance that I didn't have." Osceola McCarty Scholarships are now given to high school graduates who would otherwise be unable to attend college. McCarty's gift has inspired many others to perform acts of generosity, but it has confused some. She is regularly asked, "Why didn't you spend the money on yourself?" She answers simply, "I am spending on myself."

These two people—one a distinguished scholar and writer and the other a poor scrubwoman with a fifth-grade education—responded nobly to the different challenges and opportunities presented to them. They chose to do what they believed was the right thing to do. One endured a living hell and chose to hold on to and deepen his sense of self as a consequence. He transformed his own experiences into something helpful to others. The other committed herself steadily and patiently over years—indeed, decades—as she scrubbed and wrung out other people's clothes. Frankl's story shows how devastating circumstances can bring out what a person is really made of. Frankl chose to meet adversity heroically rather than cave in to despair or cowardice. McCarty's story illustrates, by contrast, a person of character consciously choosing to give of herself to others. She was free to do whatever she wanted to with her hard-earned money, and she chose to support others. But regardless of the challenges they faced, these individuals each lived the kind of life and became the kind of person that made their admirable response possible. Because of their strength of character, both were able to meet with hardship and remain focused on what was most worthwhile for themselves and others.

Viktor Frankl's and Osceola McCarty's stories are extraordinary but not unique. The world is filled with individuals who are likewise ready to respond with character, though their challenge hasn't yet come. We all know dozens of people whose character is disclosed in quieter, more hidden ways. There is the father struggling with an alcoholic wife, his own dreary job, and a very uncertain future who never complains and always has a good word or deed for others. There is the promising high school athlete who in a freak accident severs her spinal cord but never succumbs to self-pity and instead spends her free time working with handicapped children from her wheelchair. And then there are the myriad ordinary people who have never done anything particularly dramatic but have gotten out of bed every day and done the very best they could at school, at work, in their families, and in their communities. They are ready for what life brings them. They have good character.

Defining Character

As Antoine de Saint Exupéry puts it in *The Little Prince,* "It is only with the heart that one sees rightly; what is essential is invisible to the eye." Character is one of those essentials. *Character* is one of those familiar words that often turns out to be difficult to pin down. Like all abstractions, you can't see character; you can't touch it; you can't taste it. Tom Wolfe titled his 1979 book about the daring and skill of the young men who pioneered our space program *The Right Stuff.* When we are around individuals who have the right stuff—that is, who have good character—we know it.

The English word *character* comes from the Greek word *charassein,* which means "to engrave," such as on a wax tablet, a gemstone, or a metal surface. From that root evolved the meaning of *character* as a distinctive mark or sign, and from there grew our conception of character as "an individual's pattern of behavior . . . his moral constitution." After the toddler stage, all of us have a character, a predictable way of behaving that those around us can discern. Each of us is marked by our own individual mix of negativity, patience, tardiness, thoughtlessness, kindness, and the like; however, a developed character—that is, good character—is much more than established patterns of behavior or habits of acting.

Good character is about *knowing* the good, *loving* the good, and *doing* the good. These three ideals are intimately connected. We are born both self-centered and ignorant, with our primitive impulses reigning over reason. The point of a nurturing upbringing and education is to bring our inclinations, feelings, and passions into harmony with reason.

Knowing the good includes coming to understand good and evil. It means developing the ability to sum up a situation, deliberate, choose the right thing to do, and then do it. Aristotle called this *practical wisdom*.[3] Having practical wisdom means knowing what a situation calls for. For example, it means knowing not to get into a car when the person behind the wheel has been drinking. It is about students' ability to plan their weekend in such a way that they can get their homework done, spend time with their family and friends, complete their paper route, and get the lawn mowed or the basement cleaned. But practical wisdom is not just about time management; it is about prioritizing and choosing well in all spheres of life. It is about the ability to make wise commitments and keep them.

Loving the good means developing a full range of moral feelings and emotions, including a love for the good and a contempt for evil, as well as a capacity to empathize with others. It is about wanting to do what's right. Loving the good enables us to respect and love people even when we know their actions are wrong. In other words, it allows us to "love the sinner but hate the sin."

Doing the good means that after thoughtful consideration of all the circumstances and relevant facts, we have the *will* to act. The world is filled with people who know what the right thing to do is but lack the will to carry it out. They know the good but can't bring themselves to do the good.

What is "the good"? Cultures differ somewhat in how they define it, but there is a huge overlap of common understandings. Some form of the Golden Rule, for example, exists in almost every culture. Clearly, respect for the dignity of others is a fundamental good. Additionally, in the world's literature, religions, philosophy, and art we find a huge deposit of shared moral values. The good, then, is a cross-cultural composite of moral imperatives and ideals that hold us together both as individuals and as societies.

Those ideals that tend to cut across history and cultures and show up most frequently are the Greek cardinal virtues: wisdom, justice, self-mastery, and courage. They are called *cardinal,* from the Latin *cardo,* or "hinge, that on which something turns or depends," because most of the other virtues are related to one or more of them (see Appendix B). Wisdom is the virtue that enables us to exercise sound judgment, engage in careful consideration, and maintain intellectual honesty. It also enables us to plan and take the right course of action in our pursuit of the good. Justice is an outward, or social virtue, concerned with our personal, professional, and legal obligations and commitments to others. A sense of justice enables us to be fair and to give each person what he or she rightly deserves. Self-mastery, by contrast, is an inner, or individual virtue. It gives people intelligent control over their impulses and fosters moral autonomy. A ten-year-old who throws frequent temper tantrums or a teenager who spends six hours a day in front of the television and cannot complete his homework are examples of individuals who lack self-mastery. Lastly, courage is not simply bravery but also the steadfastness to commit ourselves to what is good and right and actively pursue it, even when it is not convenient or popular.

Knowing the good, loving the good, and doing the good involve the head, the heart, and the hand, in an integrated way. We are all too familiar with the cerebral moral theorist, who can cite Aristotle, Kant, Confucius, and the Bible chapter and verse but is too busy to console his crying four-year-old by reading her a bedtime story or to run an errand for a neighbor recovering from back surgery. We may also have met the bleeding-heart moralist, who sees injustice and victimization at every turn but is too paralyzed by the dark side of humanity to take the first step to do anything about it. Then there are those who only mechanically fulfill moral "obligations." We may find students, for example, who meet service requirements—ten hours of volunteer work at a hospital or twenty hours organizing an annual clothing drive—yet fail to reflect on, care about, or truly commit themselves to an ethic of service. Some students will even admit to such mechanical participation in service clubs and programs, saying, "It's just a requirement" or "I need it for my resume."

Character demands more from us than merely an intellectual commitment, a heartfelt desire, or a mechanical fulfillment of responsibilities. As our friend James Stenson has put it, a person of character is a person with integrity, someone who says what she means, means what she says, and keeps her word. This link between our character and daily actions is reflected in Lord Macaulay's remark that "the measure of a man's real character is what he would do if he knew he would never be found out." Another measure of character, we would add, is what a person does under pressure—for example, the pressure to cheat to keep a certain grade point average. When we spend time with people, their integrity and character are revealed to us, and often these are quite contrary to what they would like us to think. There is a story about a man who traveled high into the Tibetan mountains to gain wisdom from a famous guru. After sitting at the guru's feet for ten minutes and listening to him describe how wise he was, the man finally broke in and, turning away, said, "I must leave you, for what you are speaks so loudly that I cannot hear your words!" As the fox in *The Little Prince* said, what is essential is often invisible to the eye, but eventually it becomes evident to the heart.

We may be too close to ourselves to see our own character, but those who are around us for any length of time usually have no trouble at all perceiving it. Samuel Johnson captured this uncomfortable truth in one of his "Rambler" essays: "More knowledge may be gained of a man's real character by a short conversation with one of his servants than from a formal and studied narrative." Our character is our way of acting or manner of being—who we are. We all have patterns in our behavior, and often we are quite unaware of them. Some of us are like the student in our classroom who is totally unaware that he compulsively smooths his hair and says "like" as every other word.

Character, then, is very simply the sum of our intellectual and moral habits. That is, character is the composite of our good habits, or virtues, and our bad habits, or vices, the habits that make us the kind of person we are. These good and bad habits mark us and continually affect the way in which we respond to life's events and challenges. If we have the virtue of honesty, for example, when we find someone's wallet on the pavement, we are characteristically disposed to track down its owner and return it. If we possess the bad habit, or vice, of dishonesty, again our path is clear: we pick it up, look to the right and left, and head for Tower Records or the Gap.

Our habits and dispositions, this mix of our virtues and vices, inform the way we respond to the myriad, unfolding events of life. In turn, they determine whether others come to trust us or mistrust us. When people come to know us, they come to know our character. Thus when Socrates urged us, "Know thyself," among other things he was directing us to come to know our habitual ways of responding to the world around us. But he was not suggesting that self-awareness be an end in itself. He, and most of the world's great thinkers who followed him, wanted more from us than mere knowledge of the habits that make up our character. They have called on us to be aggressively reflective and to acquire the right habits, to sharpen our intelligence and engrave strong, moral characters on ourselves.

Human beings are different from other life forms. Plants respond to the sun. Sunflowers even lean their heads to follow the sun during the course of the day. Salmon perform an astounding feat: after spending several years wandering around the ocean, they swim hundreds of miles upstream to the exact place of their conception. Certain species of birds fly a third of the way around the globe to a particular spot and, months later, turn around and come back to the spot from which they left. But they are all reacting instinctively.

Human beings, in contrast, have relatively few instincts. Unlike the rest of the fauna and flora with which we share the earth, we have fewer hard-wired responses to events. Nor are we tabulae rasae, or blank slates, as was once the view of some psychologists and philosophers. More and more we are becoming aware that certain personality traits, such as shyness, are part of our genetic inheritance. Most of what we need to function well in the world, however, is acquired through learning. And fortunately, we possess a huge capacity for learning.

Although there is much for human beings to learn, nothing is more important for our personal happiness and the health of society than the dispositions and habits that constitute good character. Throughout history, it has been recognized that personal character counts. The scholar consumed by self-interest and the financial wizard on his third wife are by now cultural clichés. In contrast to such figures stand people of generosity and perseverance, such as Osceola McCarty or the widowed father who quietly, carefully, and against great odds raises three marvelous children. Their stories warm our hearts. Memories of the self-sacrifice of a Mother Teresa and the fortitude of a Viktor Frankl loom large in our collective memory. Serious people agree with Heraclitus' short, arresting sentence, "Character is destiny." If we are each to be fully human, then, we need to form a strong moral character. Our success or failure in this task will determine our destiny—and that of our nation.

Achieving Character

The purpose of this book is to attempt to answer the question, "How is good character formed or achieved?" Primarily within the context of schools, the task of all of us—rich or poor, bold or shy, young or old—is to engrave on our essence the strong marks that constitute good character. We are the architects and artisans of our own character. We don't enter the world with habits, good or bad. Sadly, bad habits, such as selfishness, laziness, dishonesty, and irresponsibility, are easy to pick up. We slip into our vices effortlessly, like a comfortable pair of shoes. Acquiring good habits takes work! But it is the most essential work for each of us. The nineteenth-century British writer William Makepeace Thackeray captured much about the nature of this process in four lines:

> Sow a thought and you reap an act;
> Sow an act and you reap a habit;
> Sow a habit and you reap a character;
> Sow a character and you reap a destiny.

The central theme of this book is captured not so much by this agricultural metaphor, however, as by our engraving metaphor: we all actively engrave our own character on ourselves. Like a craftsman etching a metal plate or a sculptor shaping a stone into a fine statue, so, too, each of us is called to make our life into a work of art. Each of us, then, must consciously decide to act to acquire particular habits and gradually, through time and effort, to make deeper and deeper marks on our hearts and minds.

The choice to become an artist is a personal decision, one that sets us on a journey to become skilled and competent at our craft. Our will, our determination, to follow through with that journey is critical. Although natural talent plays a part in the flowering of a great painter or pianist, dedication and hard work are key ingredients as well. Abilities need to be developed and honed; flaws must be identified and systematically reduced. Amid the wild cheers and flood of bouquets at a great soprano's crowning moment, only she is aware of the thousands of hours spent practicing scales and endlessly rehearsing. There is an old saw about a tourist in New York City who asks a native, "How do you get to Carnegie Hall?" The hurried New Yorker yells back over his shoulder, "Practice! Practice! Practice!"

Effort and practice alone don't make a fine artist, though. The artist needs a vision, a standard of perfection toward which he or she aims all this effort. An artist needs a vision of the good. The parallel here, of course, is between becoming an artist and becoming a person of sound, moral character. In each journey of becoming there are events: a conscious choice, some kind of deliberation and action, the elimination of those things that keep us from achieving, (usually) a long period of practice, and finally, competency and achievement.

Taking Responsibility for Character Development

Becoming a great artist or a person of character is the individual's responsibility. No one can do it for someone else. But although there are here and there a few self-taught artists, we know of few people of character who are totally self-taught. Developing one's character is a social act. We exist and are raised within a social milieu—within a web of human connections. Indeed, human beings require the support and love of others just to stay alive, at the very least in our early years. Having few instincts, we rely on others for food and shelter and to learn the survival skills we need to maintain our lives. Character, too, needs to be nurtured, and the people with whom we enter into this human web play a key part in our learning to become flourishing people of character.

Although the importance of others in the acquisition of character may seem utterly obvious, there are advocates of various approaches to character education who downplay the importance of other people. Some educators, drawing on the powerful (but largely discredited) views of the French philosopher Jean Jacques Rousseau, would go so far as to eliminate contact with adults, since adults infect children with their corrupt morality. Others see efforts by adults to mold children's character as no more than pernicious indoctrination. One leading text in the field refers disparagingly to "the cold hand of orthodoxy," referring to the imposition of one generation's moral values on the next. Although we acknowledge the existence of negative influences and the capacity of individuals (and entire societies, for that matter) to thwart their children's development of character, we disagree with this anti-adult view. Children need the help of adults for more than food and shelter. They need adult tutelage not simply in algebra and agriculture. And they especially need it to understand and acquire the strong moral habits that contribute to good character.

Young children come into the world as bundles of joy for their parents and bundles of potentiality for themselves. Infants are their own suns, with the rest of us whirling around them. Their first tasks are to understand what it is that is whirling around them and to learn how to get their little solar system to serve their own ends: to obtain food when they are hungry, get changed when they are wet, be held when they want to be held, and be comforted when they are hurting. Even though they are delightfully innocent and curious about the world around them, infants and toddlers are thoroughly self-absorbed. Growing up means learning that those other beings out there have desires and needs as well. Children need to discover the balance between concern for self and concern for others. Becoming a person of character, though, means moving well beyond simply finding that balance. It means gaining control of one's own clamoring desires, developing a deep regard for others, and being ready to put aside one's own interests and sometimes even one's needs in order to serve others. Clearly, children need help to see this and to act on it.

Earlier we offered the image of character development as the engraving upon oneself of one's own moral essence, often with the help of others. The individual becomes the sculptor of his or her own best possible self. Becoming an artist or a person of character is a developmental process. It takes knowledge. It takes effort and practice. It takes support, example (both good and bad), encouragement, and sometimes inspiration. In short, it takes what we are calling *character education*.

Most complex learning takes time and much guidance from a teacher. The teacher can be any one of a number of people in a person's life. Using our metaphor of the artist, the teacher often needs to encourage the young artist to pick up the engraving tool. At times she needs to actually hold the child's hand and guide his movements. She needs to be there to explain and encourage, to nudge and correct and rejoice with the child when he makes progress. Gradually, the young artist becomes able to perform on his own, often with the teacher watching from the back of the studio. Later the artist has true independence. At that point, the seasoned artist is ready to take his turn as teacher. The route of the artist to maturity is the same as an individual's path to moral maturity. It is not merely an individual achievement; it is a social achievement.

Who, then, is responsible for the character education of the young? Without a doubt, a child's family has the primary responsibility. So, too, do neighbors and friends. "But character and competence," Mary Ann Glendon explains, "have conditions residing in nurture and education. The American version of the democratic experiment leaves it primarily up to families, local governments, schools, and religious and workplace associations, and a host of other voluntary groups to teach and transmit republican virtues and skills from one generation to the next."[4] So despite the fact that some modern educational theorists and practicing teachers and administrators may disagree, we believe that character education is a central mission of our schools.

The Irrational Fear of Indoctrination

Many critics and educators are convinced that character education must be avoided because, at its base, it is nothing more than brainwashing. Critics of our conception of character education claim that it amounts to imposing particular values or personality traits on young people or crude manipulation of children by the dominant powers in their lives. They see it as top-down education or, worse, "indoctrination"—and there are few words in the English language that can send a chill through an American administrator or teacher like the term *indoctrination*.

In his record of a conversation with John Thelwall on July 27, 1830, Samuel Taylor Coleridge captures the absurdity of not indoctrinating a child to act virtuously:

> Thelwall thought it very unfair to influence a child's mind by inculcating any opinions before it should have come to years of discretion, and be able to choose for itself. I showed him my garden, and told him it was my botanical garden.
>
> "How so?" said he, "it is covered with weeds." "Oh," I replied, "that is only because it has not yet come to its age of discretion and choice. The weeds, you see, have taken the liberty to grow, and I thought it unfair of me to prejudice the soil towards roses and strawberries."[5]

For several decades now educators have been fearful about indoctrinating students rather than educating them. They believe that the leading teaching methodologies, such as the inquiry approach, discovery method, and cooperative learning, add value to our schools because they "don't indoctrinate." Also, much of the sharp criticism of the public schools as "tools of the state" and "manipulators of the young" that was so prevalent in the late 1960s and 1970s is still alive today in our education textbooks and teachers' programs. Certainly, there is a real danger that schools can be used to miseducate children and even manipulate their moral values, but this criticism needs a fuller examination than it has received.

First of all, educators cannot teach children everything, from pre-Socratic philosophy to the latest conspiracy theories pulled from the Internet. Our efforts must be guided by an examination of what is most important for students to learn during their school years. This is the ultimate curricular question and one that places very strong obligations on school boards and educators. Because of the limited time available to them, teachers must select from a universe of knowledge only a small portion and then grapple with finding the most effective ways to help students understand and appreciate it. And then they must indoctrinate, or "instruct in doctrines, theories, beliefs, or principles," as *Webster's* puts it.

It is each school board's duty to identify the knowledge base and moral values its students will learn. To decline this responsibility is to put not only students at risk but ultimately our entire society. It is our firm belief, however, that fear of indoctrinating students with moral values and principles is a major reason why so many educators and schools are reluctant to embrace character education. There is an implicit hope that somebody else—the home, the church, the Boy Scouts or Girl Scouts, someone!—will do this teaching. However, as we shall see, for educators the responsibility to teach our core virtues and moral values simply comes with the territory.

All cultures, including our own, recognize the need to help children become members of society. To do so means that we must instruct them in doctrines, theories, beliefs, and principles—*Webster's* very definition of *indoctrination.* Down through the ages, we have been aware not only that children will die without adult protection and care but also that children need education and training before they can take their place in society. A mother sternly telling her three-year-old not to play so roughly with his baby sister is clearly engaging in top-down education. A seventh-grade teacher who puts a stop to a wolf pack's taunting of a new student is instructing her students about the moral values of civility and charity. A church that engages its high school youth group as cooks and servers in a homeless shelter is indoctrinating the young in an ethic of service. Indeed, every act of education by one person of another can be conceived of as top-down education. This simple fact of life needs to be understood and appreciated.

Clearly, though, indoctrination is currently misconceived of as the force-feeding of the ruling classes' most self-serving ideas and values, such as racial or gender superiority, to impressionable minds.

The word also implies to some the use of irrational means to pass on certain ideas to impressionable minds. This is not what we mean here. And it should be pointed out that the most seemingly "progressive" classrooms, where students are led to do projects on "less repressive forms of government than democratic capitalism" or on "more humanistic alternatives to surviving than by eating our fellow creatures (birds, beasts, and fish)" can, in fact, be deeply indoctrinating. Teachers and entire schools can be guilty of wrongly teaching certain moral values. We know of teachers who have inappropriately used their classrooms to gain disciples for their pet political causes. The novel and film versions of *The Prime of Miss Jean Brodie* give brilliant portraits of this pedagogical perversion, as the teacher, Miss Brodie, uses her strong and commanding personality to intellectually seduce her impressionable students with all her views, from politics to music. Checking such abuses is a key responsibility of educational supervisors. Long ago, Plato wrote in *The Republic* about our responsibilities to foster character in our children. "We don't allow them [children] to be free until we establish a constitution in them, just as in a city, and—by fostering their best part with our own—equip them with a guardian and ruler similar to our own to take our place. Then, and only then, we set them free."

The art of educating, whether within the family, a school, or a corporation, is to find a balance between not giving the learner enough guidance and holding his engraving hand so tightly that he becomes frustrated or discouraged. Clearly, too, education is a joint responsibility, of both the teacher and the learner. Each partner's overall responsibility shifts with the increasing age and experience of the learner. The mother must take a firm hand with the three-year-old bopping his sister with her dolly. The seventh-grade teacher must win the hearts of her wolf pack by teaching them empathy. And the church youth group's leaders must rely primarily on their good example to encourage their high schoolers to serve those who are less fortunate than they.

The Case for Character Education in the Schools

Before getting into the issue of the school's—particularly the public school's—place in character education, we need to set that issue in context. First, the primary responsibility for each child's character education lies with his or her parents. History, law, and common sense affirm that parents are first in the line of accountability. Family members, both immediate and extended, have varying degrees of responsibility to help young people develop good habits and a sense of right and wrong. Traditionally, neighbors and community members have had a responsibility to watch over and help the children and young people in their neighborhood. One of the most pernicious features of modern American life, however, is the attenuation of this sense of moral connection and, therefore, moral responsibility among people living in the same community. Nevertheless, the connections are still there.

Religious groups, too, have traditionally played a major part in ethical training and in helping their members shed vices and acquire virtues. For example, in a recent survey 90 percent of the national sample answered the question about their religious affiliation by naming the particular group to which they belong. Clearly, religious groups are stakeholders in their members' character education. Then there is the government—local, state, and federal. Government is highly invested in promoting a citizenry of character as opposed to a citizenry of moral disasters and weaklings. A citizenry without character leads to two inevitable alternatives: social chaos or a policeman at every corner. There are many stakeholders, then, who bear responsibility for educating the young in the community's highest ideals. Why, then, should our public schools have to get involved? What is the case for character education in the schools?

It may seem odd to some that a case has to be made for developing our children's characters in school. However, having labored long in the educational vineyard with teachers, district leaders, and parents, and drawing on our own studies and surveys as well as those of others, we know that many teachers and administrators are quite ambivalent about getting the schools involved in character education. In fact, many are vehemently opposed to it. Thus the need to make our case.

The first argument in favor of character education in the schools can be called the argument from intellectual authorities. The world's great thinkers from the West, including Plato, Aristotle, Kant, and Dewey, and from the East, including Confucius, Laotzu, and Buddha, have all been strong advocates of giving conscious attention to character formation and focusing our human energies on living worthy lives. Even a casual dipping into these sources confirms their deep preoccupation with questions such as "What is a good and noble life?" "What do people need to be truly happy?" and "What do people need to keep from self-destruction?" Broadly speaking, their answer to these questions is to know what a good life is and to work to conform oneself to that ideal—an educational project.

Socrates long ago stated that the mission of education is to help people become both smart and good. In recent decades the second part of that definition has suffered in American schools and colleges. In the midst of what has been called a knowledge explosion, and faced with increasing questions about what in this noisy, modern world is the good, educators have blinked. They have argued that, given this overload of information, the best the schools can do is to teach students how to access it all. The focus, then, has turned to process skills—reading, writing, and data storage and retrieval. Although these skills are important, this emphasis on process has left to others the teaching of our culture's core moral values. That part of the educator's mission has been taken up by some enormously talented and persuasive "teachers"—the popular media and the hard-sellers of our consumer society. Meanwhile, educators have too often left students adrift in a swampy sea of moral relativism and ethical anesthesia. In contrast, great educators of the past, from the ancients to Maria Montessori, knew that people need to learn to be good and that their schooling must therefore contribute to their becoming so. Thomas Huxley wrote in the nineteenth century, "Perhaps the most valuable result of all education is the ability to make yourself do the thing you have to do, when it ought to be done, whether you like it or not; it is the first lesson that ought to be learned." This is not all there is to character education, but it is a good start—training our will. Such demanding messages do not fit well with the feel-good theories in vogue in many school systems today, however.

The second argument in favor of character education is that of our nation's founders. This, too, is a reasoned argument from authority. Those who carved out the United State from the British crown risked their lives, their families, and their fortunes with their seditious rebellion. Most of them were classically educated in philosophy and political science, so they knew that history's great thinkers had generally held democracy in low regard. Democracy contains within itself the seeds of its own destruction, they had said: allowing people to, in effect, be their own rulers would lead to corruptions such as mobocracy, with the many preying on the few and political leaders pandering to the citizenry's hunger for bread and circus. The founders' writings, particularly those of Thomas Jefferson, James Madison, John and Abigail Adams, and Benjamin Franklin, are filled with admonitions that the new republic must make education a high priority. They stressed education not merely for economic reasons but also because the form of government they were adopting was (and remains) at heart a moral compact among people. To work as it should, democracy demands a virtuous people. Jefferson wrote about the need for education in order to raise "the mass of people to the high ground of moral responsibility necessary for their own safety and orderly government"— to give them the ability to participate in a democratic society. The founders called for schools where the citizens would learn the civic virtues needed to maintain this intriguing but fragile human invention called democracy. In 1832—a time when some of the founders were still alive—Lincoln wrote, "I desire to see a time when education, and by its means, morality, sobriety, enterprise and industry, shall become much more general than at present." Then as now, the educational requirements of our system of government were still aborning.

The third argument is the law-based argument. In fact, however, this is more of a "reminder" than an argument since the state codes of education clearly direct schools to teach the moral values that support democratic life. Still, though, some educators are nervous about character education because they fear it may run contrary to students' rights to free expression and religion, and therefore schools could be sued for their efforts. Visions of subpoena-waving lawyers dance in their heads. There is little or no basis for such worries. The current nervousness among school administrators appears to have resulted from community uproars and a few suits in the 1970s over value-free moral education programs. Still, the state codes of education, which direct the operations of our schools, overwhelmingly support actively teaching the core moral values that provide the social glue of civic life. Currently, all fifty states have revised or are in the process of revising their curricular standards, which dictate what is to be taught and when. Recent research by Lynn Nelson at the University of Northern Iowa found that although only a few states have educational standards that address character education directly (Alabama, Connecticut, Hawaii, Indiana, North Dakota, Oregon, Tennessee, and Utah), forty-six states report addressing character education indirectly. By "indirectly" they mean through outcomes and standards that focus on the responsibilities of democratic citizenship or on particular attributes of civility. No state codes of education or standards outlaw, forbid, or in any way discourage character education.

Fourth is the vox populi argument. In addition to the world's great thinkers, our nation's founders, and the law, we have another source of guidance in American society: public opinion. We are clearly the most polled people on the face of the earth. We are polled about everything from the popularity of TV personalities to the sex lives of politicians, from the plight of Bosnia to the guilt of nannies. But though polling can get out of hand, it does give politicians and other decision makers a way to understand what we, the little people, are thinking.

For many years now, the Gallup organization and other polling companies have been asking the American people about our views on the performance of the public schools and related topics. Our answers do not paint a pretty picture. Americans are not pleased with American schools. Polls reveal major dissatisfaction with the lack of discipline in our classrooms. Apparently, people believe the schools are disordered and make relatively few demands on our children. Against this is the 90 percent or more of adults who support our public schools' teaching honesty (97 percent), democracy (93 percent), acceptance of people of different races and ethnic backgrounds (91 percent), patriotism (91 percent), caring for friends and family members (91 percent), moral courage (91 percent), and the Golden Rule (90 percent).[6] This voice of the people, added to the support provided by the wisdom of the past and our laws, should provide educators with the confidence and public trust they need to energetically engage in character education.

The fifth and final argument in favor of character education is the inevitability argument. Simply stated, this argument asserts that children cannot enter the educational system at age four and stay until age sixteen or seventeen without having their character and their moral values profoundly affected by the experience. Children are impressionable, and the events of life in school affect what they think, feel, believe, and do. All sorts of questions bubble up in children's lives: Who is a good person and who isn't? What is a worthy life? What should I do in this or that situation? Sometimes their questions are never even asked out loud. Clearly, the answers children arrive at are heavily influenced by their experiences in school, with their teachers, their peers, and the material they study.

Further, schools place great demands on children. Children are expected to treat one another with civility, to put aside their playthings or television viewing or sports to do schoolwork, and not just to go through the motions of doing schoolwork but to do it to the best of their ability. As we discuss fully in Chapter Seven, becoming a good student (that is, doing one's work to the best of one's abilities) is one of the great ethical challenges the majority of our children face during their youth. How they respond to this challenge has a huge effect on their character formation. Therefore, both the events of one's school years and the self-confrontation that being a student provokes will inevitably have an impact on a child's character.

We are witnessing the schools' reawakening to what was historically one of their most essential tasks, the formation of character among the children in its care. There are many signs of this reawakening and many reasons for it. Among them is our increasingly clear need to build a society shaped by citizens who know, are committed to, and can act on the key moral values and principles on which our democracy is based. Another reason is the frightening statistics about crime, poor academic achievement, promiscuity, substance abuse, and sheer unhappiness among the young. Another is the very real unpleasantness of running schools without a positive ethical environment. Schools that are mere sites of training and information transfer, where students know they are simply compelled to attend, are barren and sterile places. Teachers and administrators who chose a career in education to help young people get a good start in life regularly report feeling burnt out and disillusioned by the hassle and bureaucratic drudgery of it all. The answer to these ills is, we believe, character education. Although this is a bold promise, we must hastily add that we are not talking about superficial changes or quickie workshops or purchasing new curricula.

There's no such thing as character-education-in-a-box. True character education means an approach to schooling that is fundamentally different from what currently exists in most of our schools. It means, as Steven Tigner puts it, *taking our students seriously as persons* and helping them become informed and responsible moral agents.[7] What we attempt to lay out in the remainder of this book is a very different mission from what is presently dominant in our schools, an educational mission that focuses on helping students know the good, love the good, and do the good.

| **Views, Values, or Virtues?**

How can we help students develop the strength of character they need to lead their lives well—to make good choices and honor their commitments? For students to choose nobly, they need some direction. It's easy to say that the schools should help provide this direction, but what approach should they take? Where does character development fit into the curriculum?

People's moral compasses are shaped by a number of different factors, from their family, faith, and friendships to their experiences, such as hard work, suffering, and joy. Some argue that the *views* we have on an array of different issues provide our moral starting point. Others contend that our *values* constitute our moral compass. In this chapter we argue that *virtues* are what orient us appropriately and strengthen our character. These three terms—the "three *Vs*" of views, values, and virtues—are often used interchangeably, but in reality they serve very different purposes. This, in turn, has led to a great deal of confusion for those trying to implement character education in their schools.

In choosing which one to emphasize in the classroom, we must be aware of where each road leads. As the traveler's axiom states, "You're never gonna get there if you're not sure where you're goin'." Our aim in this chapter is to point educators toward what we believe is the right road, a road that leads to the *keystone* of character education. Although views, values, and virtues all play an integral part in schooling, only virtues provide the true moral support critical for building character.

The "Three Vs" in the Classroom

We begin with an illustration of character education in three class-rooms. All three are eleventh-grade English classes discussing Mark Twain's *Huckleberry Finn*. All three teachers are intentionally trying to integrate character education into their curriculum. The classes have reached the part of the novel where the bounty hunters searching for Jim, Huck's friend and companion on the raft, approach Huck to ask him if he has seen the runaway slave. In what many critics have recognized as an ethical moment of truth for Huck, he decides to lie to the hunters to keep Jim from being captured. With this act he goes against all he has learned from his father and society. Twain has Huck conclude that he is going to "throw his lot in with the Devil."

Scenario One: The Views-Driven Approach

Ms. Hadyn begins the lesson by asking her students to complete the following in-class writing assignment:

> Our book, *Huckleberry Finn*, is increasingly becoming controversial. Many school districts around the country have banned it, and some public libraries have been pressured to remove it from their shelves. Critics claim that the book is filled with racial slurs, insults, and stereotypes that are deeply offensive to African Americans and all people concerned with equality and harmony. Others rebut this claim, stating that the book is not only an American classic but also a biting satire of our country's former racial laws and attitudes. The very fact that Huck would have to struggle to make a decision about whether or not Jim is someone's personal property is a telling reminder of the profound indignities and mistreatment African Americans suffered under slavery. What are your views on this con-

troversial topic of banning *Huckleberry Finn*? Write a brief argument for your point of view, and state the reasons for your position.

She gives the students twenty-five minutes to write their papers, and when they are finished she starts the discussion. After giving the students some more background on the controversy surrounding the book in various parts of the country, Ms. Hadyn invites them to state and support their positions.

Teacher: Yes, Sarah?

Sarah: I think it's a racist book. And quite honestly, I've been wondering why we're reading it. I mean, just look at Jim's full name: "*Nig*"—I can't even say the word!

Teacher: Lots of people are upset about this. All right, anyone else? Todd?

Todd: I agree with Sarah. If I were an African American and had to read this, I'd be insulted. And having to be reminded that my grandparents or great-grandparents were slaves. . . . Well, it's just too much.

Teacher: What do you mean, "too much"?

Todd: Well, being in class with white kids whose ancestors owned my grandparents would be hard. It would make me mad and want to get back at them. It's just not right.

Teacher: Okay. Larry, you've had your hand up for a while.

Larry: Hey, we're going over the top. This is a satire. Twain was on Jim's side. He was showing how crazy slavery was. Those bounty hunters were the bad guys.

Todd: That's what you think! Not everyone takes it that way. For some, there's a lot of insults in this book.

Teacher: Fine. Thank you. Can we hear from someone else? Rosa?

Rosa: Well, I'm Hispanic. And although I can see the discrimination point, I think we're missing the point. Isn't Jim sorta the hero of the story? Isn't he Huck's teacher?

The discussion continues for the rest of the period, and the teacher keeps a running tally on the board of the various points raised, under the headings "Pro-Ban" and "Anti-Ban." As the period draws to a close, she explains that in a democracy it is important for people to take positions on controversial issues and defend their views. She says that this is particularly true for issues like racism that affect people's lives and futures. One student asks what Ms. Hadyn's own view is on whether the book should be banned. "Well, first of all," Ms. Hadyn says, "I would never have taught it if I believed it should be banned. And though I'm sensitive to the criticisms of it, my own view is that this is an American classic and one that points out for inspection the racism that has been part of our past. I think the good done by this book outweighs the harm." Several students are eager to dispute her. As she is about to acknowledge them, the bell rings. Students head for the door, many of them still vigorously arguing their views.

Scenario Two: The Values-Driven Approach

Mr. Klopper announces at the beginning of his class that they are going to do a "mind-stretching" exercise today. He tells the class that although they probably all identify with Huck and Jim as they attempt to run away, he wants the class to consider the events around the bounty hunter scene in a different light. "Close your eyes and imagine the following," he instructs. "The bounty hunters are just poor men hired by the equally poor farmer from whom Jim has run away. The farmer is a good man, struggling to keep his own family fed. He was always generous to Jim and his wife and children. Without Jim, the slave he inherited from his father, his whole livelihood is in jeopardy. Furthermore, Jim's wife and children desperately want him back. He never told them he was going to run away. His wife is crestfallen, and the children cry themselves to sleep every night."

After adding these imaginary elements to the story, Mr. Klopper breaks the class down into four groups and asks them to take up the perspectives of Jim, Huck, the farmer/slave owner, and Jim's wife. He then asks the students in each group to put themselves in their character's shoes and discuss what they believe is the right thing for Huck to do. Further, Mr. Klopper instructs the students to give two justifications for their decision. After fifteen minutes of spirited discussion in the groups, the teacher asks spokespersons from each group to explain their group's opinion and how they justify it. The students get quite involved in the exercise, rooting for their character and making light of the other group's reasons.

"Now for the real mind-stretching," Mr. Klopper explains. "We are going to do a little switching around. I want the 'Jim group' to consider the case from the farmer's perspective, and vice-versa. And the 'Huck group' should now consider the situation of Jim's wife, and vice versa. This time you only have ten minutes to pre-pare." The process is then repeated, with each side again report-ing its conclusions.

With ten minutes left in the period, Mr. Klopper announces, "I want you to write an answer to the following question: 'If you were in Huck's shoes, and you were aware of these other three per-spectives, what would you do when the bounty hunters came, and why?' You have until the end of the period to complete your re-sponse." The students begin writing immediately. After the bell rings, they leave their papers on the teacher's desk. Several stu-dents ask Klopper, "Who was best? Which group argued the best?" He smiles and says, "I'd have to say it was a tie." Moans and ques-tions follow. "What would you do, Mr. Klopper? Would you turn Jim in?" As he gathers up his material and glides toward the door, he says with a smile, "No! No! That wouldn't be fair. Make up your own mind." The moans continue as the door closes behind him.

Scenario Three: The Virtues-Centered Approach

Mrs. Ramirez begins her class by asking what her students re-member about the purpose of satire as a literary device. Several students offer responses. "It pokes fun at institutions to show their corruption," one offers. A second student recounts Jonathan Swift's use of irony and exaggeration in "A Modest Proposal," which makes the outrageous yet calculated proposal that the Irish consider eating their young children as a solution to the economic depression: "Yeah, Swift shows how cruel the British were to the Irish." After a brief discussion of political cartoons and satire in TV sitcoms, Mrs. Ramirez returns to Mark Twain. "Well, you should know that we are reading not only one of the most popular American novels ever written but also one of the greatest satires in American literature. Although satire holds people, customs, and institutions up to ridicule, it is often driven by a moral purpose. The author is trying to get people to see the absurdity or immorality of something by presenting it in a satiric manner." She tells them that with the passage they are now discussing, about Huck's being tempted to turn Jim in, they have come to a critical juncture in the novel: "Huck makes a moral decision and acts on it. Now I want you to reflect on his decision and write about it. I want you to think about what this decision reveals about Huck, about the kind of person he is becoming. Based on what you know about Huck thus far—that is, he's a young boy, just beginning to grow up—and what you know from our previous discussions about virtues, which virtue is Huck beginning to show in this scene? Or is Huck simply acting out of enlightened self-interest? Please give evidence from the text to support your response." She tells the class that they have twenty minutes to make their arguments, "so think hard and work fast. When you've finished, we'll read a few and discuss them."

After some head scratching, a bit of staring blankly into space, and some visits by Mrs. Ramirez to a few questioning students, everyone settles down to write. The teacher returns to her desk and writes as well. At the end of twenty minutes, Mrs. Ramirez invites the students to share their papers.

Mrs. Ramirez: What kind of person is Huck becoming?
    Deborah: I think Huck is really changing. He stands up for what he believes is right, even if he has to lie.

Steve: Yeah. Huck shows a lot of guts; he's changed a lot from the beginning of the novel.

Mrs. Ramirez: How has he changed, then?

Steve: I'd say he's gained courage.

Danielle: I don't think so. Huck needs Jim, and he doesn't want him taken away. That's all. He's not thinking about the consequences, like whether or not Jim will ever see his wife and children again. I think Huck's acting out of his own self-interest.

Mrs. Ramirez: One could even go so far as to say Huck is being cowardly in not turning Jim in; he's not facing up to the law and its consequences, right?

Norma: No, I don't think he's being a coward at all.

Mrs. Ramirez: Why not?

Norma: For the first time, Huck realizes that Jim is a person, not property. It reminds me of the people who willingly hid Jews in their homes during the Holocaust and then lied to the Nazis. Huck shows respect for Jim—*and* courage.

Mrs. Ramirez: Let's look at Huck's situation again. What's motivating him? Is he acting from self-interest, or is something else driving Huck's decision to lie?

The discussion goes on. Students offer additional evidence from the novel to support Huck's showing signs of loyalty and friendship as well as courage. The "enlightened self-interest" case is refuted with the argument that if Huck were really interested in his own welfare, he would not have risked the danger he puts himself in as an accomplice to a runaway slave. Toward the end of the class, one of the students asks Mrs. Ramirez what she thinks Huck shows in this scene. "First, as you have discovered," she explains, "there is no single answer to the question. In one way or another, Huck shows signs of all the character traits you mentioned. But my sense is that the desire for justice is what moved him to action. It dawned on him how unfair it would be for Jim to be sent back. I could make a strong case as well for respect, which has a lot to do with justice. I think what was happening to Huck on the raft was that he was beginning to see what is wrong with the way people around him saw Jim as just a slave, as someone's property. Huck has grown to see Jim as a person, worthy of respect and fair treatment." With that the bell rings, and class is dismissed.

These brief scenarios show us how three different classrooms and teachers might approach one question, all under the banner of character education, in varying ways. Although we strongly favor the general approach of the third scenario, the classroom centered on virtues, the other two are not without merit. Each approach contributes to the effort to foster character development through the curriculum. Ms. Hadyn helps her students to be sensitive to the effects of racism, including the effect that just *portraying* racism in literature can have on some people. Mr. Klopper involves his students in the practice of taking different perspectives, challenging them to understand the points of view of others. Both of these approaches lack a moral anchor, however. Neither approach helps students appreciate the difference between a morally good decision and a morally weak one: every moral choice is up for grabs, just one of a set of views or values. When such approaches become the *only* or *primary* way of addressing moral issues, character education has no anchor.

The Problem with Emphasizing Views

The first scenario, of a views-driven classroom, captures the way character education is conceived of and carried out in many American classrooms—as a discussion among viewpoints on controversial moral issues. The teacher believes in helping students develop a moral compass and believes she is advancing this goal by helping them acquire strong views on social issues. It is pedagogically effective. She works from a text and uses the curriculum to help students grapple with important issues. She has them confront the issue on their own and arrive at their own point of view. And because she believes that students should come in contact with well-thought-out views, and perhaps further believing that her view on the banning issue is correct, she shares it with her students.

An exemplar of the views-driven instructional approach is one of America's most popular teachers, Oprah Winfrey. Her highly successful method has not only sired numerous imitators on television but also hundreds of thousands in our classrooms. The Oprah method goes something like this:

1. Find a hot issue, one that will generate interest (ideally passionate interest).
2. Present the issue in as stark and dramatic a fashion as possible. Try as much as possible to keep the issue black or white, with little or no gray area.
3. Get people to formulate their views and to take sides on the issue.
4. Have them present their views in a confrontational (my-side-against-your-side) manner.
5. Act as a referee. Make sure all sides are heard and the situation remains charged but not out of control.
6. Try to stay neutral (except when you believe you have the correct view) and nonjudgmental (except with views you consider way out of the mainstream).
7. Congratulate people for their interest and participation, not for the merit or truth of their positions.

Although the Oprah approach makes for successful television (that is, her program draws large audiences and sells more commercial products), it makes for questionable education—and dubious character education. The aim of this approach is both to get students to form views and opinions on a wide range of topics *and* to encourage them to hold specific, socially acceptable views on certain topics. However, focusing on views naturally tends to feed controversy. For instance, although it is difficult to generate much excitement by expressing concern for the less fortunate of the world, it is quite easy to do so by asserting that the United States ought to open wide its borders to them. Few like to talk about abstract principles, such as duty to one's country. It is much easier to take things to a personal level, such as by asking whether everyone should be required to give two years of military service.

There is nothing wrong with generating controversy in the careful pursuit of truth. Controversy can prompt reflection, thought, and insight—but it can also provoke anger, resentment, and a contentious spirit that spills out of control. Every community has its shared views and its competing views. In our country there are a number of so-called hot-button issues that are of great interest to people, particularly adolescents. For instance, during junior and senior high school many students are fascinated by the occult, by the effects of drugs and alcohol, by sexuality, and by all the controversy that surrounds these themes. The more controversial the topic, such as homosexual marriage, a scandal surrounding a public figure, or the use of animals to test drugs, the more interest they have in it. 'Twas ever so. Certainly there is a place in school for discussing society's unfinished business, our unsettled questions. Indeed, such discussions can heighten students' awareness of the moral domain and help them appreciate the complexity of many moral issues. An overemphasis on controversial subjects can harm rather than help a school's character education efforts, however. Such subjects can end up generating more heat than light. At worst, they can leave students with the impression that ethical issues are "just too complicated" and "ultimately, just a matter of opinion." Too often, the moral significance of an issue is reduced to a smorgasbord of divisive claims and counterclaims, and the moral principles that underlie those claims remain unexamined.

The Problem with Emphasizing Values

Our second scenario illustrates a values-driven lesson. The concept of "values" has been a tricky and troubling one in recent American education. Values are what we desire, what we want, and what we ascribe worth to. Values tend to be idiosyncratic. They can be reduced to a matter of taste or feeling rather than representing the product of thought and deliberate choice. Furthermore, values can be good *or* bad. What matters is not their content but the fact that we prize them. And often we are a little schizophrenic about our values. For instance, we may value the image of ourselves as "lovers of poetry" but rarely buy a book of poetry or even read a poem. Or we may be quite vocal about the vulgarity of soap operas but in fact spend several hours a week watching prime-time soaps. Human beings have all sorts of values, and we apply them to many different areas of our lives. Some values are no more than matters of preference, like a taste for designer clothing or good wine. Some values are related to one's ethnic background and traditions, such as the French citizen's concern for his language. Some stem from our religious beliefs, such as our attitudes toward the Sabbath. We also have aesthetic values, such as a love for Beethoven or bebop. Some are social values or manners, like the desire to take care of one's personal hygiene and to eat with knives and forks. And then there are moral values, such as those guiding how we treat others. We will take up moral values shortly.

Over the past twenty years, schools have focused heavily on values, instituting "values education" and "values clarification" programs as a primary vehicle to address morality and ethics with students. The problem with values-driven character education, however, is not simply the question of which values should be addressed (our taste in music or our moral values with respect to warfare) but also what we believe about the authority of these values. The current cultural climate holds that values are not only a matter of personal choice but also a personal right, not to be limited by some sort of "moral authority." Each person is free to define his or her own values. This works fine when we limit ourselves to questions of taste, as in "I really value evenings by the fire" or "I like dry white wine," but such subjectivism can become pernicious in the moral realm. Does anyone have a right to value, say, being able to use manipulation and power to get their way with people?

When the question "Is this the right thing to do?" is pushed, the answer comes, "It's certainly right by me!" In short, values are perceived as relative. But relative to what? The cultural relativist might answer that they are relative to the different rules and mores of different cultures. In effect, different communities and nations have arrived at their own conclusions about what is right and what is wrong. Over time they have forged agreements on rules of conduct. From a values perspective, then, what is right or wrong depends on the particular cultural context with which one is dealing. Can we say in such a climate that, for example, enslaving another person is wrong or teenagers shouldn't be having sex? "Maybe yes, maybe no," comes the answer.

For the cultural relativist, rules are man-made and thus quite arbitrary. Adherents to this view have confusedly alleged that if everything is relative, there are no moral principles, no universal *good*, to count on. In our ethnically, culturally, and religiously diverse society, we have moved swiftly from cultural relativism to personal relativism. In the world of personal relativism, the individual is king. Although she may choose to obey the law as her only moral norm, whatever else she does is a matter of personal choice. And if a person should choose to break the law, what matters most is that she doesn't get caught. Morality becomes a purely personal matter. The only moral standard that remains is that there *are* no absolute moral standards or norms. There are just individual values. Confronted with an ethical problem, we are responsible for solving it only in the way that suits us best. We are our own private judge and jury.

Writing in *Back to Virtue* on this problem of cultural and personal relativism, or what he calls the moral worlds of collectivism and privatism, Peter Kreeft explains: "Their effect (privatism and collectivism) is that we live in two separate worlds. Our feeling life, our inner world of 'values' (no longer real goods), is set against the outer world of behavior, a world governed by social 'mores' (no longer morals). 'Values' are like thoughts, like ghosts, undulating blobs of psychic energy. 'Mores' are like brute facts, like machines, ways people do in fact behave, not ways they ought to. We are like ghosts in machines."[1]

In this prevailing intellectual environment, the most morally educative act teachers feel permitted to perform is to help their students clarify their own values—their "inner world of feelings." They are also free to socialize students to embrace conventional mores and socially accepted values. Neither act fosters character, the integral *moral* education of the head, the heart, and the hand. Instead they promote subjectivism and a mechanical morality that changes with the fashions of the day.

The teacher in scenario two, the values-driven classroom, is concerned with his students' values. He wants them to come to their own conclusions about what is the morally right thing for Huck to do. And he adds all the emotional detail to help them see that there may be many different answers, depending on what they *feel* most strongly about. Mr. Klopper took an important step toward developing his students' character; however, as many American educators do, he based his character education effort not on giving his students hard, intellectual evidence, grounding them in the truths of our society's collective moral wisdom, but on the doctrine of privatism—"whatever you feel is important." His method reflects something that is as close to educational dogma as it gets: the idea that adults have no right to impose their moral values on the young.

Mr. Klopper is similar to Ms. Hadyn, who is also intent on helping her students form their own views. The main difference between the two is that Ms. Hadyn asks her students for reasons based on evidence rather than reasons based on an emotionally charged response to hypothetical details. Both believe that it is more important for their students to arrive at their own perspective than to accept someone else's truth. But worse yet, they are inculcating their students with the same dogma: there are no universal truths or values. The best students can do is to come up with satisfying views, with their own feelings about an issue, to clarify their own "undulating blobs of psychic energy." By focusing on controversy and emotional responses, these teachers have ignored the moral basics. And, as we have discussed in Chapter One, there *are* moral basics.

The Benefits of Emphasizing Virtues

In scenario three, the virtues-centered classroom, the approach to character education is different. Mrs. Ramirez's approach is a mix of reflection and guided discussion. Keeping the students close to the text of the novel, she wants them to reflect on Huck's actions and thoughts. Additionally, she wants them, as much as possible, to make connections between the work under study and important life lessons. She poses the question about what kind of person Huck is becoming and asks them to base their conclusions on evidence from the story. She does not want them to blurt out the first thing that comes to their minds or to rush to judgment. Like Ms. Hadyn in the views-centered classroom, she gives them time and requests that they commit their thoughts to the discipline of written expression. Only once they have thought and written does she engage them in discussion. Mrs. Ramirez does not conduct an anything-goes free-for-all but sets up a logical thought process to lead students—by eliciting their responses—toward a specific goal. She believes there are important moral truths that must be understood.

Each of these three teachers is skillful in his or her own way. Each is attempting to engage students in serious issues. Each believes he or she is integrating character education into the curriculum. Clearly, each one excites students and gets their "ethical juices" flowing. Yet, only one teacher actually gets to the heart of things. Without a conception of virtue, without a sense of what it may mean for a person to live in an honorable or contemptible way, the views one holds, no matter how well they may be defended, are empty. Without a clear sense of the good, personal values and the ability to show empathy remain hollow. Only one teacher helps students to see why Huck's decision to lie is good, despite appearances. Her students come to see the power of virtue in shaping an individual's life. Only this teacher helps her students understand that character comes not from acquiring particular points of view or values but from developing a set of ideals upon which to base one's life.

The Search for Meaning in Life

Detached from a conception of the purpose of life, virtues become merely nice ideals, empty of meaning. "What is the purpose of human life?" Although this is an extremely abstract question, for centuries it has consumed philosophers, theologians, great writers, holy women and men, and individuals across cultures and from all strata of society. If we could arrive at an answer to this question, it seems natural that it would direct everything we do, from how we spend our minutes and hours to what we try to accomplish through our family lives and careers. Certainly, too, the answer would inform our educational efforts. Needless to say, however, it is a question that is rarely asked in schools today.

Just because they have not come to grips with this ultimate question doesn't mean our schools have been purposeless. In fact, they have been driven by a cacophony of purposes, from vocationalism to mental health, from mastery of the basics to computer literacy. Clearly there is a good to each of these educational efforts, but each purpose seems to have its turn in school, is tried—often with great fanfare—found wanting, attacked, and then put on the educational ice floe.

Raising questions about the ultimate purpose of life is out of fashion, particularly in our public schools. But the absence of these questions puts at great peril our educational system's goal of drawing the very best from students. One reason for educators' reluctance to ask about our purpose in life is that the U.S. public school system is designed to serve children from a variety of cultures, creeds, and origins. Since individuals of different cultures answer this question in different ways, those taking the lead in our public schools have gently pushed this question aside. The failure to contend with this anchoring question, however, has resulted in enormous confusion and drift. We have replaced the more probing questions about what it means to live well as a human being with secondary questions about how can we help our students to become successful, wealthy, and well liked. But in our view, fundamental reform and increased public support for our schools depends on bringing more sturdy questions back to the surface.

We should not fear raising this age-old question about the purpose of life. To ignore it would be miseducative. Further, throughout history there has been a fairly consistent answer: happiness, or living well. Thoughtful observers of the human condition have continually noted this same quest, the quest for happiness. As Baruch Spinoza said, "What everyone wants from life is continuous and genuine happiness." At the turn of the century, William James observed, "How to gain, how to keep, how to recover happiness is in fact for most men at all times the secret motive of all they do, and all they are willing to do." We all appear to have a drive toward happiness that we can observe in young children, in elderly retirees, and in ourselves. The real questions, then, are "What is happiness?" and "What brings happiness?" Answers range, of course, from the saccharine claim of Charlie Brown that "Happiness is a warm puppy" to the cynical comment of A. Edward Newton that "the formula for complete happiness is to be very busy with the unimportant."

A serious question, "What is happiness?" really invites us to ask, "What does it mean to live well—to lead a fully human life?" And it is here where there are quite different answers and real divisions. A large percentage of Americans would probably respond by saying that living well means having a good family, a satisfying and well-paying job, or good health. Another percentage, being intimately connected to their faith tradition, might add that true happiness means being close to God or some related condition. There are many outside of religious traditions, though, who understand the good as living in harmony with nature or making of their own lives a work of art. Although differences in people's ultimate goals do exist, there is a strong consensus among people holding different life goals on the means of achieving them. The devout Southern Baptist who is trying to follow Jesus and the agnostic struggling to make her life a work of art both agree that they should treat the underprivileged with care, be honest in their dealings, and respect the rights of others. Further, as citizens of the same nation, they usually agree on certain moral standards and virtues that are instrumental in advancing the common good. It is a basic tenet of public education in this country that people of very different theologies, or no theology at all, can come together in their communities and agree on teaching their children these means to happiness and to living in harmony together.

As a community we may be able to agree on core virtues, such as justice, responsibility, courage, and compassion; however, we are still left to grapple with the purpose of life question. F. Washington Jarvis, headmaster of the over-350-year-old Roxbury Latin School in Boston, illustrates this challenge well in "Beyond Ethics," an article he wrote for the *Journal of Education.* Jarvis describes a conversation he had with a former high school star, noting that "glittering prizes crowned his accomplishments in school." Jarvis cites the student, now a successful businessman in his early thirties, as saying:

> You know, ever since I was in school, all my days have been like this one—never enough time to do everything I need to do. I worked

incredibly hard in school. I worked incredibly hard in college and in business school. And I work incredibly hard at my job. Occasionally, along the way, from time to time, I've asked myself, "Why am I working so hard, why do I want this life?" But lately I've been asking myself that question a lot more often. All the time when we were in school you used to talk to us about ethics, about how we should live. That's good, your words did affect us. I've volunteered as a Big Brother and as a tutor and I've taken all the seminars on cultural awareness et cetera. But you really should talk more about why we should live. Ethical questions are important, but the even more important question is whether there is any purpose and meaning to things, whether all this hard work is worth it, whether life is worth living.[2]

Meaning—*the point of it all*—nags at us. And it certainly nags at our students. In the small community of South Boston alone there were seven completed suicides and over seventy attempts by teenagers in 1997. Last summer the *New York Times Magazine* featured a special report on "cutting,"[3] an obsessive-compulsive habit that many adolescents, especially girls, have in which they punish themselves by inflicting pain on themselves—cutting their thighs and arms with razors or burning their skin with cigarettes. By wounding themselves physically, they attempt to escape a deeper pain, that of loneliness, despair, and sometimes anger. Whether our students come from wealthy suburban neighborhoods or live in the projects, they are hungry not only for a sense of belonging but also for a sense of purpose in what they do and what they experience. If adults who have children in their care do not help to provide them with the moral knowledge and truths that people, over generations and generations, have squeezed from our successes and failures, then young people will fend for themselves and find direction elsewhere.

Teachers, whether in the classroom or on a field trip to a nursing home, cannot help but influence a student's groping with questions of human purpose. Students should come away from their education with the understanding that pursuing an answer to these fundamental questions is of the utmost importance. The school that ignores the centrality of these questions or trivializes them because they don't want to offend anyone is, indeed, making a statement to students, that these questions are not really that important.

Although clearly the public schools should not advocate a *particular* ultimate answer, they can offer a generic one—one such as that offered by Aristotle and echoed by many others down through the generations: "Verbally there is very general agreement; for both the general run of men and people of superior refinement say that it is happiness, and identify living well and faring well with being happy."

As educators we have an opportunity to help students exercise wisdom in making sense of "the pursuit of happiness" or "living well and faring well." We need to make it clear that "the pursuit of happiness" does not entitle us to simply having a good time, enjoying warm and fuzzy feelings, or leading a life free from toil and suffering. These sought-after *goods,* although not bad in themselves, represent a caricature of human happiness. Since happiness can present itself to us in a variety of guises—a bottomless box of Godiva chocolates, an Alfa Romeo, a romantic cruise for two around the world—our educational efforts should help students discern what is truly good and therefore most worth our time, energy, talents, and interest. In the words of Victor Frankl, we need to discover "a reason to be happy."

In the 1993 film *Groundhog Day,* Bill Murray plays Phil Conners, a self-centered, cynical weatherman who finds himself caught in a time-warp: every day is Groundhog Day in Punxsutawney, Pennsylvania. At the end of his second February 2 day, he breaks a pencil by his bedside and awakes in the morning to find it in its original condition. This is his sign that his actions have no permanent consequences. A jubilant Phil declares, "I'm not gonna live by the rules anymore." He gorges on cream puffs, doughnuts, and bacon for breakfast; seduces multiple women; makes exorbitant purchases; and even stops flossing his teeth. After days of wanton self-indulgence, he finds himself feeling empty—as if he is lacking something. He turns his attention to Rita, his kind and beautiful producer. If only he can "win" Rita over, Phil believes, *then* he will be happy. He spends days studying her preferences, her likes and dislikes. But Phil ultimately fails because he doesn't understand her character. "I could never love someone like you," she exclaims at the end of one night, "because you'll never love anybody but yourself." After days of despondency and suicide attempts, a "new" Phil Conners sets out to *deserve* Rita. He spends his days reading great literature, studying piano, helping the troubled and the homeless. He spends less time with Rita, however, and more time serving other people. Through his efforts to improve and focus less on himself, he earns Rita's loving respect and the happiness of a "fully flourishing life." This movie humorously illustrates what it means to come to know the good, love the good, and finally do the good. Phil Conners finally discovers a reason to be happy.

Educators can provide opportunities for students to discover the enormous range of reasons individuals have to be happy. For example, one of the most powerful activities in a high school in our community is a sophomore year project. All the tenth graders have to research and report on the heroic qualities of someone living. Before gathering evidence and documentation and beginning writing, however, the students spend a great deal of time and energy grappling with questions such as, "What makes someone a hero or heroine despite their inevitable flaws?" and "What is a worthwhile life?" Students, teachers, and parents report that this project has a strong and lasting impact.

The Connection Between Virtue and Living Well

The word *virtue* comes from the Latin *vir,* which has a root meaning of "force" or "agency." In Latin the expression *virtus moralis* became the established equivalent of the Greek expression *arete ethike,* "moral virtue" or "character excellence." The Greek word *arete* means "excellence." The novelist Pearl Buck wrote, "The secret of joy in work is contained in one word—excellence. To know how to do something well is to enjoy it." Virtue actually enables us to do our work better and to enjoy it more as a consequence. It helps us to become better parents, better teachers, better students, better friends, better colleagues, and better spouses. What distinguishes virtues from views and values, then, is that virtues are cultivated from within the individual and actually improve character and intelligence. Views are simply intellectual positions, and values evoke neither a moral commitment nor the promise of leading a good life. Additionally, unlike views and values, virtue is not passive. Virtue is both the disposition to think, feel, and act in morally excellent ways, and the exercise of this disposition. Furthermore, it serves as both a means and an end of human happiness. As a means, virtues are those habits and dispositions that enable us to live out our responsibilities more gracefully. Hemingway describes the virtue of courage, for example as "grace under pressure." As ends, virtues such as kindness, courage, wisdom, compassion, and responsibility represent ideals of human life worth striving for. Martha Washington sums up the connection between virtue and happiness in this way: "The greater part of our happiness or misery depends on our dispositions [our virtues], and not on our circumstances. We carry the seeds of the one or the other about with us in our minds wherever we go." Teachers and schools have a place in bringing those seeds of virtue to fruition.

This struggle for virtue is, in a way, the everyday wisdom that many of us continually forget. We see it in the serene face of Nelson Mandela, whose sacrifices and sufferings have transformed the once truculent revolutionary. Literature is filled with characters, such as *The Scarlet Letter*'s Hester Prynne, whose acceptance of their plight strengthens and ennobles them. It is there for us to see in the life of George Washington, who at sixteen took himself in hand and forged himself into the strong and virtuous leader he became as a man. It is there in the life of the teacher Annie Sullivan, whose dogged persistence and compassion opened the mind of a deaf and dumb child, Helen Keller, who in turn brought a brilliant sustaining light to many others. The goal of life is to become a fully human person, that is, a person who is capable of pursuing the *good* in the context of everything one does—from being a competent computer technician to raising one's children. Helen Keller herself stated it succinctly: "Many people have a wrong idea of what constitutes real happiness. It is not obtained through self-gratification, but through fidelity to a worthy purpose."

Earlier we defined character education as the effort to help students know the good, love the good, and do the good. In short, it is about helping students mature into persons of integrity—persons of intelligence and moral character. It is necessary, therefore, to help students wrestle with and understand the *good*—that is, what is true and worthwhile in life as well as what is right. To do this, we need to help them develop knowledge of the good and intelligent judgment so that they learn to choose well among competing and attractive options in life. Simultaneously, we need to help them love the good—concern for the needs of others, fidelity to one's commitments, a job well done, true friendship—and the habits necessary to attain it. Loving the good is about educating students' feelings and passions so that they love the right things for the right reasons (for example, so that they learn to do their homework for the sake of learning rather than simply a grade, or that they join the KEY club to give to others rather than to gain recognition). As human beings our motivations are frequently mixed; loving the good helps us to recognize and refine them. In a way, it becomes the engine of our moral growth. Moral maturity, in the end, is about leading a good life. To do this we must act, we must fulfill our obligations. Therefore teachers must help students see that doing the good is the bottom line.

Again, Pearl S. Buck can provide us with a helpful insight: "You cannot make yourself feel something you do not feel, but you can make yourself do right in spite of your feelings." A few years ago, when one of us was teaching in a suburban high school, an incident involving a bright and popular thirteen-year-old girl drove this point home. Sweet and well liked by teachers and peers, she was an animated participant in class discussions and activities. In class one day, however, her math teacher confiscated a two-page note that she had obviously been working on for some time. After class, the teacher asked to meet with her at lunchtime.

Before the meeting, the teacher read the note and discovered that this young woman had been viciously and cruelly maligning one of the less popular girls in the class, a girl who was extremely self-conscious about being overweight. The sheer meanness of the note and the obvious history of cattiness it revealed were both alarming and disappointing to the teacher. When the offending student came to meet with her teacher, she was visibly ashamed and upset. The teacher simply said, "I read your note about Jennifer," and the girl dissolved into tears. A sober but fruitful discussion ensued. The young woman's shame turned to resolve when she acknowledged that she would be devastated if others were to talk about her in such brutal terms and, even worse, alienate her from her peers as a consequence. For the remainder of the school year, she not only stopped her cattiness toward this student but actually sought out ways to make her feel genuinely included among her own friends.

It sometimes takes a startling event like this to awaken students to the disharmony in their lives. All too often, we see discordant responses in our students, who may weep bitterly at the cruel injustice they see in a film or read in a story but turn right around at recess and bully the classmate who can't sink a basketball or taunt a classmate who stutters. There are numerous opportunities throughout the school year for teachers to help students see where they can take steps toward developing virtue.

To attain a virtue is hard work. To cultivate the virtue of generosity, for example, first we need to see (with either our heart or our head) the *need* for generosity. Then we need to struggle against the competing impulses of selfishness and laziness. Finally, we need to do something generous. But one generous act does not a generous person make! Aristotle, in answering the question "How does a man become virtuous?" said, "a man becomes virtuous by doing virtuous acts." Occasionally giving five dollars to a charity won't do it. It has to be a habit of giving of oneself and a disposition to react generously to those around us. Generosity has to become second nature to us. Cultivating virtues in our own lives is also a matter of reclaiming ground lost to vices. Vices, too, are habits, or settled-in dispositions. Unfortunately, they come easier to us. We seem to slide easily into habits of laziness, selfishness, carelessness, and the like. These habits become engraved on our character effortlessly. It is a different story with virtues. Anne Frank summed this up nicely: "Laziness may appear attractive, but work gives satisfaction. Virtue is worth the effort."

An education that fosters virtue must also introduce students to society's moral standards and ideals. In common parlance, these are called shared moral values. And this takes us back briefly to that word that has recently been so troublesome for schools: *values.*

Deciding Whose Values to Teach in Public Schools

As we suggested earlier, one of the most dangerous fancies floating around the world today is that everyone has different moral standards and principles. The notion is carried further in suggesting that everyone is entitled to define his or her own moral standards and values. This may be fine if people's racism or dishonesty stays locked up in their own hearts, but once it "goes public" and individuals act on those moral "values," then we have a problem. When the popular 1960s slogan "different strokes for different folks" spills over from aesthetic values to moral values, social harmony is threatened. Our stroke may be "black supremacy" and yours may be "white supremacy." We need to lean on *common* moral values. Such values are a community's social glue; they enable people to live together in harmony.

Although some cultural anthropologists and sociologists might disagree, children are not born into this world with many moral values. However, we are social beings. From birth to old age, we are interdependent. All but a handful of us live in some sort of a community, and we cannot avoid contact with others. Lest we sink into barbarism, we need to educate our children to understand and incorporate the community's shared moral values and standards into their own lives. But accepting that premise brings us quickly to the question, *"Which* moral values? The values of my community, or yours?"* How, in a public school system in a nation as ethnically, religiously, racially, and socially diverse as ours, can we possibly teach moral values without offending one group or another? Without an answer to this, character education becomes a highly suspect operation, if not impossible. We believe, however, that there is a strong and compelling answer to this question.

The answer is much simpler for educators in private and religious schools. People are free to attend or not attend a particular nonpublic school. If a religious person signs his daughter up in a school with a strong atheistic spirit, then he is free to take her out. There is something of a consumer-vendor relationship, which is freely formed and easily broken. The situation is different in the public schools, where many, if not most, children are compelled to attend because their parents lack the wherewithal to pay for private schooling. The public schools need to be aware of and sensitive to the religious and moral values of families. Christina Hoff Sommers, professor of philosophy at Clark University, reminds us of our grounds for doing so:

> We are born into a moral environment just as we are born into a natural environment. Just as there are basic environmental necessities, like clean air, safe food, fresh water, there are basic moral necessities. What is a society without civility, honesty, consideration,

self-discipline? Without a population educated to be considerate, and respectful of one another, what will we end up with? Not
much. . . . We live in a moral environment; we must respect and
protect it. We must acquaint our children with it. We must make
them aware that it is precious and fragile. . . . We must make students aware that there is a standard of ethical ideals that all civili-
zations worthy of the name have discovered.[4]

That said, public schools can be secure in teaching well-
established moral values and standards, the social glue we need to
survive together peaceably. For example, the moral value to treat
other people with respect is basic to a well-ordered society and essential to a well-run school. Beginning with the cardinal virtues we
outlined in Chapter One, there is a core of common-ground values that quickly come to the surface when educational communities come together to identify them. These lists of core moral
values and standards may vary slightly from one community to the
next. The way in which one community articulates patriotism or
service may be somewhat different from how another community
defines them, but there is nevertheless a large overlap in the content that emerges. The Chicago public schools, for instance, have
identified ten core values that they believe are essential: caring,
courage, courtesy, fairness, family pride, kindness and helpfulness,
honesty and truthfulness, responsibility, respect, and a work ethic.
In the Tempe Union School District, in Phoenix, Arizona, we find
a different list, with enormous overlap. How do these large districts, serving thousands of students, arrive at consensus on these
matters? First they establish the need to have a foundation of core
values in their schools. Then they invite parents, teachers, students,
clergy, and community members to meet and discuss shared moral
values and virtues. Finally, they give names to the habits and dispositions they want the school to foster in their children.

Perhaps this sense of a common core of moral values and standards is easier to understand in a more homogeneous nation, such
as Denmark or Japan. In a country as diverse as the United States

(and one in which that diversity is highly cherished), the issues—on the surface, at least—seem troubling. But Americans have no stronger moral principle than "all men are created equal." We affirm that all of us share a common humanity, and with that affirmation come shared rights and shared obligations. As Americans, we live under the Constitution and the Bill of Rights. Our laws bind each of us, and each of us is entitled to due process under the law. Certainly the schools should teach our founding documents, since they represent the social covenant under which we live together. But is that all there is?

The late C. S. Lewis spent much of his academic life wrestling with the question of whether or not the cultures of the world—both modern and, especially, ancient—shared moral principles and values or whether various cultures lived under vastly different ethical systems. Having studied the histories and holy books of Hindu, Egyptian, Greek, Roman, American Indian, Buddhist, Babylonian, Christian, Hebrew, and many other cultures, he came to the definite conclusion that in all these enduring societies and cultures there was a way, a common road, that they all shared. Although different cultures emphasized different standards or values, there existed a common core. Lewis called this common way the Tao, after a term used in the writings of the sixth-century B.C. teacher Lao-tzu.

In the appendix of his 1947 book *The Abolition of Man: How Education Develops Man's Sense of Morality,* Lewis lists many of the moral principles and values of these cultures as evidence for this common way, or Tao. The statements below highlight some of these moral facts of life:

- Human kindness is essential to a fully functioning society.
- We owe a special love, loyalty, and support to our parents and our families.
- We have a special relationship to future generations, especially our own children.
- Married people have certain rights and responsibilities in relation to each other.

- Some degree of honesty is needed for a society to function smoothly.
- We are obliged to help the poor, the sick, and the less fortunate.
- Basic property rights must exist in any organized society.
- Some things exist that are worse than death, such as treachery, murder, betrayal, and torturing another person.
- Our own inevitable death colors how we view life and, coupled with the promise of our posterity, gives the continuum of life its meaning.[5]

These moral values and principles make up the *good* that we propose students come to know, love, and do. It takes virtue, then, to live according to these principles. American public school educators can consciously and confidently teach this inheritance. Indeed, this Tao is the legacy and the responsibility of all the world's educators.

Philosopher Andrew Oldenquist has stated the case nicely from an anthropological perspective:

> If we were anthropologists observing members of a tribe, it would be the most natural thing in the world to expect them to teach their morality and culture to their children, and moreover, to think that they had a perfect right to do so on the ground that cultural integrity and perpetuation depended on it. Indeed, if we found that they had ceased to teach the moral and other values of their culture, we would take them to be on the way to cultural suicide: We would think them ruined, pitiable, alienated from their own values and on the way out.[6]

Character education, then, is not a frill or another passing fad. It is an essential task of a society to make sure that its children forge the necessary virtues and moral values that advance human life. To use Oldenquist's phrase, to do less is to commit "cultural suicide."

Chapter Three

Building a Community of Virtue

New York City, home of Carnegie Hall, Times Square, the Brooklyn Bridge, the Statue of Liberty, the Yankees, and the Mets, is celebrating its one hundredth anniversary with an outpouring of civic pride. And New Yorkers have reason to celebrate. Although it is certainly not without its flaws, the Big Apple is the "comeback kid" of American cities. Within ten years, New York City has gone from the murder capital of the nation and a town with a well-earned reputation for filth and inefficiency to an again-thriving tourist and economic Mecca. And behind the glitter and the crowing of the city's politicians are some solid changes, particularly a dramatic decline in violent crime and the rebirth of the city's neighborhoods.

What accounts for this surge in the moral life of the city? In his discussion of "defining deviance down," Daniel Patrick Moynihan, the senior senator from New York and an urban sociologist by training, points out that cracking down on the little things effects positive change in the moral life of a city. Getting the prostitutes and hustlers off the streets was the first step. Next went the intimidating beggars and squeegee men. Then it was loitering and drinking on street corners and stoops that was targeted. When the New York Police Department started taking graffiti, vandalism, and shoplifting more seriously, drug dealing in the streets plummeted. Mayor Giuliani remains committed to the "little things approach" and has recently asked for increased vigilance against jaywalkers to enhance safety in the streets. The police chief has written about making public places "learning environments."

Behind all these improvements is a citizenry that decided to change, to take its city back. Big Apple residents are rejuvenated and have invested themselves in restoring a stronger spirit of community. A case in point is the Bronx's Crotona neighborhood, which was devastated by tenement fires in the 1970s but has recently been brought back to life by its inhabitants. The *New York Times*[1] reports that it is thanks to scrappy community advocates like Mr. Astin Jacobo (a community overseer who grew up in Crotona), church groups, and organized tenant associations and housing programs that new construction has come to the neighborhood. The resulting new homes and modest gardens are the surest signs that after years of abandonment, this neighborhood is poised to rejoin a city that, in the latter part of the 1990s, is enjoying the bounty of more jobs, less crime, and growing optimism.

What are some other sure signs of a flourishing city or community? Clean parks and sidewalks, provisions for the homeless and vulnerable, a high percentage of registered voters, thriving church communities, and energized civic associations are among the key indicators. These indicators suggest that both a community's citizens and its public servants have a stake in and benefit from the city they inhabit. Good cities emphasize their citizens' responsibilities and protect their rights, enabling them to flourish both individually and collectively. Peace, prosperity, and freedom may be blessings, but they are also hard-earned achievements. That all this is a matter of degree is clear from the recent *celebration* that Brooklyn had gone a full week without a murder.

The early Greeks laid the foundation for our understanding of what a city is. The Greek city, or *polis,* consciously cultivated particular habits or virtues among its citizens, habits that the Greeks had learned were necessary for life in the city, or "civilized life." A city was more than a shared physical space. It was a group of people—citizens—who shared a vision of what constituted a good life.

It was a safe place, particularly compared with the spaces outside the city walls, where people were vulnerable and had to stand alone against barbarism. And the Greeks were quite conscious that a just city did not come to be by chance. Then as now, good cities required a solid political and moral architecture. The *polis* was not merely a haven from barbarism and vulnerability but also a center of civic life and learning. To flourish, a society must rest upon a covenant of shared principles between citizens who are ready to fulfill their civic obligations. Personal and social responsibility, combined with allegiance to shared ideals, are integral to the moral fiber of the body politic. Therefore an education in one's culture and civic duties is essential.

History has shown us that societies, from classical Athens and Rome to twentieth-century Berlin and Sarajevo, fall when their moral framework crumbles. When a people or government fails to attend to what holds their city together, when citizens have little regard for the common good, when political leaders betray or distort the moral ideals and principles for which they supposedly stand, then as Yeats prophetically pointed out, "Things fall apart; the centre cannot hold / The best lack all conviction, while the worst / Are full of passionate intensity." History is full of examples of the dire consequences of that intensity, from the burning of Atlanta to the bombing of Baghdad.

Like a city, a school is "a thing made." It is a social construction, and as such, it can rise or fall. School communities are themselves microcosms of the city they inhabit. They, too, must be communities of virtue, built on a solid frame. This frame, similar to a city's moral and political architecture, arises from a school's set of core beliefs and principles (who its people are) and its driving purpose or mission (what they stand for). These principles are either upheld, in the same way that a city upholds its laws, ensuring order, safety, and equal opportunity for its citizens, or they are lost and thwarted in the face of competing priorities. When the members of a school community have ownership in core beliefs and principles and are committed to them—like the citizens of Crotona in the Bronx—there is a rebirth of learning and pride in the school. In contrast, when students, teachers, and parents are cut off from what goes on in their school or are not invested in it, the moral life of the school begins to fall apart.

Communities of virtue are both made and sustained by the moral ethos of the school, by its distinctive climate or atmosphere. The word *ethos* is borrowed directly from the Greek and means "character, a person's nature or dispositions." And the ethos of a school is a profound character educator. Building a strong moral ethos in classrooms and throughout an entire school community is what this chapter is all about. For as our colleague Charles Glenn puts it, "Only a school of character can aspire to foster character in its pupils."

The Teaching Power of a School's Ethos

As Gerald Grant put it in *The World We Created at Hamilton High,* "Much of what we have become as a nation is shaped in the schoolyard and the classroom."[2] Since environment has a profound impact on children's development, we need to pay strict attention to our schools' environments. School absorbs an enormous chunk of our children's lives. Beginning when they have barely moved from the Big Wheel to the tricycle and continuing on through their adolescence, children spend the majority of their waking hours in the environment of a school. Like the citizens of the Greek *polis,* members of a school community incur specific obligations that shape the way they habitually behave.

We are social beings and forge our lives in a social context. Classroom and school environments give rise to a variety of social relationships: among students, teammates, and cast and choir members; among teachers, administrators, and staff; between students and teachers; between students and bus drivers, cafeteria staff, and custodians. The connective tissue that sustains these relationships—whether it is trust, encouragement, mutual respect, cooperation, collaboration, and selflessness, or mistrust, fear, power, manipulation, competition, and antagonism—has a powerful character-shaping influence. In sum, the ethos of a school has both an inevitable and a potentially permanent educational power.

Unfortunately, sometimes the principles that govern a school's ethos do not draw out the best in its students. Sometimes, indeed, they provoke the worst. Students quickly pick up on the tacit values at work in their school community and build their patterns of behavior around them. For example, survival skills are cultivated in environments where older children bully younger children. Manipulation and cheating are heightened in schools where rank in class and academic achievement are prized above all else. There is no such thing as an ethos-less school. Within a given school community students will either learn to develop and thrive as persons of strong moral character or to slide by, manipulate the system, cave in under pressure, and compromise their family, their faith, or themselves.

With over 850 students in pre-K through second grade, Easterling Primary School, in Marion, South Carolina, serves a large population of youngsters. But that is the least of the school's challenges. Six housing projects feed into Easterling. Says Principal Zandra Cook, "Our children associate with people every day who do not live by the codes we live by here in the Easterling Primary School. The greatest challenge we face is to ensure that our children learn to transfer those skills and habits of character into environments that don't support them." Building students' confidence in their ability to make a difference is at the heart of Easterling's mission. "We tell our children," Cook continues, "when you know what's right, do what's right, and you can be a leader." All reports suggest that this message is getting through to Easterling students.

Actions That Support a Community of Virtue

How can schools support a community of virtue among their students? The following paragraphs provide a few suggestions.

There are a number of initiatives we can take to build a community of virtue. When these actions are intentional, we help to raise everyone's awareness about what matters most in our school community. A community of virtue is supported by a developed sense of the common good and a commitment to advancing it. The common good is those social practices that affirm our common humanity and provide for the betterment not only of individuals but also of all people. Advancing the common good is a basic project in a democratic society. And it is also the "unfinished" project that young people need to be invited to take up.

Aiming Higher

Without goals, we flounder. Without demanding goals, we settle for mediocrity. Schools must hold high expectations, both for academic performance and for character, and work consistently to help students live up to them. In Phoenix, Arizona, for example, the Mountain Pointe High School motto, "Purpose, Pride, and Performance" resonates throughout the school, bolstering everything from students' academic goals to their class discussions, soccer practices, and championship pep rallies. One student summed up her experience at Mountain Pointe this way:

> There are three things I live by. These three things have only been there for a few years, but I hear and see them every day: "Purpose, Pride, and Performance." *Purpose*—the word that reminds me of why I am here and what I have to accomplish. *Pride*—what makes me stand tall each time I hear my name. *Performance*—the actions I take to move forward in my life. I have had four years at Mountain Pointe High School to live by these vows, and they have definitely

made me a better person. I may not be a "perfect" role model, but I feel I have accomplished more at this school than I have anywhere else.

Creating Resonance

A friend of ours returned from a piano lesson the other day and exclaimed proudly, "I'm working on 'digging in.'" "What do you mean?" we asked, puzzled. "My piano instructor said that anyone can make pretty sounds by gliding along the surface of the keyboard," our friend explained. "But to make beautiful music, you have to dig deep into the notes. . . . Then the sound resonates." Building a community of virtue is not simply about aiming high or having lofty goals; it is about "digging in." There is an intense concern to see that in all aspects of school life—from the cafeteria to the playground, from the classroom to the faculty lounge—virtue is modeled, taught, expected, and honored. In a school with a strong moral ethos, virtue and the opportunity to practice it resonates throughout the community.

Instituting Meaningful Service

"Community service," "service learning," "mandatory service hours," and the like are high on the agenda of educational reform. In today's highly politicized atmosphere, we caution schools not to approach service superficially. We do not want our students simply fulfilling a requirement or beefing up their resume. Service can become an empty ritual, or worse. And although it can be a powerful learning event for students, service is not simply about engaging our students in productive work. We need to help them reflect on why it is important to take responsibility for the school community and to take care of those who are less fortunate than they are. The school community is an ideal place to invite students to give more of themselves. There are numerous opportunities to work as a class: removing graffiti, planting a garden, managing the school recycling program. Giving older students an opportunity to read to or tutor younger students not only helps them acquire the habit of service but also builds friendships between grades. Further, it gives the younger students a close look at older, service-rendering role models.

Mound Fort Middle School, in Ogden, Utah, has transformed its ethos completely by linking its efforts to improve literacy with a service program. Six years ago the faculty agreed they needed to focus aggressively on reading, because most of their students were illiterate. In addition to bringing in reading specialists to train the teachers, students were trained to read aloud. Now students practice and share their skills each week by reading stories to the elderly in a local nursing home and to children in the neighboring elementary school. Not only have scores skyrocketed, says Principal Tim Smith, but also violence in the school has plummeted. Perhaps one of the most telling results of this schoolwide effort comes from a parent who was astounded to discover her previously television addicted, thirteen-year-old son reading to his little sister instead of watching his favorite shows.

Encouraging Student Ownership

To build a community of virtue, students must have a stake in its construction. They must "buy in" rather than be forced in. They need to understand and embrace the principles behind their school's moral code. Regardless of how a school community chooses to label its code, it should be grounded in principles everyone understands and embraces. When students have ownership of their code, anyone in the school community can ask them with confidence, "This is our school, so how can we solve this problem together?" "What might you do differently next time?" "What do you think is the best thing to do?" Moral maturity and freedom require more than mere adherence to the law; they require an understanding of the why and wherefore of its rules and regulations—the principles that make it worthy of their allegiance.

Bailey Gatzert Elementary School, in Seattle, Washington, serves a diverse student population. Five years ago, says one veteran teacher, "the playground was like a battlefield." There has since been a radical improvement in student behavior and academic performance, due largely to the school's Four Promises program. Everyone in the school community promises to act in a safe and healthy way, to respect the rights and needs of others, to treat all property with respect, and to take responsibility for their learning. It was not the four promises alone that effected change. The administration, teachers, and playground staff were also committed to teaching children how to play fairly. Additionally, the in-school counseling and family support workers join the staff in constantly referring to these four promises. By invoking the notions of honor and commitment, however, the school has tapped a deeper motivation than compliance with rules and regulations. When students feel ownership of their school's ethos, teachers are not the ones who say, "We don't do that here!" Students will become invested in a world they help create.

Remembering the Little Things

The moral life of a community is made up of many little things, and a community of virtue attends to those little things. On the academic front, everything from helping students see the importance of finishing their work neatly, completely, and on time to teachers' keeping their word about quiz dates, deadlines, and grading criteria falls under the umbrella of "the little things." Emphasizing the school's appearance is another constant invitation to grow in virtue. Hanging student work attractively, putting tables and chairs back where they belong, leaving the blackboard clean, and returning books to the library are among the long list of daily responsibilities that should be shared by everyone in the school community. Just as paying attention to the little things helped change the moral life of New York City, it will also improve the moral ethos of a school community and foster pride in its members.

Building Close Relationships

Warm friendships and close relationships are part of the connective tissue that sustains a community of virtue. In recent decades, schools have attempted to break down the walls between people through sensitivity training in an array of areas, from ethnic, religious, and cultural diversity to sexual orientation and gender identity. This was and continues to be done to promote tolerance and healthy relationships. But, quite frankly, we have found just the opposite to be the end result of these efforts. Programs that point up our differences rather than celebrate what we have in common can, in fact, be a hollow experience, ignored by teachers and mocked by students. As one student put it, "after we went to our diversity seminars, everyone split for lunch and sat at tables with students from their own ethnic groups."

We agree that tolerance of civil dissent is critical to public discourse in a democracy. Tolerance is not a virtue in and of itself, however. Children as well as adults seek not to be tolerated but to be trusted and respected, to be understood and befriended. Tolerance demands very little of us. We may tolerate—put up with—a man sitting next to us on a train who is speaking very loudly, but that doesn't mean we respect him. Furthermore, if we teach our children to tolerate all differences, they may never learn that some things in life—such as genocide, character assassination, or torture, for example—are simply intolerable. With overzealous efforts to sensitize them to differences, we may end up desensitizing them to important moral distinctions. As Ogden Nash aptly put it in "Yes and No" (in the 1936 collection *I'm a Stranger Here Myself*):

Sometimes with secret pride I sigh
to think how tolerant am I;
Then wonder which is really mine:
Tolerance or a rubber spine.

Lynn Lisy-Macan, principal of the Brookside Elementary School, in Binghamton, New York, built her school's character education effort on the cohesiveness resulting from closer bonds among the people in her building. "I saw a real need to work on relationships with each other—teachers with teachers and teachers with students," she explained. Their focus has proved fruitful. "There's a certain feeling here at Brookside. Kids hold doors for adults. They speak to adults, and they are respectful. . . . There is a strong sense of community in the way children interact. As a staff we're making strides, but as adults it's hard to change. . . . We still fight, but I believe our foundation is stronger. Students and teachers feel closer. There is a strengthened connectedness. . . . We used to call character education a program. Now it's part of our culture."

Caring Enough to Correct Others

In an address to his students at the opening of the fall term, F. Washington Jarvis, our headmaster friend, explained to an auditorium filled with junior and senior high school students, "People who take the time to criticize you are often, in my experience, the ones who love you the most."[3] We live in an era of "positive thinking" and "warm fuzzies." It is also an era that underestimates the resilience and realism of youth. To build a community of virtue, we certainly need to take the time and the interest in our students (and colleagues) to offer a word of encouragement and sincere praise when it is warranted. But we also need to be ready to correct them—and be skilled at doing so—and offer advice that will help them grow in virtue. Helping a student get an objective picture of the consequences of his rude behavior is not easy. Trying to do it entirely through positive comments is impossible.

Conditions That Create a Negative Ethos

Movies, newspapers, and the nightly television news have given many of us a negative stereotype of our urban schools. Images immediately come to our minds of children trying to learn in hostile environments, of danger lurking outside the schoolhouse door (and inside it, too), of disruptive boys and girls, indifferent teachers, and ineffective administrators. The attention given on TV to burly police officers, metal detectors, and surveillance cameras wrongly suggests that our urban schools are nothing less than junior state penitentiaries. This is not only a hackneyed image but a gross and destructive one as well. In fact, many urban public schools have a wonderful and constructive ethos. Suburban and private schools, meanwhile, tend to benefit from the opposite stereotype. Yet more than a few of these schools are afflicted with serious moral problems. Ethos varies enormously from school to school. What follows is an anecdote that illustrates how easily we can be deceived about the ethos of a school.

We heard an account some time ago from a high school teacher who had been tenured for many years in a quite comfortable suburban school district. Her high school was famous as a "lighthouse school" because of its reputation for excellence and its students' high academic, artistic, and athletic achievement. She told of an encounter with a senior, a boy she had taught when he was a freshman and at the time of this incident was teaching in a senior English elective. In was late in the school year, and concerned because he was becoming more and more withdrawn, she asked him to see her during a free period in her room. She was aware, too, that although he was one of the school's most outstanding students, he had recently lost a competition for the school's top college scholarship. The teacher acknowledged that although he had been one of her students for over a year and a half, she really didn't know him that well. She knew that he was very disciplined, as he had to balance a job at a 7-11 with his commitments to the debate squad and the wrestling team, which he captained. The teacher had heard, too, that the reason he worked was because there was no father at home and he needed to help out. Apparently, he had started a lawn maintenance business when he was in the eighth grade and now was able to make real money during the summer months. She related that she just wanted to give him a "little pep talk to get him out of his funk."

Their talk started slowly, with her asking a number of probing questions. After several monosyllabic answers and long pauses, he stared at her and said sardonically, "I mean no disrespect, but you don't get it, do you? You think you know what is going on in this school, but you're like the rest. You don't have a clue." Offended and somewhat defensive, she challenged him to back up his charge. And he did. He was clearly outraged by the unprincipled behavior of the majority of his classmates and some of the school's teachers. When she pushed him for specifics, he first got red in the face and then related chapter and verse about the prevalence of cheating and plagiarism among his classmates. The young woman who had been awarded the scholarship was apparently a notorious cheater. So were several others among the school's academic cream. He also insisted that although most of the teachers let it happen because they were too lazy to seriously monitor exams or adequately correct written work, he knew of three teachers that students claimed had caught them cheating but just wouldn't go to the trouble of making them pay the consequences.

He claimed that the vice-president of the student council had told him late one night when they were away at a debate tournament that since the ninth grade a handful of their classmates who had over and over been elected to prestigious positions in student government and various clubs had cynically set out to garner those positions. And they had been astonishingly successful. A debate team mate said that one of the school's history teachers had acted as an informal political advisor to these kids and seemed to get a big kick out of their political intrigues and machinations. He spoke of how teachers and administrators backed down whenever one of the well-connected kids got in trouble and pointed out how ironic it was that they always had to "make an example" of other kids. He talked about how much effort went into educating the talented kids while the rest just got scraps of attention from teachers—"unless, of course, they're important to the team." It came pouring out for a half hour. Finally, he said, "Lookit. I've got to get to work. But come on. Face it. The kids all know it. This place is a moral garbage can." The teacher could say nothing to the boy. She was stunned and paralyzed and as embarrassed as she had ever been.

What, then, contributes to a school with no soul, a school in danger of becoming a "moral garbage can"? The following are a few of the warning signs.

No Shared Vision or Ideals

When a shared vision or set of ideals is not embedded in a school community, then "Who cares?" and "Why bother?" become the silent mantra of many students. When disrespect ("dissing" peers and adults) is common, when "please," "thank you," "excuse me," and holding doors are all just remnants of a stuffy propriety that's gone out of style, when cheating and "getting by" are the norm, we can say with sad confidence that the school ethos does not foster respect, thoughtfulness, and diligence. We suggest posting the school's vision and mission statement prominently and referring to it frequently in both class meetings and faculty meetings.

Competition Run Amok

Cutthroat competition—on the sports field, in spelling bees, or in the AP calculus classroom—undermines community. Coaches who habitually fight with referees or storm off the court, swearing, after a loss send a clear signal to students: winning is what counts the most. Students who are both pushed to "look out for number one" and systematically rewarded for doing so are trained to be selfish and arrogant rather than cooperative and understanding. Character-building schools recognize students for their improvement, commitment, and sportsmanship, not simply for their successes and wins.

Little Opportunity to Serve

When students are not expected to remove the toilet paper from the trees in front of the school after a big victory or to monitor a class of younger students at recess, when teachers accept homework hastily done with a sigh ("at least she turned it in"), then a subtle message is reinforced: school is your right, not your responsibility. If students are not given an opportunity to "adopt a grandparent" at a nearby nursing home or to tutor a younger student, then they miss a chance to develop responsibility, generosity, and compassion. In a community of virtue, service is simply a way of life, not an occasion for bells and whistles. Meaningful service has its own intrinsic rewards.

No Traditions

Traditions are the backbone of school spirit, and school spirit is essential to loving the good. Schools without traditions are communities without heart, without a spirit of family, without a respect for history in the making, without a desire for memory making. A school community that does not take advantage of opportunities to celebrate and honor virtue, achievement, and service cannot provide a true framework for building character. Schools of character institute memorable traditions, annual events involving family and school community members, that potentially mark young people for life.

No Student Voice

Schools that do not welcome students' dialogue, inquiries, and recommendations deprive young people of the opportunity to develop self-knowledge, integrity, good judgment, and the ability to deliberate soundly. It's a mistake to tell students that their school or classroom is a democracy—it cannot and never will be. But children need to learn how to participate in a community and to prepare themselves for democratic citizenship. When schools make mere compliance with rules (rather than students' moral maturity) a priority, they sow the seeds of passivity rather than virtue. On the other hand, students become committed to an ethical community through such activities as drawing up classroom constitutions or refining school policies on open lunch.

Neglect of School Grounds and Property

A school's appearance is not everything, but it does make a strong statement to students, teachers, families, and visitors. If the front steps of the school are littered with candy wrappers and cigarette butts, if the school foyer features last year's student work, if scraps of paper and plastic cups litter the hallways, and if it is generally expected that "somebody else" will pick it all up, then students and teachers alike become indifferent to their school community. In character-building schools, students take pride in their classrooms and school grounds. They participate in lunchroom cleanup and the upkeep of the playing fields, and so on.

Ineffective Character Educators, or "Miss-the-Mark" Schools

Society's deepening worry about our children in recent decades has inspired some educational efforts notable for their good intentions, their ability to capture headlines, and their complete inability to create schools of character. Without thoughtful consideration of what character education means, schools may occasionally play pretty music, but their haphazard efforts never truly resonate in the lives of their students. Following are three approaches that run such a risk.

The Social Services Mall

Particularly in large middle and high schools, the school community can be conceived of as a social services agency rather than an educational institution. Increasingly, teachers of all disciplines and grade levels spend long hours (and their school's limited financial resources) attending professional training programs on drug and alcohol abuse, pregnancy prevention, and AIDS awareness. Additionally, students spend class time on small-group and private sessions in which they receive "peer support" and psychological counseling. The fires of social problems rage fast and furious, and these schools strive to keep up with all the technical and curricular support available that promises to put out the blaze. These deeply moral issues are often presented and dealt with in a value-free manner ("Here are the facts, now you make up your own mind"), hindering any real moral or intellectual growth.

The Substitute Nanny School

A second popular model that holds firm in a number of our elementary schools is that of the school as child care provider. Given the depressing trends in youth crime and the declining moral influence and very existence of the nuclear family, many public schools have done their best to offer a safe haven for children for six to nine hours a day. Providing early morning and afternoon child care as well as government-subsidized meals, the school community's function becomes one of keeping kids off the streets and out of trouble rather than educating them. Although it is a worthy goal to provide material needs for children whose parents cannot do so, it is not the schools' essential mission. This approach can lead to students' sensing that they are simply being parked in school for the day. In such schools, the goals of character development and academic growth are frequently given little attention.

The Achievement-at-All-Costs School

Some schools take an extremely laissez-fare approach to community building. Ignoring the need to build character and schoolwide esprit de corps, they believe their sole purpose is to drill students in academics. Such schools can become nothing more than hard-driving information dispensers. Often they take the stance that parents, religious groups, and youth organizations have sole responsibility for children's moral development. They are much more concerned with the "three *R*s" and technology training than with character education. Their fundamental belief is that if the schools provide the academic knowledge and skills training people need to succeed in the workplace, then they are doing fine by their students.

None of these approaches, either alone or in combination, provides a positive character-forming influence. But there is an alternative model—the school as a community of virtue—in which academics and character are developed hand in hand. Fusing these two goals creates a synergy in which each objective advances the other. Thus we believe that a community of virtue provides a much richer context for students' intellectual and moral growth than do any of these other approaches.

"Lesser Places" Where Character Education Takes Place

In addition to the obvious place—in the classroom—character education of some sort or another can occur in a number of other, unexpected places in the school. Just as attention to the "little things" contributes to the moral life of the community, so does attention to its "lesser places." What follows are discussions of potentially miseducative environments in and around the school, each accompanied by a set of questions that invite the reader to transform these lesser places into corners of character building.

The School Bus

Many students are bused to and from school every day, and here they learn yet another moral code. Some schools have assertively addressed "bus issues" with their students. But more often than not, taunting, ridiculing, yelling obscenities, and just plain harassing other students are characteristic pastimes on the ride to and from school. Some parents complain; some bus drivers initiate a zero-tolerance policy concerning swearing and horsing around. On many buses, however, the intervention occurs long after the emotional (and sometimes physical) damage has already been done. Here again, children learn to either fight back or retreat from trouble. Others steel themselves and step onto the bus with fear in their guts. Threatened by their assailants not to tell their parents or teachers what has happened or they'll get it worse next time, children who are picked on on the bus have yet another reason to dislike school. The code of the school bus is survival of the psychologically fittest, or as one student told us, "It's put down or be put down."

To turn a bad bus climate around, consider these questions:

1. Are the bus drivers treated as important members of the school community? For example, are they recognized at annual assemblies or thanked by parents, students, and school staff?
2. Does the school respond immediately to a problem on a bus by calling a meeting with the students involved and their parents?
3. Are the bus drivers supported and recognized by the school as character educators? Are they encouraged to uphold the school's code of expectations and virtues on the bus?

4. Do parents back the school and the bus driver when they are asked to speak with their child about misbehavior on the bus?
5. Do older students look out for new and younger students who are riding the bus for the first time? What can be done to foster this kind of Big Sister, Big Brother tradition on the bus?
6. Do students feel safe on the bus? If not, why? Are these issues being addressed proactively?

The Hallways

In one urban school we've visited, students walk silently through the hallways, in single file, accompanied by stern-faced teachers armed with walkie-talkies. The teachers look more like prison guards escorting inmates through a penitentiary than teachers leading sixth graders from class to class. A college senior recounted for us her experience in a private high school that prided itself on its students' intellectual achievements and its impressive list of Ivy League acceptances. All the students knew that there was one hallway you shouldn't walk down alone because a particular group of boys liked to play "gang rape" in a closet down that way: "They didn't actually rape anyone. But they liked to bang on the walls and make a lot of noise, sometimes pulling a girl in to get a few good screams going as well. . . . I couldn't figure out why they got such a kick out of it. That is just one example among many of the sick things kids did and got away with. None of the teachers knew; or if they did, they didn't do anything about it."

Here are a few things to ask yourself about your school's hallways:

1. Do teachers and administrators make eye contact with students and greet them in the hallways?
2. Are the hallways clean and safe?
3. Do the adults in the school make an effort to keep student work posted neatly?

4. Is there zero tolerance for vulgar language and gestures? Are public displays of affection tolerated? Are these issues discussed among the faculty and staff so as to promote a coherent character-building effort, or simply as disciplinary problems?
5. Are the hallways clear during class time? Could adults circulate the hallways more frequently—not necessarily as police agents but as reminders to students that the adults in the building care about where they are and how they are spending their time?

Study Halls

Monitoring study halls is among the least desirable jobs teachers have to assume, especially in schools where students have two or more study halls a day. In some schools, students perceive quiet study halls as either a cruel punishment or an exciting challenge to see what they can get away with. Everything goes, from roaming the halls under the pretense of going to the lavatory to flipping through *Seventeen* magazine, *TV Guide,* or, yes, even *Hustler.* The lessons here are many: "You don't have to take the study hall monitor seriously, because she's not your teacher." "You can do whatever you want." "Study hall is a free zone."

Ask yourself these questions to help turn your school's study halls around:

1. Are students being assigned adequate (and engaging) homework, so that they have something to do when they arrive in study hall? Are students taught that using study halls well is an effective way to learn to manage their time and improve their study habits?
2. Are students required to arrive in study hall with books, pens, papers, and necessary supplies? Is there a reasonable way for students who want to work on a group project to do so without distracting the rest of the class?

3. Are the study hall monitors alert to what students are doing in class? Do they permit note writing or inappropriate magazines?
4. Have the teachers met to discuss the issues and challenges of leading a quiet study hall? Have they worked out a policy and set of expectations in keeping with the school's core virtues?

The Lavatories

Another frequent "free zone" is the lavatory. "Everybody knows that smoking ain't allowed in school"—except in the bathrooms. Starting as early as the fifth grade, students learn many creative ways to smoke in school. A popular one is to climb up onto the toilet, light up, and blow the smoke into the vents. If an adult happens to enter, a quick drop and flush eliminates the evidence immediately. What else goes on in this free zone? For younger students, the boys' and girls' rooms offer students their first encounter with four-letter words and dirty drawings. Students are maligned by a few words etched on stall doors—"For a good time call . . ." Fights start, gossip soars. Not too long ago, it was reported that some sixth-grade boys had taken obscene Polaroids of willing sixth-grade girls and then sold the kiddie porn to other boys in their school.

Here are a few points to consider to help turn your school's lavatories around:

1. Are the bathrooms in the school safe, clean, and in working condition? That is, are the doors on their hinges, do the lights and faucets work, and do the windows open?
2. Are there adequate supplies of soap, paper towels, and toilet paper?
3. If the walls are covered with graffiti, can each class participate in a "bathroom beautification" project, scrubbing or repainting the walls? Activities like this can conclude with a picnic, pizza lunch, or sundae party sponsored by the PTO.
4. Are the bathrooms properly monitored by adults or responsible students to ensure that smoking, gossip, vandalism, and other inappropriate activities are nipped in the bud?

The Playground

The playground is a powerful place in elementary school. Here the rules of the student community are forged. Students pick their best friends to be on their kickball team. Some students are always picked last or left free to drift to the sidelines as loners. A stray student punches another child and leaves him bruised and crying. When the bell rings, all scramble to line up and file back inside to their classroom. At least two students have taken a moral lesson away from the playground: "Might makes right" and "No one cares about me, so I've got to look out for number one."

If this sounds like your school's playground, ask yourself these questions to help turn it around:

1. Is the playground an inviting and clean area in which students can play safely?
2. Can a few games or sports be organized and overseen by older students or playground monitors to minimize exclusion and maximize student involvement?
3. Do teachers and monitors take time out to discuss positive and negative playground incidents (with individual students or the whole group, depending on the situation)?
4. Do monitors and older students stop fights, foul language, and littering immediately?
5. Can different grade levels be assigned to clean up and spruce up an area of the playground as a class project?

The Cafeteria

In the 1970s cult film *Animal House,* John Belushi popularized "food fights" in schools across the country. Projectile food remains high on the list of fears harbored by teachers on lunch duty. In many elementary, middle, and high schools, lunchtime is for the most part sheer bedlam. Cafeteria employees brace themselves before the crowds descend on them. Fifth graders jostle younger students to get ahead of them in line. Shouting is the accepted mode of discourse. Territorial about their tables, children rush to save seats for their best friends. Although it's understandable that children need to release pent-up energy at lunch, the pushing, shoving, name-calling, and generally raucous behavior seen in a great number of cafeterias fosters an élan of aggression rather than self-control and courtesy. Lunchtime becomes more an effort to fend for oneself than to celebrate time together as a community.

Here are some questions to help you tame a rowdy cafeteria:

1. Are the school's core virtues and code of expectations posted in the cafeteria?
2. Do teachers and other adults in the school speak with students and visit tables for friendly conversation during lunchtime?
3. Are students assigned jobs in the cafeteria on a rotating basis? For example, different students could be responsible for reminding classmates to throw their trash away when they're finished eating, distributing drinks or lunches, sweeping the floor, wiping down tables, or pushing chairs back under the tables when lunchtime is over.
4. Do the cafeteria monitors remind students to speak and act with courtesy and to wait their turn in line?
5. Are there logical consequences for serious misbehavior in the cafeteria?

The Faculty Room

The teachers' room is perceived by some younger students as a mysterious adult hideaway or a hallowed ground upon which they dare not tread. Although the office space and facilities for teachers vary widely from school to school, it is clear that the faculty lounge can have a pervasive culture of its own. We are concerned here with the teachers' room that looks more like a swill pit than a place of work. When the faculty room becomes the seat of gossip and complaints about students and parents and administrators and fellow teachers, when dirty jokes are more common than collegial exchanges about lesson plans and units, then the health of the school community is being infected from within.

If this sounds like your faculty lounge, ask yourself these questions:

1. What steps can be taken to make the faculty room a more inviting place to work?
2. Can teachers and staff use more professional discretion and care when discussing issues related to students and their parents? Would a faculty honor code or pledge facilitate such a commitment?
3. What initiatives can be taken to promote collegiality and awareness of other teachers' work and talents? Are there planned social events for the teachers and staff?

Examples of Schools of Character

Not all schools of character look the same. What follows are two pictures of very different schools that have taken *who they are* and *what they stand for* seriously and built a community of virtue that expresses their distinctive character.

The Hyde School

In 1966 Joseph W. Gauld, concerned that America's schools were failing to inspire excellence in students, founded the Hyde School—a private boarding high school that is perhaps best known for its success in working with "troubled" youth. Today the Hyde School has two campuses—one in Bath and the other in Woodstock, Connecticut—and a national reputation. Five other schools have adopted some elements of the Hyde "character first" curriculum.

The Hyde School is based on the principle that we each have dignity and a "unique potential that defines a destiny." Helping students achieve this potential means putting "character first." All students are expected to develop these traits:

- The *courage* to accept challenges
- The *integrity* to be truly themselves
- *Concern* for others
- The *curiosity* to explore life and learning
- *Leadership* in making the school and community work

At Hyde, character development is fundamentally a family affair. "We do not take kids unless parents make a commitment to go through our character development program," says Gauld. Parents gather monthly for parent meetings, retreats, and family weekends. Hyde asks parents to look within themselves, find their strengths and weaknesses, and strive to better themselves, for their own sake as well as for their child's. "You have to start with the principle that parents are the primary teachers and home is the primary classroom. . . . If you get to the parents, you get to the kids," says Gauld.

The Hyde faculty know—and students quickly learn—that achieving excellence is not easy. A sign hanging in the school simply reads, "The truth will set you free, but first it will make you miserable." Says Gauld, "I learn the most about myself by facing challenges." Students are not the only ones held to the school's high standards of truth and responsibility; teachers and staff are as well. Students are expected to accept challenges—including mandatory participation in athletics and performing arts. The "building blocks" of excellence in a Hyde education are as follows:

1. *Motions.* The individual is expected to follow the motions of responsible behavior.
2. *Effort.* The individual begins to take pride in meeting his or her given challenges.
3. *Excellence.* The individual begins to pursue his or her best. One discovers and acts on a unique potential.

How does the Motions-Effort-Excellence model look in practice? Malcolm Gauld—the founder's son and the current headmaster—describes taking over the Hyde women's soccer program in the mid-1980s: "The program was in shambles. The girls not only did not want to play soccer but held great disdain for Hyde's mandatory sports policy." At the first practice, he called the girls together and said:

> Okay, I know that many of you would prefer not to be out here. I'm not going to waste my time explaining why this will be good for you or why I think you could begin to develop a love for soccer or athletics. For the next two months, we are simply going to do the things that soccer players do. What do soccer players do? They show up on time. They bring their cleats and leave their purses at home. All of you will be expected to wear special Hyde Soccer T-shirts, which I will order. In short, I expect you to behave like soccer players and keep your attention on task while you're out here on the field.

Although initially he met with great resistance, the coach held them accountable for the motions of responsibility he had outlined. After several weeks, a group of girls made the step from the Motions to the Effort phase, displaying a positive attitude and a greater work ethic at practices. At the end of the season, three girls asked to join a local winter league—they wanted to move up to the Excellence stage. The following season, the three players at the Excellence level served as exemplars for the rest of the team, and a group of Effort-level girls wanted to compete for starting positions. Soon, 90 percent of the players displayed a norm of consistent effort and hard work. This was the beginning of a tradition of championship soccer teams.

When you walk through the halls of Hyde, you may see a student scrubbing the floor or cleaning a bathroom. "All students have jobs here," says Gauld. Students are expected to take responsibility at every level—including taking responsibility for other students. The concept is called "brother's keeper." One student described it this way: "If I respect this person and I love this person, then I want them to go after their best. If it's someone who's going out and drinking, they're not going after their best. I'm going to hold them to that. You view it more as 'How can I help this person?' than 'How can I snitch on this person?'" Says Gauld, "America is a freedom-of-choice society; [Hyde] is a 'choosing-well' environment." At Hyde, students, faculty, and parents believe that "we're trying to make the best choices possible, and it's my responsibility to let you know when you are not making good choices."

The "Hyde Solution" goes beyond rhetoric: it embodies a fundamental commitment to individual character development. At Hyde, the purpose of academics is to allow students to develop their unique potential—to help them answer the questions, "Who am I? Where am I going? How am I going to get there?"

Easterling Primary

During an in-class discussion about honesty, a second-grader at Easterling, visibly upset, explained to her teacher, "Mommy made me wear these shoes out of the store. I told her it wasn't honest. But she told me to shut up and do as I'm told." As noted earlier in the chapter, Easterling Primary School may serve little people, but its challenges are big. The school song—"Where Little People Do Big Things"— truly captures the spirit of this Title 1 school in rural Marion, South Carolina.

The whole school environment reflects Easterling's belief that "children are our highest priority." Easterling is, as Principal Zandra Cook and others report, "one big family." In each classroom, children cooperatively design job charts and assign responsibilities. The classrooms are warm and inviting. Everywhere you turn, it is evident that people care. "Even the janitors see children as primary" Cook explains. Furthermore, she adds proudly, "Easterling is a beautiful school." The children's work is displayed on banners in the hallways at all times. A garden designed by an environmental architect in honor of an assistant who died adorns the front of the library.

A magic carpet and fairy tale scenes decorate the library walls. Painted by a volunteer outside the community, "Wee Fox Cafe" (the Easterling mascot is the Wee Fox) is emblazoned across the large awning that serves as the entrance to the cafeteria, and each of the dining room walls brightly features one of the four seasons.

What is the key to their character education effort? "Everything meshes," Cook answers decisively. "We try to integrate everything, to make sure that it's consistent. The children have to understand. This is what makes us strong." Easterling has been diligent in their effort to make things "mesh." The first meshing point is the staff's involvement. Easterling has a faculty character education team, and "they take their job very seriously." The whole school began strategic planning for character education three years ago, and they continue to assess and refine their efforts. Since it opened, Easterling has been surveying parents on their needs and values. As a result, the school's motto, rules, and "common core of human values" represent shared priorities:

Wee Fox Motto

I will treat others the way I want them to treat me.

Wee Fox Rules

1. I am honest
2. I cooperate
3. I show respect
4. I am responsible

Common Core of Human Values

respect

responsibility

justice

kindness

honesty

loyalty

In addition, these values are made a vital part of daily life at Easterling. Teachers weave this core into all their curricular activities. Manners and social skills are taught through the Spanish and drama classes, where students role-play how to "voice an opinion in a kind way or to listen attentively." Schoolwide assemblies and multicultural luncheons provide an occasion for students to appreciate one another's differences. It's not just about costumes and food, however; it's about exploring the history and culture of diverse ethnic groups in an engaging way.

Parent outreach is a third significant feature of Easterling's character education effort. Easterling provides a variety of workshops for parents, on topics ranging from discipline to the content and methodology of its Heartwood Values–based literature program and its Second Step curricula, which teach children to problem-solve and empathize. Consequently, Cook reports, "Our parents know very well how to delve into characterization while reading a story to their children. They know to ask their children, 'How did so and so solve this problem?' or 'What traits did this character possess?'" A parent resource center with books and tapes on child development is open to all families. In keeping with the school's emphasis on early learning, prevention, and parental support, a parent-community group disseminates approximately thirty hospital packets a month to parents of newborns. Easterling's home-school liaison even makes house calls in the school's van, which was purchased with money awarded through the Target 2000 initiative. "We work very hard with our parents," Cook explains. Easterling Primary believes that "the family is the primary influence in society."

Next to parent education, perhaps the most powerful way the school promotes parents as character educators is through its morning television program. Each Friday, fathers visit the school to read stories on the air. "The children love it," Cook says enthusiastically. In fact, the school's daily television program is an effective tool for showcasing models of good character in the school.

Each week, for example, a second grader is selected by his or her peers as "Citizen of the Week" and appointed to co-anchor the program for those five days.

The school has also effectively meshed the business community into their coordinated effort. "We have someone from a business visit each day," Cook explains. Visiting business leaders remind children that "working together, caring for what you do, attendance, consideration for others, and working hard" are essential to being a good employee.

What are the results? Total disciplinary actions are down significantly from last year. But more important, Cook says, "We see a difference in the children's understanding of what character is. They don't know manners, how to express their feelings appropriately, before they come here. No one talks to them much. What we see now is their ability to handle things, to work cooperatively without arguing. We see growth. . . . Especially in children with emotional and behavioral problems, I have seen remarkable changes."

The first of the core beliefs articulated by Easterling Primary reads, "We have an obligation to make a positive difference in the lives of others." Clearly, Easterling Primary is making that difference.

The Framework for a Community of Virtue

What does it take to change the ethos of a school and develop it into a community of virtue? What follows are what we believe to be the key elements and factors that need to be in place:

A Relevant Mission Statement

Revisit your mission and vision statements. Do they articulate shared principles and ideals, such as *who we are* and *what we stand for*? Revise them to reflect the centrality of character in academic and personal development.

Core Virtues

Identify the core virtues that are consistent with your identity and purpose as a school community, specifying those habits that you would like to see practiced among all the members of the school. Most school communities choose to engage in a democratic process of discussing and selecting these core character traits. These virtues (such as respect, perseverance, loyalty, self-discipline, and kindness) will become your starting point in shaping a strong moral ethos.

Partnerships with the Home

Invite parents to collaborate with teachers in a joint effort to help students acquire virtue and develop integrity. Schools need both the commitment and the trust of parents to help children become morally responsible. Parents and teachers must work together to help students understand what it means to take pride in their work and to be personally accountable for what they choose to do or not to do. They can also jointly assist students in their development of intellectual virtues and skills, such as diligence, concentration, listening, planning, and organizing.

Teamwork

Divide teachers and administrators into either grade-level or subject-area teams. Have these teams brainstorm possible ways to create a stronger moral ethos in the classroom. Together they should carefully go over the school's curriculum, assessing its moral richness (or poverty). Then they should work together to develop and exchange lesson plans that tap the moral dimensions of a particular story, event, experiment, or topic. Science teachers need to ask themselves, for example, how conducting a science lab can become a character-building experience for students. Teamwork with one's lab partner, responsibility and care for the instruments and materials used in the experiment, diligence in striving to get the best possible results are among the many lessons that can be included in a science lab.

A Formal Launch

Introduce your character education initiative at a formal assembly for the entire school community. Parents, as well as school, political, and religious leaders, should be invited to celebrate this new effort. This is not intended to serve as a pep rally but rather as a forum to acquaint the community with the school's mission statement, core virtues, policy revisions, and plans for implementing character education schoolwide.

Regular Meetings and Assessment

Make character education a priority item in regular faculty meetings. Discuss and assess the school's moral ethos as well as students' internalization of its core virtues. Individual teachers and staff members should regularly reflect on the following questions:

- Do I strive to integrate the core virtues into my teaching and professional development?
- Do my professional and social relationships with colleagues, students, and parents reflect the principles of character and integrity we hope to instill in our students?
- Do I consistently demand academic and personal excellence from my students?
- Do I foster opportunities for moral reflection during formal and informal classroom activities?

Involved Staff

Involve your library, custodial, administrative, and cafeteria staff, as well as volunteers and bus drivers, to achieve greater resonance. Their work, example, and daily involvement with students should embrace character education. Bus drivers should insist on courteous behavior. Cafeteria workers should expect students to clean up after themselves. Librarians can work with teachers to feature books of characters that inspire students.

Involved Students

Give students a stake in the school's character education initiative. Engage students in creating classroom constitutions and defining behavior expectations. Make sure they know that the school counts on their insights, feedback, example, and leadership in sustaining a community of virtue. Invite students to fill out surveys each year with candid comments on the school's climate, academic classes, and extracurricular activities. Invite them as well to describe how they use their time and their level of engagement in school life. Students need to see that the quality of friendships and relationships in the school is key to the quality of life at the school. Therefore, the school's mission and core virtues should be regularly and carefully reviewed with them.

Integrated Extracurricular Activities

Athletics, performing arts, and clubs all provide opportunities for students to practice the school's core virtues. Students need to see that there is a larger purpose than fun and games behind these activities—to help them develop good habits and good character. The language of virtue and high expectations should be maintained in all of the school's sponsored activities, events, and field trips.

Relevant Evaluation

Some people like to begin with the hard-and-fast data: academic achievement scores, attendance records, number of disciplinary actions, student surveys. We suggest that it is more important to return to your mission statement and core virtues, to reflect on where your school is and where it is heading as a community. What can be done, for example, to promote greater collegiality and support among all the adults in the school? Take a look at absenteeism in your school (among both students and teachers), the condition of the school grounds, the tenor of schoolwide events, the atmosphere in the cafeteria, the language and social interactions in the hallways, the state of the lavatories—to what extent do these corners of your school's life represent who you are and what you stand for?

At this point we would like to risk introducing yet another metaphor, one that may help you to answer this question. In the last decade, American corporations have transformed themselves and become the envy of the world. They have done it in large part by transforming their ethos. In the corporate world, a strong ethos is what distinguishes a mediocre business from an outstanding one. A company's ethos is inspired by its core values and purpose. The extent to which these are embedded in the staff's thinking has a great impact on their job satisfaction and productivity. Three best-selling business books, Collins and Porras's *Built to Last,* Tom Chappel's *Soul of a Business,* and Stephen Covey's *Principle-Based Management,* speak precisely to this point. The first identifies the habits of visionary companies. The second emphasizes the importance of involving all stakeholders in the process of building the corporate culture. What matters most in a successful corporation is not its competitive edge but the community and commitment it creates. Evaluation, then, is not only about assessing results; more importantly, it is about how the company is doing in relation to its identity and purpose. The problem with mediocre corporations is not the lack of a mission but a mission that is not shared deeply. And this, Covey argues, is "the seedbed of most other problems."

Like outstanding corporations, the schools of character we have found are able to state with confidence *who they are* and *what they stand for.* It is these shared ideals and principles that govern these

Chapter Four

Cultivating Character Through the Curriculum

C. S. Lewis tells a story, an allegory, of a mythic country where the educational leaders decided to drop mathematics from the course of studies. This was a popular decision with almost everyone except the mathematics teachers. Students cheered, and the general populace, awash with painful memories of cosines and unbalanced equations, went along with the policy. And all was sweetness and light in this country—for about a dozen years. Then people started noticing that trolley fare collectors never seemed to get the fares right. Confusion and tension abounded as shopkeepers and their customers haggled over incorrect change. The chorus of complaints was ignored until the tax collectors discovered that people were making so many mistakes that the tax system would grind to a halt. Of course, the no-math policy then came under serious review, and mathematics was quickly returned to the curriculum. The target of Lewis's allegory was the British educational authorities, who at the time were supposedly contemplating dropping religion from the curriculum. (They did not.)

Lewis's little story illustrated a truth that is too often forgotten: there is a direct, cause-and-effect connection between a society's education system and its social progress or decline. The Duke of Wellington allegedly announced that "the battle of Waterloo was won on the playing fields of Eton." The power of education to shape not only an individual but also a nation is increasingly being appreciated. And it is not the form of an education that is vital but what goes into it: what is taught and what is learned.

The content of an education is, of course, the curriculum. The concept of the curriculum frequently suffers from multiple loose interpretations, however. A great deal of the meaning of *curriculum* is clarified if it is accompanied by an adjective. For instance, the *formal* curriculum is the planned course of study for a particular subject or, more usually, for the entire school. In most good schools, the formal curriculum is written down and available for inspection by all. It represents what students can expect to be taught and what (with work) they can expect to learn. Beginning in the early grades, though, most schools offer activities for their students on a voluntary basis. Beyond this are the extra, voluntary activities that most schools offer beginning in the early grades. Sports, band, dramatics, and the computer club are all examples of these *extracurricular* activities.

Other curriculum-related terms have received much attention in educational circles in recent years. The *hidden* curriculum, for example, refers to the largely unintended outcomes of schooling. The hidden curriculum encompasses a range of information, from each student's popularity and position in school society to attitudes about competing or cooperating with others. A school's or classroom's rules are sometimes considered part of the hidden curriculum. Students learn a great deal about how to behave in society from how they are taught to behave in school. Chapter Three was essentially about becoming more aware of the hidden curriculum and replacing its negative aspects with positive educational experiences for students.

Another term is the *null* curriculum, which refers to the universe of knowledge and skill that is absent from the official curriculum. In Lewis's story, educators took mathematics out of the formal curriculum and consigned it to the null curriculum. Clearly, since our schools have limited time and there is so much to teach, most of the world's knowledge must remain in the null curriculum.

The concept of the null curriculum is useful in considering changes to the formal curriculum. For instance, until recent decades sex education, driver's education, and drug education were in the null curriculum, but a conscious decision was made to make them part of what is explicitly taught in school.

"The curriculum," then, is the answer to the question, "What should our schools teach?" However, it is also society's answer to a much deeper and more important question: "What is most worth knowing?" The broad framework of a curriculum is a statement of what knowledge, skills, and moral principles students ought to acquire during their time at school. In effect, it is a statement about the kind of people (competent, trustworthy, intellectually curious) the schools should produce. It is a statement of what can be expected of graduates, both academically and personally, when they leave school for the next level of education or to enter the world at large. The larger question is, of course, followed by a host of lesser but still important ones, such as, "When do we teach this principle or that skill?" and "How do we teach it?"

The daily professional life of educators—be they teachers, administrators, or specialists—overflows with pressing questions that affect the lives and futures of students. "Should I teach a particular concept or skill?" "What is the best way to help students understand gravity?" "How do I know they have really learned decimals and percentages?" "Our mathematics department chairperson will be having her baby soon; how can we find a replacement in the middle of the year?" "What can we do to teach our students to behave more civilly in the auditorium?" "What are we going to do about our poor reading scores?" And on and on. We have never met an educator whose plate is not spilling over with pressing questions. The density of these smaller questions, plus the pace of life in school, may explain why the big questions are so rarely asked and even more rarely given the attention they deserve.

In our combined fifty years of attending faculty meetings, spending time in the teachers' lounge, and going to educational conferences, we have witnessed teachers' great dedication and commitment to the curriculum and the enormous effort they invest in both developing it and working from it. With every lesson a teacher plans, she inevitably has to ask herself, "Why is this lesson on the food chain important?" or "What will my students learn from this take-home lab on soil types?" "How can I teach narrative plot structure more effectively?"

One question, however, is rarely asked or discussed among groups of teachers and administrators: "What is most worth knowing?" We know of few faculties or curriculum committees that have deliberately grappled with this mega-question of what in the universe of facts, theories, concepts, literature, music, and the arts is *most* worthy of the attention and retention of students. Very few have asked, "What knowledge and abilities do they need to lead good lives, to participate well in society and appreciate the heart of our civilization?" Schools are centers of action, and teachers rarely have the luxury of being able to wrestle with such questions. We believe, however, that this kind of reflection and dialogue among educators must be encouraged. Although the question of what is most worth knowing appears rarely to be asked in educational circles, this does not mean it has gone unanswered: the de facto answer is the curricula taught in this country's sixty thousand schools.

Most European nations have a central ministry of education. France has perhaps the most centralized of educational systems, characterized by the alleged fact that the minister of education can look out his window at 10:30 in the morning and know that all the fourth-grade students in France are putting away their arithmetic and taking out their reading books. In the United States we have fifteen thousand educational authorities, or school boards, each acting as an authority on the curriculum whether they realize it or not. Although each of these local authorities operates within guidelines set by their state and answers to the state board of education, they all have great freedom and latitude.

The local school boards' greatest power is their authority to answer the what's-most-worth-knowing question. In our system, local districts implement the general educational goals set by the state departments of education, and they can override them in a variety of ways. Also, they can add their own goals, such as developing a high level of music appreciation among their students or adding special vocational skills to complement a local industry. As we saw in Chapter Three, schools can become driven by social goals, such as stamping out smoking and unsafe sex. They can center their curriculum on emerging technologies, such as computers and data processing. They can focus their curriculum on the process skills of learning, on "the basics," or on myriad other themes or emphases. Depending on which expert one speaks with, this local autonomy is either the bane or the genius of American education. Nevertheless, our system's local autonomy allows schools to change their curricula and direction with great speed. Change is a two-edged sword, however, and can be used for true educational reform or the opposite.

An updated, trans-Atlantic adaptation of C. S. Lewis's mathematics story could be written about the American schools that decided two or three decades ago not to "impose moral values" on their students and to leave character education to someone else. The stunning statistics about out-of-wedlock births, drug use, homicides, suicides, cheating, and general unhappiness among American students suggest that we have failed to sow the education fields with our best moral principles and virtues, and we should not be surprised by the resulting weeds and general barrenness. Said another way, we have transferred moral and character education into the null curriculum, and we are now dealing with the results. Cause and effect.

Adding Character Education to the Curriculum

Where does character education fit into the curriculum? The simple answer is this: everywhere. Since education seeks to help students develop as persons, character development is part and parcel of the whole enterprise. Teaching, as Alan Tom reminds us, is a moral act. We believe that learning is a moral act as well. And most certainly, the classroom exists as an ethical community. Character education, then, with its twin goals of intellectual and moral development, should be implicit in all of the school's undertakings. In this chapter, however, we focus specifically on how we can use the formal curriculum to help students develop the virtues that make up good character.

With the growth of the information superhighway, the volume of knowledge deemed worthwhile has been increasing day by day, and all this information is competing to find its way into the curriculum. With this surge and pressure, there is a danger of churning out students who are rapid processors of information but may not necessarily be more reflective, thoughtful, and able to give sustained consideration to the information that matters most. An education that reduces learning to mechanics, skills, and facts is a shallow one—an education that leaves students blind to the moral, intellectual, and cultural fabric of our civilization. The late Josef Pieper contended that "man's ability to see is in decline." Perhaps we are less inclined to penetrate to the meaning of things, to see beyond externals, than we once were. Perhaps our moral vision is in decline. In the miasma of trivial information, mass media, and getting and spending that characterizes our world today, the moral significance of our work, relationships, actions, and experiences becomes blurred. We need to penetrate to the moral questions and ideals embedded in the curriculum and help our children realize that being a good student is a commitment and a responsibility that can indelibly mark their character. Where do we begin?

The great thinkers of both the West and the East have focused on the nature of the individual and the human condition. Their penetrating insights into humanity have helped us see both our human frailties and our potential for greatness. One of the stronger indictments of humanity comes from Hobbes, who summed up our state with the comment "Man is a wolf to man." A constant theme in philosophy is growth and development, the capacity people have to improve themselves, their relationships with others, and their world. The great thinkers have attributed this change, this advancement, to education and culture, which represent the heart of civilization. Education presupposes improvement, but not merely mechanical, cognitive, or social improvement. Education—particularly education that embraces character—is more comprehensive than that. The aim of character education through the centuries has been to help individuals become better human beings—intellectually, morally, and socially. Through character education, we gain the necessary knowledge, understanding, experience, and competencies to lead a richer life. Character education, then, is the vehicle for both personal and societal development. To omit character education from the curriculum is to ignore our potential for growth as civilized persons.

Character education, then, seeks to cultivate wisdom—the practical intelligence and moral insight we need to make good choices and lead our lives well. D. Bruce Lockerbie of Paideia, Inc., articulated this goal nicely in an address to teachers: "It's not information, data, or facts alone I seek and try to convey; it's wisdom in dealing with these facts and wisdom in applying these facts to my dealings with nature and human nature. I'm not as interested in dispensing knowledge on how to make a living as I am in helping young people learn how to make a life. . . . A little knowledge is a dangerous thing, but a lot of knowledge without character means disaster."[1]

The curriculum is a primary source of our shared moral wisdom. It carries our moral heritage. Stories, biographies, historical events, and human reflections provide us with a guide to what it means to lead a good life and possess strong moral character. This moral heritage also includes encounters with human failure, tragedy, injustice, and weak and sinister characters. In effect, the curriculum can be used to sharpen our students' capacity to see what is most important, that is, knowledge of what it means to lead one's life well or poorly.

How do we achieve this goal? First, we need to examine the curriculum. Does it include encounters with complex lives—with individuals who have taken a stand for a noble ideal and lived by their commitments? Does it include individuals like King David and Scrooge, who lived both contemptibly and virtuously? And do teachers invite students to explore what accounted for their change in character? Does the curriculum engage students with a rich enough landscape of compelling images and ideas?

If the curriculum does provide a textured landscape, what are we doing to reveal that texture, to give students an eye for detail and nuance? Do we allow the moral themes to surface, and do we treat them with as much seriousness as we treat learning how to write a paragraph or multiply fractions? Do we help our students see learning in general as a moral responsibility and one that is enhanced by habits such as diligence, intellectual honesty, good judgment, courage, and persistence? Let us examine our practices and aims. Do we give priority to results? In the press of the school calendar and the need to "cover material," we can all fall prey to expediency, to simply getting through this unit and that lesson on time. We need to step back and take a long hard look at what we are trying to accomplish and what our students are learning.

If we want students to understand virtue, we must teach it. And this does not mean instituting a separate course. Although at the middle and high school level an ethics course can be quite useful, what we are advocating here, for all grades, is the deliberate integration of the concept of virtue into every subject taught. In math, social studies, and even gym, we must tell the human story, our shining moments and our dark ones. We should put before young people, those who are to take up the burden and the torch, stories about fascinating lives for whom virtue was far from boring. Women are often given short shrift in the curriculum. Joan of Arc, Susan B. Anthony, Jane Pittman, and Nien Cheng, for example, are just a handful of the women of character whose lives have made more than a mark on history and can make a lasting impression on the hearts and minds of our students. Their stories nurture the moral imagination and plant the seeds of aspiration in young people. Narrative and art have long served as profound teachers, helping us not only to identify models of vice and virtue but also to engage the larger questions: "What is the meaning of life?" "Will being good make me happy?" "What does it mean to be human?"

Questions such as these often get crowded out of the curriculum by a variety of other appeals for our students' attention. The content of the curriculum—whatever it is—always has tough competition, not only from special interest groups in the community but also from society at large and from students' own peer culture. Among the lessons battling for our students' hearts, minds, and wallets are those taught by popular icons, by the fashion industry, and by the mass media. When students aren't engaged by the curriculum in school, they are more likely to be seduced by the culture of easy pleasure. Of course, if we want students to become thoroughly engaged, then the academic curriculum must be taught in a compelling way, such that it engages the head, the heart, and the hand.

In 1997, the Bronx mourned the loss of an outstanding and beloved young high school teacher, Jonathan Levin, who was knifed to death in his apartment, apparently for his ATM card. The assailant was a former student, a young man Levin had tried to mentor years back by offering him personal advice and academic support. However, another more penetrating curriculum dominated this student's life, gangsta rap. Two worlds crowded into the New York synagogue for Levin's funeral. On one side sat Levin's beloved students mourning the loss of their teacher. Mourning on the other side sat Levin's father, CEO chairman Gerald Levin, and his associates—the leaders of the corporation that produced gangsta rap. Columnist Jim Sleeper brilliantly captured the poignant irony of this scene: since the murderer was both a former student of Levin and a faithful disciple and performer of gangsta rap, it wasn't clear "which of the two grieving worlds [had] raised the predator."[2]

This anecdote raises a difficult question: what is the reach of the school's curriculum in the face of such seductive forces in our students' lives? There is no easy answer. Jonathan Levin was a committed teacher who spent time outside of school with the young man who would one day kill him. He tried to engage his student in worthwhile pursuits. Clearly, a number of variables are at work shaping the moral trajectory of our students. Nevertheless, the best we can do—and we are obliged to do it—is to connect them with the most vital moral lessons in the curriculum, and to do so in a thoughtful and compelling way. If we find that the curriculum we are teaching is thin gruel for moral reflection, then we might want to initiate a team meeting to examine how we can enrich the subjects we teach so that they give our students the opportunity they deserve to understand and appreciate our shared moral wisdom.

Bringing Our Moral Heritage into Focus

The French existential philosopher Jean-Paul Sartre wrote, "all literary work is an appeal. . . . You are perfectly free to leave the book on the table. But if you open it, you assume responsibility for it." Educators are likewise responsible for the books they ask their students to open. There are four lenses we can use to draw the moral dimensions of the curriculum into focus: moral literacy, moral imagination, moral discourse, and moral integrity. Using these lenses, teachers and students can together focus on what's most worth knowing.

Developing Moral Literacy

Taking our cue from E. D. Hirsch's concept of cultural literacy, we believe a deliberate effort needs to be made in this country to promote moral literacy. We need to combat the widespread loss of heroes and moral ideals in the hearts and minds of our students. Young people need a meaningful frame of reference, a knowledge of individuals who bring the moral journey to life for them—individuals whose lives teach vital and memorable lessons. Ignoble lives also have impact. We learn from bad examples as well. From Napoleon, Theodore Roosevelt, and Joseph Stalin to Indira Gandhi, Madame Curie, and Elizabeth Cady Stanton, we need to help our students come to *know the right people.* They need to know people like Louis Slotin.

Shortly after World War II, Louis Slotin was working in his laboratory at Los Alamos, New Mexico. Slotin was one of the team of scientists who had been responsible for the development of the atomic bomb. After the Axis powers surrendered, he and his team continued to work together, searching for peaceful uses for atomic energy. One day in 1946, Slotin was conducting an experiment to measure the radioactivity of plutonium. His method was to move smaller pieces of plutonium closer and closer together and each time take measurements. The work was exacting and potentially dangerous. However, instead of using expensive equipment, Slotin used an ordinary screwdriver to gradually nudge the pieces closer together. At a critical moment, the screwdriver slipped out of his hand, moving the pieces together and immediately setting off the alarms indicating that a deadly chain reaction was beginning. As the laboratory filled with radioactivity and the alarms blared, Slotin's team stood frozen, realizing the deadly consequences of what was happening before their eyes.

Without a moment's hesitation, Slotin reached into the protected area and with his bare hands separated the pieces of plutonium, thus preventing the chain reaction from going further. Knowing that he had, in effect, just taken his own life, he quietly told his seven coworkers to mark their exact distance from the plutonium so that their degree of exposure to the radioactivity could be determined. This done, he apologized to his coworkers and told them what turned out to be exactly true: that they would live and he would die.

Educators, like parents, have to be concerned with helping students come to know the right people. Individuals like Slotin are worth knowing about. Our students need to be familiar with Beethoven's passionate determination to continue composing despite his hearing loss. They need to know about star athletes like Brian Piccolo, who battled leukemia while maintaining his courage, loyalty, and optimism. There are numerous children, too, that students should hear about, like Max Warburg and Karen Killilea, whose heroism in the face of cancer and cerebral palsy, respectively, made them role models at the early age of ten. Knowing the right people can help a student come to see his or her own capacity for greatness even in the midst of adversity. As children's author Katherine Patterson put it, characters in stories may be "more real to us than the people we live with every day, because we have been allowed to eavesdrop on their souls."[3] We should tell those tales that capture the hidden and forgotten stories of human courage: the story told in *Giants of the Earth* of the Norwegian farmer Per Hansa and his family, who struggled to survive in the 1880s and 1890s against incredible odds—locusts, droughts, loneliness, and treachery; or the story of Jane Addams, who gave her life to the poor and miserable of Chicago's slums; or of Harriet Tubman, an escaped slave with a huge price on her head who returned again and again to the slave states to lead her people to freedom.

Memorable lives cast a certain spell on us and can have a profound influence on the kind of person we become. The French writer A. D. Sertillanges describes it as the "ring of a soul": "Many saints, great captains, explorers, scholars, artists, became what they were for having met an outstanding personality and heard the ring of a soul."[4] A colleague of ours commented recently that her son had read the biography of Justice Thurgood Marshall in the third grade and decided then that he wanted to become a Supreme Court justice. He is in the eighth grade now, and his aspirations are still unwavering.

And we need not shy away from introducing students to the negative—to lives motivated by greed, selfishness, and hypocrisy. Persons of ignoble character also teach valuable lessons. By studying the life of Hitler or performing Macbeth's dagger soliloquy, students can explore the lust for power in today's world and examine qualms of conscience in their own lives. What matters here is that we provide our students with balance and realism. If we tip the scale too far to the dark side, we run the risk of promoting moral skepticism, cynicism, and even depression in our students.

We are reminded of the well-established American literature curriculum one of us was required to teach to a particular group of eleventh graders. Several of the students were dealing with troubling personal struggles—divorcing parents, regular visits with a probation officer, a drug and alcohol problem. The prospect of teaching Arthur Miller's *Death of a Salesman,* about Willy Loman's miserable life and eventual suicide, followed by his even less uplifting play *All My Sons,* seemed both absurd and insensitive. Selecting and resequencing within the curriculum is not a matter of censorship; it is a matter of providing a balanced diet. The curriculum should never contribute to squelching students' faith in the power of individuals to change their lives.

Exciting the Moral Imagination

Educating for virtue means more than just pointing out exemplary lives. Young people need to know that developing virtue also brings with it adventure and enjoyment. They need to experience the imaginative side of character education as well as the intellectual one. Children need to be among the farm animals in *Charlotte's Web* or stranded on the island with the other boys in *Lord of the Flies.* The stories we tell, the history we explore, the issues we research and address in science class—all these things fill students' imaginations with a storehouse of experiences, images, and events. And these images and experiences—vicarious and real—have tremendous staying power; they have the power to transform. As Dostoyevsky points out at the close of his epic novel *The Brothers Karamazov*, one good memory, especially a memory from childhood, is enough to change a person even at the end of her life. And as Cynthia Ozick, author of *The Shawl* and other children's stories on the Holocaust, puts it, "What we remember from childhood, we remember forever."

Why does imagination have such a powerful effect on character? What is its connection to moral desire and action? William Kilpatrick summarizes the relationship well: "[I]magination is one of those keys to virtue. It is not enough to know what's right. It is also necessary to do what's right. Desire in turn is directed to a large extent by imagination. In theory reason should guide our choices, but in practice it's imagination much more than reason that calls the shots. . . . Children's behavior is shaped to a large extent by the dramas that play in the theaters of their mind."[5]

The staying power of those images—be they from pictures or words—that play themselves out in the theaters of our students' minds is great. Research confirms that repeated viewing of violence and sex have deleterious effects on young minds. Children as well as adults are often haunted by traumatic memories. And increasingly, senseless violent crimes committed by children as young as eight years old are being attributed not only to neglect or abuse but also to exposure to violent murders and hard porn on TV. Although some children have the family support and moral wherewithal to keep their heads above water, others become victims of this empty, hostile, and persistent assault on their imagination and memory.

How can the curriculum serve to ignite students' *moral* imagination? Teachers need to select stories that captivate young readers, stories that enlighten, entertain, and move our students. As Louise Rosenblatt explains, stories offer the "gift of transport": "To enter a story, we must leave ourselves behind, and this it may be argued, is precisely what is needed to get a proper perspective on ourselves. The willingness to let go of self-concern is a requisite for both moral health and mental health."[6] Good stories, then, enlarge our students' minds and hearts. They help them to shed their preoccupation with self and to see what they have the potential to give or to do. In other words, stories not only nourish the imagination, they nourish the soul. Barry Lopez captures this nicely in his children's classic *Crow and Weasel*: "'I would ask you to remember this one thing,' said Badger. 'The stories people tell have a way of taking care of them. If stories come to you, care for them. And learn to give them away where they are needed. Sometimes a person needs a story more than food to stay alive. That is why we put these stories in each other's memory. This is how people care for themselves.'"[7]

What does exercising the moral imagination do for students? First, it can help them develop empathy. We teach students to empathize by asking them probing questions and engaging them in activities that will give them an opportunity to walk in someone else's shoes. Empathy is the capacity, as Atticus Finch so memorably put it, to "climb into another person's skin and walk around for a day." (*To Kill a Mockingbird*, by the way, is one of the most frequently taught novels in the eighth and ninth grades. If it is taught well, the moral education this book can provide is profound.) Empathy fosters the intellectual virtue of understanding and the capacity to fully consider another person and his or her circumstances. Empathy connects us with others. Younger students reading a story like *The Selfish Giant*, for example, will explore why the giant vindictively bars the children from the garden. Empathy also allows students to experience incredible circumstances, such as Anne Frank's life in hiding, vicariously. Such experiences encourage students to resolve in the quiet of their hearts to stand up for the threatened and the vulnerable.

Second, tapping the moral imagination gives students the courage to consider moral questions. It provides a setting, safely detached from students' own lives, where they can comfortably ask, "What is the right thing to do?" Students can more confidently ask this question of a character in literature or a figure in history than they can of themselves in their own situation; however, asking it of these others points students toward an understanding of good and bad choices, obligation and irresponsibility, integrity and hypocrisy. If it is asked frequently of lives under study, students will eventually acquire the confidence to ask this question of themselves and their peers.

What follows is a series of questions we have used with K–12 teachers across subject areas to help them tap their students' moral imaginations. They can be used as prompts for reader-response exercises, journal writing, or in class discussion.

1. Which character (in the book, novel, play, biography you are reading) would you most like to be like? Did this character face a difficult challenge? How did he or she overcome it?

2. Which of his or her character traits would you most like to have in a friend? Why?

3. What have you learned most from your encounter with this character?

4. Which character would you least like to be like? Why? What have you learned from this character?

5. Identify and briefly describe your favorite or least favorite character in the book. On the back of this page, write one of the following:

   An original poem that captures the personality and qualities of this character

   A journal entry from the point of view of this character that chronicles his or her thoughts and reflections about a significant event or experience in the book

6. Write a letter to a friend that describes a memorable scene from the story. Be sure to explain why it was so memorable to you.

7. Discuss something meaningful you have learned from this particular book. Be as specific as you can.

Stimulating Moral Discourse

Since virtue is about cultivating strength of mind as well as strength of character, students need to practice reflection and rational inquiry throughout their experience with the curriculum. In other words, they need to be stretched discursively, dialoguing with their peers, their teachers, their readings, and themselves about moral themes and questions. As Americans we are keen on preserving lively discourse in the public square. Such thoughtful exchange requires training, and it begins in the classroom, where dialogue serves as a means to ascertain the truth of the matter. Socrates, the great teacher and lover of wisdom, used dialogue to pursue the truth. Picking up on this, excellent teachers stimulate their students' passion to explore. Thoughtful dialogue is not only a powerful way to investigate a topic but also a wonderful way to foster friendships within a classroom. By engaging students in moral discourse, they learn to take moral themes seriously and to take others seriously, listening to and considering thoughtfully what each of them says.

What follows is a short description of how moral discourse unfolded among a group of fourth graders in a large urban public school who were reading Eleanor Coerr's *Sadako and the Thousand Paper Cranes*.[8] An extremely diverse group—over six cultures were represented in the classroom—engaged in a fruitful discussion of heroism and sacrifice. The teacher's prompting and feedback illustrate what we mean by using moral discourse to "help students see."

Sadako is the true story of a ten-year-old Japanese girl who contracts leukemia after being exposed to radiation from the atomic bomb dropped on Hiroshima. To inspire courage, Sadako's friend, Chizuko, gives her a golden paper crane and tells her that if she folds one thousand cranes, legend says that she will recover. She made 644 cranes before she died. The fourth graders began their study of the story by reading the prologue aloud. It concludes by saying that Sadako is now a hero for the children of Japan.

The teacher instructed her students to record what they learned about Sadako as they read each chapter. She urged them to find out as much as they could about Sadako so that they could eventually answer the question "Why is Sadako a hero?" The teacher faithfully responded to her students' daily written observations with comments such as "I wonder why Sadako doesn't cry in front of her family" and "How is Sadako changing physically and emotionally?" As a result of this written dialogue, the students' insights into Sadako's character became richer. Their written reflections spilled over into their class discussion. After reading that Sadako's mother stayed up all night to make Sadako an expensive silk kimono, the teacher asked the class, "Sadako will probably never be able to wear the kimono. Why did her mother take the time and spend money she didn't have to make it for her?"

Roberto: I think she wanted Sadako to feel normal again, to be like the rest of her friends, who had kimonos.

Kim: Yeah, Sadako wanted to be a normal kid. She loved to run, but when she got sick she couldn't run anymore, and she couldn't go to the school and be with her friends. I think her mom wanted to do something special—you know, to make her feel better.

Teacher: So the kimono was a way of saying "I care about you?"

Monique: Yeah. Sadako couldn't wear it outside, but she knew that her mom made it, and that helped her.

Teacher: What do you mean?

Monique: When someone does something nice for you, when you know someone loves you, it makes you feel better, even if you feel really bad.

Later that afternoon, the class read aloud the Japanese folk tale "The Crane Wife." The students recognized the theme of sacrifice in the story and began to use that word to describe the actions of Sadako's mother.

At the end of the unit on Sadako, the teacher shared her reflections with us: "We tearfully finished the final chapter together. The children's final messages to Sadako were moving, from 'May God watch over you. You never lost hope' and 'The courage and spirit you had was very strong, and I want you to know that you are a heroine in my eyes too' to 'If you were alive I'd visit you every Sunday.'"

Clearly, these children learned to see quite a bit about the meaning of sacrifice, caring, and friendship and about what it means to be a heroine. (See Appendix L for a mini-unit on *Sadako and the Thousand Paper Cranes*.)

Sometimes heroism or another particular virtue isn't so easy to identify in a character, especially when it is muddled by our inevitable human weaknesses. "The more I see of the world," Lizzy Bennett quips in Austen's famous *Pride and Prejudice*, "the more dissatisfied I am with it; and every day confirms my belief of the inconsistency of all human characters, and of the little dependence that can be placed on the appearance of merit or sense." Students need to learn how to see through appearances. Moral discourse helps them to distinguish between celebrities and heroes, between getting an assignment done and doing one's best, between infatuation and love, between ridicule and good humor, between honesty and bluntness, between friendship and companionship, between discretion and secrecy. Moral discourse is a powerful way to help students make these distinctions—and to make sense of "the inconsistency of all human characters." A group of fifth graders learned to consider these distinctions in their unit on the European explorers. During a discussion about the courage it took to embark on their journeys, the teacher pointed out that greed, too, was a driving force for some of them. With this prompt, the children pondered the question "How does motivation affect courage?" After an extended dialogue, the students were able to see the difference between true courage and ambition. At the end of the unit, they put together booklets combining their research and reflections.

Perhaps one of the most powerful ways to promote moral discourse beyond the classroom is to assign intergenerational interview projects. In a unit on World War II, for instance, students can be assigned to interview a relative or friend who is a veteran of war or was a civilian during wartime. Helping students formulate interview questions and inviting them to share their findings is an effective way to engage them. Many of the children we've known have returned to class saying that they had never before had a conversation like that with their grandfather. Others are enormously impressed with what it took to endure the challenges of everyday life during the war. Some classes organize trips to veterans' hospitals and collect oral histories. These encounters not only make for highly involving research and writing projects but also stimulate friendships across generations. We cannot overestimate the power of conversation to foster character within and beyond the classroom.

In addition to thoughtful dialogue, moral discourse needs to be informed by moral concepts and definitions. The language of virtue should not be reduced to empty rhetoric—words emblazoned on brightly colored posters or sacredly hung in the front foyer—without clear definitions that are understood by all. Schools that take moral conversation seriously take the time to define these terms with age-appropriate language and examples. For instance, responsibility may be introduced to kindergartners as doing one's part and putting things back where they belong. For a middle school student, the definition of responsibility can be expanded to include personal accountability for one's work and actions (doing what's right even when no one else is watching or when you don't feel like it). Clear definitions of virtues (as well as moral concepts such as freedom, truth, and character), followed up with practical examples from students on how they can be put into practice, give depth and daily focus to a school's character education efforts.

Cultivating Moral Integrity

It is important that students not see morality as something remote or abstract, something that has nothing to do with them and their friends or with the here and now. Critics of character education sometimes claim that moral education is simply an effort to inculcate in students moral precepts and rules so as to secure unreflective compliance from them. They claim further that character education promotes a set of functional traits, such as unquestioning obedience and hard work, that teach students to maintain the status quo. These shallow stereotypes couldn't be farther from the truth. Moral maturity requires knowledge, reflection, judgment, and personal choice.

In Chapter One, we suggested that one of the greatest ethical challenges a young person faces is that of becoming a good student. By "good student" we do not simply mean someone who attains high marks and sits quietly with his or her hands folded. We are referring to a student with moral integrity, someone who integrates her head, heart, and hand in all she does as a student. This moral integrity is built on habits of inquiry, hard work, effort, perseverance, and the capacity to listen to and learn from others. Up to this point we have made a case for seeing the curriculum as a source and carrier of our moral heritage, something to be enriched if necessary and examined deeply. Identifying great lives, cultivating moral imagination and empathy, and raising moral questions, however, only speak to half of what the curriculum—in the hands of thoughtful and engaging teachers—can do to promote character education. The other half is about encouraging movement toward moral integrity. Students who learn to slide by or beat the system do not acquire the habits of mind and character they need for moral integrity. Instead, they acquire the skills of manipulation and perhaps even subterfuge, which may eventually become injurious to themselves and others.

Virtue is difficult. As Aristotle explains, it takes a settled disposition to habitually choose what is best and right between two extremes (for example, friendliness is the mean between rudeness and obsequiousness; courage is the mean between cowardice and recklessness). Our method in teaching math, science, or gym has to include the daily, ongoing effort to help our students apply themselves in such a way that they will eventually come to choose well, to internalize self-discipline, perseverance, diligence, and responsibility. In this way we will equip them with the inner strength—the internal constitution—they need to live well each day for the rest of their lives. The joy of achievement and self-esteem are the fruits, not the roots, of these virtues. Furthermore, moral integrity will enable our students not only to live well for themselves but also to capably judge and critique those customs, social institutions, and laws that hinder individual and social development.

Putting It All into Focus

At the Montclair Kimberly Academy (MKA), in Montclair, New Jersey, and the Benjamin Franklin Classical Charter School (BFCCS), in Franklin, Massachusetts, virtue is taught in the context of the curriculum. Many schools are making these curricular connections more explicit. What follows are just some highlights, organized under the four lenses of moral literacy, moral imagination, moral discourse, and moral integrity.

Moral Literacy

At MKA, character is an integral part of the curriculum and of the school community. "The primary approach I recommend," Headmaster Peter Greer explains, "is to take the study of a virtue and root it in a larger framework that students, faculty, and parents understand. Without such frameworks, those studying the virtue often see such study as something in which you participate around a holiday (for example, Martin Luther King Jr. Day), as a means of improving class discipline, or a class unit—sometimes drawing on several cultures. It is our opinion that these activities themselves, just won't do."[9] MKA uses two such frameworks: "citizenship" and "leading a good life." These concepts are defined in their mission statement and are familiar to all the members of the school community (see Appendix D for an excerpt from this statement).

The virtue of respect, for example, is not simply defined but is examined and practiced across the curriculum. One of the suggestions Greer makes for teaching the virtue of respect is to break it down into four parts: respect for self, respect for others, respect for the achievement of others, and respect for offices and institutions. To bring these concepts to life and to help students come to "know the right people," Greer recommends drawing from invaluable resources such as William J. Bennett's *Book of Virtues,* Welty and Sharp's *Norton Book of Friendship,* Martin Luther King's "Letter from a Birmingham City Jail," and George Washington's *Rules of Civility* (edited by Richard Brookhiser).

Similarly, character education is one of the "four pillars" upon which BFCCS was founded in 1995. The other three pillars—"parents as the primary educator of their children," "core knowledge curriculum," and "community service"—are intimately connected to it. The entire BFCCS community understands these pillars and strives to live by them. The school emphasizes one of the cardinal virtues each month, defines it, and gives students practical examples of how it can be lived at school, among their friends, and at home. Furthermore, teachers use E. D. Hirsch's core knowledge curriculum to bring these virtues to life for students.

Moral Imagination

At MKA, students are introduced to the various concepts related to virtue through a variety of media that capture their attention and engage their moral imagination. For example, when teasing was becoming hurtful in a kindergarten class, the teacher read a poem, "Teasing," that helped her students share their personal experiences. "They found it interesting that in the poem, people who do the teasing forget about it, but the hurt person stays hurt for a long time," she noted. They all agreed to be more careful about teasing.

Film clips are another effective tool for igniting the moral imagination. To set the context for a discussion of "respect for self," Greer recommends using segments of videos to help students distinguish between self-control and self-esteem. For instance, the famous parking lot scene in *Fried Green Tomatoes* shows how after a series of humiliations, Tawanda loses all control. After two teenagers slip into her parking space, she refuses to take any more abuse and bashes her car repeatedly into their Volkswagen. Students who have studied mythology liken her to the raging Achilles and recognize the absurdity of such unreasonable anger.

As BFCCS principal James Bower puts it, fostering a sense of wonder is another way to nourish the moral imagination of children. Through our teaching of the curriculum, Bower explains, "We have the power to build or preserve ideals among young children and to sustain their sense of wonder about the world. Whether it is the beauty of language, the fascination with nature, or the heroism of man, it is for us to sustain a child's belief in the ultimate goodness of the world. If we let that belief slip away from children, what have we left them?"

Moral Discourse

Georgina Perullo, a sixth-grade teacher at BFCCS, shared with us how combined units in English and social studies allowed her students to study Roman history in greater depth. In addition to reading and discussing Shakespeare's *Julius Caesar,* her class explored how the virtue of fortitude played itself out in the lives of the characters they encountered. To drive this point home, Perullo had the students find additional examples of fortitude to share with the class: "Three students brought in some excellent readings on this topic. The readings generated rich discussion, and from this the sixth graders were able to analyze the moments in their lives where courage was required. They were able to set goals and come up with solutions for dealing with difficult moments."

Moral Integrity

Before Anita Rossi, a teacher at MKA, gives her students a take-home geometry quiz, she initiates a discussion of students' responsibilities. Her students know in advance what is permissible and what is "a breach of their integrity." Even seemingly innocent remarks, she stresses, may give unfair clues to others.

To help them internalize virtue, students at MKA are reminded that "to have a good life, one must want to lead a good life every single day." In fact, Greer explains, "Each student, faculty member, staff member, and administrator is encouraged to select a positive activity and practice it every day without exception, until it becomes a habit. My positive activity this year is to look for a student who is sitting alone and go over and have a quick conversation with that student."

At BFCCS, students are encouraged to keep a character education journal where similar commitments can be made. The focus of journal reflection and writing is centered around three questions designed to promote self-knowledge and integrity: "What have I done today to put this virtue into practice?" "How have I failed to practice this virtue?" and "What can I do better tomorrow?"

A Final Word

There are a growing number of character education resources teachers can use to supplement the existing curricula. We urge you to be discriminating in selecting these resources, however. Too often, prepackaged curricula trivialize character education, offering shallow themes and activities that fail to stimulate reflective and critical thinking. Remember as well that these programs are simply instruments, tools to help your character education efforts. They cannot take the place of an ongoing effort to mine the curriculum for its moral wisdom. Although we cannot provide a comprehensive list of good programs here, we can spotlight four that increase moral literacy, ignite the moral imagination, promote moral discourse, and foster moral integrity. The four programs, identified in Appendix J, can also serve as a benchmark for evaluating others.

The curriculum is, in effect, one more way to help students see the attractiveness of a life of virtue. They need to see that there is a variety of paths they can take to develop the habits of mind and heart that will strengthen their character. Learning that actively engages students with the wisdom embedded in the curriculum is education for virtue. What we are suggesting with all of this is that students need to develop a drive to move toward an ideal—to pursue noble ambitions and give their personal best in all that they do. But achieving this drive is not simply a matter of acquiring knowledge or a set of moral facts of life. We quoted *The Little Prince* early in this book to articulate this point: "it is only with the heart that one sees rightly." Since character education is about integrated development—encompassing head, heart, and hand—the curriculum must not only help students to *know* the good, it must also inspire them to *want* to do what is good and what is right.

Chapter Five

Engaging Parents in Character Education

One of the most outstanding people we know once told us a story about her father. When she was a young girl, her immigrant father announced that he was taking her and her two brothers to the circus, which had just arrived in their small Midwestern city. Her father was a shoemaker, and such costly outings were a rarity. When they got in line to buy tickets, she saw that the price was $15 for adults and $8 for children twelve and under. Since she was fourteen and her brothers were thirteen and eleven, she feared they couldn't afford it. As they got closer to the ticket window, she said, "Papa. We're all small. Say 'One adult and three children.'" Her father nodded. When he got to the window, he said in his broken English, "Three adults and one child." Once inside the gate, she asked, "Papa, why did you do that? You threw away over ten dollars. The ticket man didn't care. Who would have known, Papa?" Her father looked at her a long time and then said, "You would have known. I would have known."

Amid all the talk here and in the popular media about character, about education, and about the situation of the young, one fact must remain central: parents are the primary moral educators of their children. Although there is a growing chorus of voices calling for the schools to take a more active role in character education, educators need to be mindful that parents have the major responsibility for their children's knowing the good, loving the good, and doing the good. This has always been the case and, we hope, always will be the case. Parents bring children into the world, feed and clothe them, and prepare them first to take their place in school and then to take their place in the larger society. Parents' emotional bonds with their children greatly enhance their power to influence their children's moral values and sense of right and wrong. However, although it is a widely acknowledged fact that parents are their children's first and most powerful teachers, parents and families as "teaching agents" have undergone radical changes in this century. Also, the relationship between the home and the school, and between a child's parents and his or her teachers, has been dramatically altered in recent decades.

The Home and the School in Perspective

Once upon a time in America, the local school was the heart of the community. A town may have had several churches, but the school was the community's "common ground" where people came together. Although the schools' principal task was to educate children, in this earlier America they were also centers of adult learning and exchange. In a world before radio and television, it was school plays, concerts, and sporting events that were opportunities to get away from chores and rather isolated lives and come together with other adults. Teachers were well known, often having taught several children in a family and even a child's parents. Also, in a world in which education was a scarce and prized commodity, teachers were respected and focal members of the community.

There have been many economic, educational, and social gains in America since that era. But there has been one serious loss: the connection between the school and the family has been dramatically eroded. Most schools now fulfill their former role as a community center only on Election Day, when they are used for voting. Adults now enjoy a much richer fare of information and social exchange, brought by the explosion of print and electronic media and increased leisure time for socializing. When parents go off to a school play or a PTO meeting or a "Back-to-School" night, they often do it out of a sense of duty. They are giving up a night of working or cards or their favorite TV programs to attend.

These changes and others, such as the strained labor-management relationship that has developed between educators and many communities, have broken down the home-school partnership of the past. More than that, there is a growing hostility between teachers and parents, between the home and the school. A January 1998 survey by NBC reported that 53 percent of Americans give our schools either a poor or a failing grade. Further, surveys of parents reveal their belief that poor teaching is widespread and that teachers either won't or can't maintain proper discipline. For their part, teachers report that lack of values in the home and parents' failure to discipline their children are among the major causes of the schools' difficulties. In this unfriendly, sometimes adversarial environment, news that a school is beginning a character education program is often met with suspicion or outright resistance. In this chapter, then, we address first the role of parents as character educators and second how parents and schools can work together to develop children of character.

Parents: The First and Most Important Character Educators

To better understand where we are now, it may be useful to consider where we came from. If we go back a hundred years, to the dawn of the twentieth century, we see a very different American family. Only about 15 percent of Americans lived in cities, and the rest lived in rural areas. Suburban sprawl was a later phenomenon. The great majority of American families were involved in farming or some related industry. Families were large, and from an early age children were drawn into the family business, whether it was a farm, a corner market, or a small shop. Parents and their children spent huge amounts of time together. Fathers were busy teaching their sons the skills they needed to take over the farm or the family trade or the shop. Mothers were busy preparing their daughters for the multitudinous tasks of a housewife and mother. Mothers and fathers and children ate most of their twenty-plus meals each week together: three times a day they had sit-down, face-to-face contact with one another.

Neighborhoods were spread out, but they were much more stable. People were born, lived, and died in the same communities. Neighbors were very important people. Whether an adult or a child, one was known by his neighbors. Neighbors felt connected to one another. The "neighborhood busybody" was only an extreme of the norm: neighbors watched over one another, especially one another's children. Parents expected their neighbors to report if Ralph was seen smoking behind the firehouse or if Lucy was seen with "that wild Carson boy." In addition, parents expected neighbors not to swear in front of their children and otherwise to uphold community standards. Churchgoing was not only a religious activity but also a social one. And what one heard from the pulpit was directed at how one behaved each day and was taken seriously.

It is too easy to become nostalgic for this early American family. Often, children's lives were warped and twisted by cruel and ignorant parents themselves living desperate lives of mere subsistence. Work became all-consuming, and children had little time or energy, and received scant encouragement, to do anything else. A woman's world was constrained and vulnerable. Although divorce was rare, desertion was common. Still, one's family—one's mother and father, brothers and sisters, grandparents, uncles and aunts, and cousins—was the central character-shaping influence, the main force, in the life of a young person.

At the threshold of the twenty-first century, the way the American family lives is strikingly different from that past world's patterns. Where once families were vulnerable to the early death or desertion of a parent, now they are vulnerable to divorce and separation. Where once parents worked and lived their daily lives in the presence of their children (except for during school hours), now they spend much less time in face-to-face contact with them. Where once a father and mother could be relatively confident that their children would follow in their footsteps, now that is very unlikely. And even when a child does plan to follow in the occupational footsteps of a parent, most of that parent's work skills will be outmoded by the time the child goes to work. Yesterday's garage mechanic, nurse, restaurant cook, and civil engineer were very different from today's. Indeed, in many homes the children have become the teachers, showing their parents how to use computers, surf the Net, and correspond using e-mail.

Where once family members looked to one another for their social life and entertainment, now the modus operandi is to "do your own thing." Parents and children have their own television favorites (not to mention often their own TVS and VCRs, in separate rooms), their own music, and their own games. The idea of having the family sit down to play Monopoly or cards for an evening has all but faded from the scene. So, too, with family dinners. Some families go weeks without sharing a sit-down meal together. "Grazing" is this era's trademark mode of dining. Someone picks up fast food on the way home from work or school and takes a few things out of the refrigerator, and the members of the family, on their own schedules, take what they need and go off to their own space and consume it. Another telling term that describes our new eating pattern is *fueling*, as in "I've been fueling on fries, cheeseburgers, and Cokes all week. I probably should switch to pizza." Finally, our homes now utterly remote from their agrarian past, there are no cows to milk, animals to feed, barns to clean, or wood to chop. And though there are plenty of chores in the modern home, somehow they often go unassigned. Busy parents often do not have the time or energy to delegate and supervise housework. All of these changes make for a very different American family, one in which the ties are fewer and looser. It also makes for a new form of family life and child raising, one that has a good number of people confused.

Strengthening Parents as Character Educators

Some parents recently shared with us that their child was suffering from the "everyone else's parents lets them" syndrome. Their eighth-grade daughter kept telling them that all her friends' parents let them watch *Melrose Place* and talk on the phone on school nights if they had "most of" their homework done and spend Saturdays at the mall and on and on. Their relationship with their daughter was becoming increasingly unpleasant, and they were beginning to feel like the Hannibal Lecters of modern parenting. Just when their confidence was at its lowest ebb and their patience had grown tissue thin, they received an unusual request from their daughter's teacher. The teacher had set up an evening meeting for all of her students' parents, with the ominous-sounding purpose of "discussing some problems that have developed recently."

This was only their daughter's second year at her school, so they had developed only casual relationships with the other parents. With no idea what "some problems" referred to, they were rather anxious about the meeting. So, too, it turned out, were the other parents. The teacher, a young woman still in her twenties, came right to the point. She was very disturbed by the quality of the children's work and their lack of effort and seriousness. She reported that homework was done mechanically and minimally and was often incomplete. She said that she did not have a solution to offer, but she really felt the need to get their insights and cooperation.

After a few defensive comments from the group of parents, one father addressed a question to the others: "My Yvonne tells us that all the other kids in this class are allowed unlimited phone calls on school nights. Is that true? Do you?" That simple question opened a floodgate and was followed by a spirited discussion of the frequency, length, and inanity of their children's telephone calls.

There were several outbursts like, "How come they have so much to talk about if they just spent the day together in school!" Then the conversation turned to hanging out at the mall, and a similar pattern of anecdotes and complaints emerged. People started to relax and to laugh. The morale in the room rose visibly. Finally, the teacher, ignoring her own agenda, suggested that they list the topics of concern to them. Sleep-overs, exclusive parties, television watching, the Internet, makeup, language codes, allowances, the "in" group and the "out" group, and chores at home filled the blackboard. It was clearly too much to tackle in one night, so the parents decided to meet once a month until they ran out of steam. The last we heard, they were beginning their second year of monthly meetings. Besides a clearer set of rules for their adolescent children, the parents moved on to more positive territory, planning weekend events and outings for the class.

The parents who told us this story reported that as a result of this experience, three things happened, besides the fact that their daughter began to talk with them more openly. First, they gained a great deal of confidence and nuggets of good advice from the other parents. Second, they became good friends with several of the parents. Third, the teacher reported a dramatic change in the behavior of her class. This story suggests a powerful role for the schools. Many parents have a lot in common and would likely become friends if given the chance. They are people of goodwill but are busy and cut off from the natural sources of advice and support that nearby brothers, sisters, and other family members provided in earlier eras. One thing that schools can do is to bring parents together and give them a forum for constructive dialogue.

Whether it comes to a single teenager or to a married couple struggling with two careers, news of a child on the way can be sobering. Often the future parents stand quite alone, cut off from their own family geographically or psychologically. Without the support and advice of their own parents and siblings, parents must grope for ways to deal with a crying baby, a withdrawn child, a lonely middle schooler, or a rebellious teenager. Although there is a good deal of advice available, they cannot get their hands on it. As one frustrated parent said to his upset and confused teenaged daughter, "Listen, sweetheart, when you were born you didn't come with a book of instructions. This is my first time around, and I'm flying blind here, myself." Child raising is for many a hit-and-miss, trial-and-error process. It is here that the schools can play a constructive and valuable role.

Social commentators and comedians regularly report that in our society you need a license for everything from driving a car to going fishing, but you don't need a license to do the most dangerous thing in the world: raise a child. The idea that, before having children, adults should attend "parenting classes" is becoming popular. Many schools and hospitals offer them. Although this is an attractive idea in theory, the Devil is in the details. Many child care experts of the recent past have offered dubious advice to parents. Still, the fact remains that many young people bringing children into the world are in need of help.

Five Parenting Principles

No institution in our culture has come under more pressure in recent decades than the family. Besieged by everything from separation, divorce, and out-of-wedlock births to a remorseless erosion of parental authority by television, peer groups, and pop culture, the family is not what it once was. Still, in traditional and single-parent families alike, the bond is there—and the tasks are there. Like schools, families are social constructions. They are made. They are also continually in flux. Like our homes, they can be improved or left to deteriorate. Yesterday's dysfunctional family can become a strong, effective unit tomorrow. However, as anyone who has ever built or renovated a house knows, it is important to have some guidelines. The five principles that follow are ideas that can serve as the basis for discussion and exchange among parents. Bringing parents together to discuss these principles (sometimes with the help of educators, who themselves are usually parents), can be very useful for them, allowing them to share examples of how to put the principles into practice.

Make Parenting Your Priority

For some time now, American parents have been on vacation from their children, from the core of their responsibilities as parents. A number of years ago, James Coleman said that two generations ago the father left the home to work in a factory or office, and then one generation ago the mother followed him out the door. The result has been less direct contact with our children. Many of us have slipped into the habit of putting our own needs and wants ahead of those of our children. Often our activities are important, fulfilling career obligations and volunteer commitments or furthering serious hobbies. The bottom line, however, is that our children need us during their formative years. When we are "doing our own thing" and are distracted from our children, they know it. They know when we are putting our work and our fun ahead of their needs. And when children don't find the support and attention they need at home, they look elsewhere.

Educators know that real learning is a direct consequence of time-on-task, of keeping the student engaged in learning for longer and longer periods. It is impossible to teach children the life lessons they need to know, particularly moral lessons, without this time on task. Mark Twain, momentarily abandoning wisecracks, said, "We are always too busy for our children; we never give them the time or interest they deserve. We lavish gifts upon them; but the most precious gift, our personal association, which means much to them, we give grudgingly." Then there is the telling wisecrack, worthy of Twain, that says, "No one on his deathbed was ever heard to say, 'I wish I had spent more time at the office.'"

Besides making the character of our children a priority and finding time in our day to focus on them, we need to seriously reflect on their development. We need to think about who they are and who they are becoming. We need to objectively analyze their behavior. Is Jacob's failure to help out with family chores just because he is particularly busy with a school project, or is he getting into the habit of ignoring the needs of others? Is Damon snapping at others because of an increasingly contemptuous disposition, or is he just having a bad day? We need to focus some of the creative energy we apply to our work and our adult life on our children. "How can I create a satisfying family event that will bring us all together?" you might ask. In short, like good teaching, parenting means throwing your whole self into it.

Accept It: You Have Authority

Democratic societies, like our own, are rightly suspicious of authoritarian people and institutions. However, suspicion of authority should not mean wholesale abandonment or rejection of it. Like it or not, parents have authority over the lives of their children. Ideally, this means they are a critical source of stability for them. Children need nurturing and direction. They need the authority and love of a parent—they need *solid* ground on which to build their character. Many of the children of the 1960s and 1970s, however, who now make up the bulk of the country's parents, are ambivalent about authority, particularly about exercising it themselves. *No* has become a dirty word—a symbol of oppression. Too many parents fear that they will emotionally scar their children by asserting their authority and saying, "No." Yet, without the ability to say no to ourselves and others, we lose self-mastery; we can neither acquire nor teach the self-discipline needed to lead lives of character. The late film star Bette Davis wryly noted the necessary link between good parenting and discipline: "Discipline is a symbol of caring to a child. He needs guidance. If there is love, there is no such thing as being too tough with a child. If you have never been hated by your child, you have never been a parent."

Many find it stressful to set limits and to discipline their children. Parents need to feel more comfortable with the authority and responsibility that come with having children. As child psychologist David Elkind has said, "We need to reinvent adulthood." Many parents try to become friends with their children, an idea that is usually at odds with being a limit setter, teacher, and caring life-guide. To seek approval is a normal human behavior, but we make ourselves vulnerable when we seek it from our children. This same notion of being a buddy rather than an authority in a child's life causes problems for many new teachers, too. New at the role, they seek approval; but children yearn for the guidance and leadership of strong, independent adults who stand for something, not grown-up playmates.

Create a Community of Good Examples

It goes without saying that parents must continually strive to be good examples for their children. No one relishes the thought of continually having to be a good example for anyone, but it is a built-in part of the job of parenting. Lincoln said that there is just one way to bring up children in the way they should be brought up: to travel that way yourself.

The routine and regularity of life in a family blur the deep reservoir of primal love that exists between children and their parents. Over and over, when high school students are asked who their hero or heroine is, the overwhelming answer is their mother, their father, or their grandparents. As parents, we sometimes forget the strength of our bonds with our children. Our irritation with their all-consuming preoccupation with making friends, their unwillingness to help out, their constant telephoning, their poor school performance, their bad manners, or their fighting with their siblings strains the surface of family life and frequently creates an adversarial atmosphere at home. It often takes a painful separation, an accident, a prolonged illness, or even a family tragedy to bring the underlying strong family bonds to the surface. And sometimes the stresses and strains of everyday life, like Chinese water torture, can even wear the bonds of love and affection away.

Children, particularly teenagers, cannot be treated like hot-house plants. They need to come to know good people and dis-tinguish them from self-serving and undisciplined people, and this is not something a parent should sit back and expect to just hap-pen. Parents need to consciously bring good examples into their children's lives. Parents should make sure their children encounter people of character, whether they be uncles or aunts or personal friends. We often need to use our imagination to ensure that such people are woven into the lives of our children, and vice-versa. Our children need, too, to hear from us why we value these individu-als. In addition, although parents should be understanding of the human failings they encounter, children should clearly understand their disapproval of certain behaviors and ways of living. In other words, parents need to teach their children how to respect all per-sons while not necessarily agreeing with the way they behave or what they believe.

Consciously Build Your Family

Often parents see a neighboring family and say something like, "Look at those Allens! Their kids have turned out so well. They all seem to enjoy one another so much. They sure are lucky." Without disparaging the role of good fortune in the genetic game of roulette we call birth, there is still probably more at work here than luck. No family is perfect. However, good (that is, supportive, fo-cused, loving) families behave differently from ineffective or frag-mented families. It is hardly an accident that they are different.

Most people who are successful in business or a career set out to do their best. They planned, often studied how to succeed and focused much of their intellectual, physical, and creative energies on their work. They *threw themselves into it.* And this made perfect sense to them. Many of these same people, however, fail to focus on what will inevitably become the main source of either their sat-isfaction or their disappointment. Behind most good families there is a conscious effort to build a strong family and raise the children well.

Although we know of no set of rules that will lead directly to a good family, one common denominator among strong families is traditions. Parents need to provide structure in the lives of their children. They do this by consistent rules and family rituals. They do this by providing a steady environment rather than a turbulent one. They do it, in particular, by establishing family traditions and sticking to them. One of the most important rituals is regular family meals together. The twenty-one weekly meals together are said to be a feature of a bygone era and a bygone economy. But the grazing and fueling approaches so in fashion today are enormously destructive. What is destroyed here is a prime opportunity for parents to teach their children—not in the formal manner of school but in the age-old kitchen way. It is around the meal table where the family story is told, where the children find out who they are and where they come from. It is around the meal table where children begin to see their parents' expectations of them and what their parents hope for them. It is around the meal table where children get a rooted sense of what is right and what is wrong. Besides the knowledge that is passed on and the emotional security that is developed there, children also get a vision of the kind of person they ought to become. In effect, they develop a moral vision for their own lives.

There are, of course, other traditions that contribute to this vision. Some of these are wrapped up in celebrations of birthdays and religious holidays. Some have to do with the annual family vacation to the grandparents or to the seashore. Some are as simple as a weekly movie or outing. Often, rituals are somewhat temporary, having to do with when Leah was in the Girl Scouts or Felipe was playing soccer. One family we know had regular "Friday night flicks" during the years their children were teenagers. Conscious that there was not much for adolescents to do on weekends, they decided that every Friday night they would rent a classic film from their own youth, such as *The Great Escape, Casablanca, The Sound of Music, Stalag 17,* and *On the Waterfront.* Every Friday night for seven or eight years, their small home was filled with kids glued to their television set. The mother once said, "Besides the fact that they love those old movies as much as we do, it was worth the price of the videos, Cokes, and popcorn not to have to worry about where the kids were hanging out on Friday night." We are not suggesting that we have to turn back the clock to find wholesome entertainment for our children. There are a host of excellent contemporary films to select from as well. Neighborhood picnics and sporting events can also draw young people together in an enjoyable way. The point is, we need to be creative about how our children spend their time and energy—and help them be creative as well about finding worthwhile things to do. Free time can either build or wear down children's character. These windows of leisure are essential for helping children to develop talents, hobbies, and skills—productive and enjoyable ways to build personal character and competence.

Besides all the benefits of doing and learning things together that family rituals provide and the important sense children get from them that they are special ("In our family, we always sing carols to our neighbors on Christmas Eve"), rituals feed a child's hunger and need for predictability and regularity. At a time in their lives of great mental, physical, and emotional change, to be part of something familiar and constant is both satisfying and reassuring to children.

Become Involved in Your Children's School Life

It is a matter of lore among teachers that as their children move into higher and higher grades, fewer and fewer parents show up for "Back-to-School" night, PTO meetings, and class picnics. On "Back-to-School" night the kindergarten classroom, with its microchairs, is crowded to overflowing. Meanwhile, up the street at the high school, the twelfth-grade science teacher has an empty classroom and time to correct that briefcase full of lab reports. There are some great exceptions to this rule: the star athlete whose parents haven't missed a practice, let alone a game, since a third-grade gym teacher told them, "Carolyn really has it. She could go all the way!" or Maximilian's parents (who gave him a briefcase his first day of first grade), who never miss a school event and whose personal crusade is to make sure Max stays at the top of his class and remains on track for Harvard. Most parents appear to lose interest in their children's schooling as they move through the grades, and this sends a message to their children.

The ability of parents to be present at school functions and to help their children with homework varies greatly. Jobs, other children, and a variety of demands make it difficult for some parents to take an active role in school activities. Every parent, however, can be aware of and sensitive to his or her child's school experience. A child's struggles with long division or loss of a best friend may seem like small potatoes compared with a parent's struggle to keep a job and keep the family financially afloat, but these struggles and losses can be titanic to children. They need to know that we take an interest in what matters to them, that we are with them, that we are at their side and on their side. Even though we may be helpless to solve their problems, they get the strength to endure and the energy to solve them on their own from our knowing and our caring.

Therefore parents need to stay in touch with what is happening in school. Again, the family dinner is key. The daily request "Tell me about your day" is children's constant reminder that the important events in their lives are important to their parents. Often, though, there is this response: "Nothin' special." That should be a signal for parents to dig a little deeper—or at least listen a little closer while running errands or washing dishes together.

One big way for parents to show their children that they take their school life seriously is to keep in contact with their teachers. Face-to-face contact is great, but for many parents it is difficult to arrange. Few parents cannot make contact with teachers by phone, however. Teachers are encouraged and strengthened by parental interest and support. And if nothing else, talking with the teacher and getting her perspective on what's happening in school will help parents better understand what their child reports about his life in school.

Schools that promote character also promote parent-student interaction. The Hazelwood School in Louisville, Kentucky, for example, has turned the traditional science fair competition on its head. Instead of assigning projects that students and some parents sink exorbitant time and money into (eagerly expecting an award), students invite their parents to an annual schoolwide event where parents and students work together on science experiments. Parents and their children learn together, and many parents have remarked that the evening affords them the opportunity to spend quality time with their children in a way that is not ordinarily possible. There are numerous possibilities for similar initiatives.

Working with Parents to Promote Good Character

The antagonism we see between schools and parents has many sources. A fundamental cause is the fact that schools change children and sometimes pull them away from their parents' world of ideas, interests, and values. Parents can even feel somewhat reduced by their children's admiration of and affection for their teachers. When her third grader announces at the dinner table that "my favorite person in the whole, wide world is Mrs. Huang!" it evokes a twang of envy in a young mother.

Besides this subtle competition for children's affection, there is also the competition for their time. Family schedules often have to bend or stretch to accommodate school schedules and class assignments. One of us was once pressed into service to help his fourth-grade son on a science project dealing with endangered species. The boy had been assigned the manatee, about which the family knew less than it did about the Federal Reserve's policy concerning Albanian currency. To make a long and painful story short, the father's stature was radically revised in the son's eyes when the report received a "D," not to mention the emotional bloodshed that occurred during the process of producing the doomed report on the doomed mammal. Let us just say that schools can inflict unintended wounds on family life.

For whatever reason, two sets of players (teachers and parents) that each have responsibility for a child, even though they also share the same goal of providing the best for her, can sometimes come at loggerheads. This is particularly unfortunate when it comes to their responsibility to help the child develop good habits, a conscience, and a steadfast character. There is, however, a vast field of common ground between them, and many schools have been actively reaching out to parents to form partnerships with the home in an effort to enhance children's moral growth. We believe parents and teachers share a common fundamental concern for children. As journalist Jeff Jacoby put it, that concern is our vested interest in the "cultivation of human goodness":

> What I care about most is not your success or wealth or popularity. What I care about most is your goodness. Whatever else people think, I want them to know you first and foremost as a decent ethical person.
>
> For what this world badly needs is more decent ethical people.
>
> Our era with its world wars and gulags and killing fields, with its rape camps and drug gangs and child pornographers, has collapsed forever the illusion that there is a limit to the atrocities of which human beings are capable. And for human atrociousness there is no cure but the cultivation of human goodness.

Certainly the activities described so far, from conducting parenting classes to bringing parents together in forums to share ideas and experiences, can be important steps toward forging a partnership between home and school. However, there are some other things that schools can do specifically to make character education a joint, cooperative effort rather than an occasion for misunderstanding or even hostility. These are discussed in the following paragraphs.

Infuse the PTO with Concern for Character

Although most teachers are concerned with developing good habits in students and strengthening their character, relatively few have a firm sense of what exactly they should do to achieve these things. More troubling is the widespread belief among teachers that they will receive little or no support for this work from school administrators, the district board of education, or parents. In effect, many teachers feel they have no mandate or authority to promote character education. And many teachers, mindful of the requirement that church and state remain separate, fear legal liability and thus shun anything having to do with teaching moral values.

Some schools have initiated character education committees, which take many forms. Ideally, each building in a school district should have such a committee. Ideally, too, the committee should include as diverse a group of parents as possible. Such a committee can serve a school community in a variety of ways. First, it can provide teachers, administrators, and parents with a forum for addressing the many issues surrounding character education. Second, it can provide teachers with the sense that they have a mandate and support to promote character development among students. Third, it can help teachers identify exactly which moral values the school should stress. Through a simple process of listing, discussing, and voting, the character education committee can identify for the school those virtues and character traits it wishes teachers and staff to focus on. It is important that the committee work in close conjunction with the entire school community throughout this process; however, once this is done, the teachers come together to see how they in their own classrooms (and also in the schoolwide activities) can teach and promote them.

Draw Up Parent Agreements

One of the most successful school reform efforts of the 1990s took place at the Allen Classical/Traditional Elementary School, in Dayton, Ohio. When the new principal, Rudy Bernardo, joined the school community in 1989, the school was plagued with many of the problems we have been discussing in this book. Achievement scores were among the lowest in the district: twenty-seventh of thirty-three. Discipline problems made it difficult to get much done in class. Graffiti marred the inside and outside of the school building. Absenteeism among teachers and pupils was extremely high, and morale among teachers and students was scraping the bottom. Eighty-four percent of the school's parents, most of them single mothers, were on welfare. In short, the Allen School fit the stereotype of the grim inner-city school. By the mid–1990s, however, with the same population of students, the Allen School had become the number one elementary school in the city of Dayton— and a beacon for school reformers.

Rudy Bernardo did many things under the flag of character education to reform his school, but he considers one of his most successful efforts to be the parent contract. Through a combination of explaining and gently cajoling, Bernardo "required" the parents of all Allen students to sign a contract with the school, stipulating that they would do a number of things. Among them were sending their children to school fed and equipped with the proper school supplies (pencils and notebooks) and seeing to it that their children had a quiet place to do their homework. Also, parents pledged to come to the school and to stay in close communication with their children's teachers. Further, they pledged to support the Allen School's core values at home. The "contract" became a covenant and a vehicle for close communication among parents, teachers, and students.

Communicate with the Community

Word that a school is embarking on a character education program often provokes a mixed response in a community. Although many parents, trustful and supportive of the school, will immediately rally behind the effort, others will be wary. Some will bring up objections such as, "Aren't they having enough trouble teaching the regular subjects? Why are they getting into this area?" or "My daughter has her family and her church to help her with her character. Why is the school getting so involved?" or "Who are these teachers to start preaching virtue and goodness. Stick to the basics!" It is vitally important, therefore, that educators stay in close communication with parents concerning character education efforts. The alleged slogan of the old Chicago Democratic party machine was to help their people "vote early and often." This slogan could well be adopted to guide the efforts of schools in these matters.

One way to initiate communication with the community is through orientation meetings that include open discussion about the school's core values and how they should be integrated into the school policies and curriculum. Two-way communication between parents and school personnel is essential here. Another way to promote communication is to invite a guest speaker to talk about building healthy relationships with adolescents or children's character development. The topic of character development will be new to many educators and parents. A third is to use (or initiate) a home-school newsletter to keep parents aware of what is currently being done to promote character in the school. Such a forum might be used to notify parents of the virtue under study that month, such as *justice*. At the Benjamin Franklin Classical Charter School (discussed in Chapter Four), a monthly newsletter not only updates parents on the "umbrella virtue" for the month but also offers narrative snippets of curricular and community service activities through which students are coming to understand and practice those virtues. It also includes "family service" and "family reading" suggestions to give parents creative ideas for re-inforcing the virtues at home. A parent newsletter could be used as well to seek parents' help in dealing with schoolwide problems, such as "put-downs" or verbal cruelty. The potential uses of newslet-ters are myriad, and each school can design one to meet the needs of its specific community.

Promote Moral Conversations Between Parents and Children

A stereotypical conversation between a parent and an older child goes something like this:

Parent: Where are you going?
Child: Out.
Parent: Who are you going with?
Child: Friends.
Parent: What are you going to do?
Child: Nothin'.

This type of exchange is symptomatic of a parent-child rela-tionship that has gone into arrest. Breakdown has occurred. Al-though this example is extreme, the conversation between parents and many middle and high school students is similarly thin. It deals with the bare essentials of life ("What's for dinner?" "Have you picked up your room yet?" "When is the laundry going to be ready?") and requests ("I want your room picked up before dinner!" "Who's gonna drive me to the mall?"). Both parents and family psychologists acknowledge that maintaining contact with children gets more and more difficult once they leave the early grades. But the understanding that comes with ongoing communication and trust is essential to being a good parent. Furthermore, to deepen this understanding parents also need to ask certain questions of themselves, "What kind of a person is my Raymond becoming?" and "Is this boy Becky is always talking to or talking about on the phone someone I can trust?"

Schools can be very helpful in initiating and deepening the exchanges between parents and their children. For example, the Loving Well Project, a literature-based curriculum created for middle school students, introduces children to the moral issues surrounding romance, love, and sexuality. The curriculum (described more fully in Appendix J) includes many homework assignments, but among the most popular are the ones that ask young adolescents to interview their parents on topics such as their first kiss and when they first felt they were in love. Although on the face of it such a conversation is not necessarily a moral lesson, it certainly provides a platform for parents to begin discussing what is a major moral topic.

This is just one example of a topic related to character education. History and English lessons are filled with topics and themes that can foster conversations about values between parents and children. English teachers can have students discuss with their parents the person that has had the most positive impact on their lives, ask them to write a short essay on a parent's hero and state why he or she thinks the individual is heroic, or talk to a parent about the biggest obstacle he or she has overcome and what helped them overcome it.

Social studies and history teachers might have students interview their parents about who they think was the most dangerous person of the twentieth century or talk to them about what could be done in their community to improve race relations and then write a short paper on their ideas. The topics are endless and the benefits many. Besides drawing parents closer to what is going on in school, it gives parents and students practice in having real conversations about their moral values, what they believe is important in life, and (frequently a topic of great interest to teenagers) what Mom and Dad were like when they were young: "Were you like me? Did you have any of the same kinds of feelings I'm having? What were you really like when you were my age?"

A Final Word

Character education is often presented as something the older generation "does to" the young. Although clearly parents have a responsibility to help children build strong character, they also have a responsibility to improve their own character. Character education is a womb-to-tomb affair. Each of us has the responsibility to become an individual of virtue. By fulfilling the requirements of being a parent, we are fulfilling ourselves as persons. In effect, our children, the source of our greatest delight (and sometimes the instruments of our worst torture) are, in fact, instruments of *our* personal growth. By being a good parent, we strengthen our own character. By strengthening our own character, we help our children develop and strengthen theirs.

Chapter Six

The Teacher's Work: Nurturing Character

Melissa was not the child Mrs. Parken worried about. She performed above grade level in every subject and was enthusiastic about school. She played jump rope with the girls and basketball with the boys, and her mom was the room mother. The sixth grader that Mrs. Parken worried about was Lucia. Lucia was a new student, in a neighborhood school that received only a handful of new students each year. Large for her age anyway, Lucia had hit puberty early. Her clothes didn't quite fit (or quite match), and her hair was never quite combed. The students could have quietly ignored her, if Lucia were quiet. But she wasn't. She had an opinion on everything and everybody, and she had a habit of jumping into conversations even when the other girls sent clear signals that she was not welcome. Soon, the teasing began, from playground taunts to guarded classroom snickers whenever she made a comment. Melissa never snickered, but she did send a few "knowing smiles"; she never teased, but she said nothing when other students did; and when Lucia approached a group of chatting girls, Melissa corroborated their silent message: "You are not welcome here."

Two months into the school year, Mrs. Parken asked Melissa to stay after school for a few minutes. "I want to tell you something I haven't told the other students. Lucia's parents were divorced recently. She had to leave her old school and her old friends to come here. She could use a friend right now. I thought you should know." Later that night, Melissa started to cry as she related the story to her mother. "I know I should be her friend. . . . But I don't really like her." "Have you given her a chance to be liked?" replied her mother. Melissa didn't sleep well that night, and she did not "befriend" Lucia the next day—but she began to watch her more carefully. She watched how she sat alone and bit her lip nervously before coming to "join" a conversation. She noticed how her shoulders tensed when the boys giggled at her during class. When she noticed that Lucia knew a lot about taking care of animals—a subject that interested Melissa as well—she asked Mrs. Parken after class if they could be assigned as project partners. The teacher nodded thoughtfully: "We could do that."

We are convinced that if you put this book down right now and reflect back on all the teachers you have had since kindergarten, you will respond to the question, "Can teachers really build students' character?" with a resounding *Yes!* Although teachers are usually thought of as being responsible for helping children better understand the world around them, they are also responsible for pointing them in the right direction. Think back on your own schooling. Think of teachers who reminded you that you could work harder, pointed out your talents, and encouraged you to develop them. Think of teachers who helped you understand and empathize with others—particularly those who were less fortunate than yourself, apparently different, or for one reason or another difficult to get along with. Teachers are far more than transmitters of information and skills or social engineers; they are examples, mentors, and special kinds of friends. The anecdote about Melissa and Lucia is just one story among millions.

As this anecdote shows, fostering virtue is not about chiseling students with harsh blows (although sometimes a stronger response is called for) but about prompting and pointing them in the right direction. Mrs. Parken awakens Melissa to a possibility— the possibility of shedding her prejudice toward a new student and becoming her friend. She doesn't force or insist; she simply makes Melissa aware that Lucia may be feeling lonely right now. Mrs. Parken also trusts her student. She chooses to reveal the relevant details of Lucia's move to Melissa, without being indiscreet. And Mrs. Parken inspires Melissa's trust in her. Melissa takes her suggestion seriously because she obviously takes Mrs. Parken (and her mother) seriously. Educating for virtue—in Melissa's case the seeds of courage and friendship were sown—is about awakening students' minds and hearts to new possibilities and pointing them in the right direction. Socrates captures this spirit of pedagogical awakening in the classic cave allegory, recounted in Plato's *Republic:*

> Education isn't what some people declare it to be, namely, putting knowledge into souls that lack it, like putting sight into blind eyes. . . . [T]he power to learn is present in everyone's soul and . . . the instrument with which each learns is like an eye that cannot be turned around from darkness to light without turning the whole body. . . . Then education is the craft concerned with doing this very thing, this turning around, and with how the soul can most easily and effectively be made to do it. It isn't the craft of putting sight into the soul. Education takes for granted that sight is there but that it isn't turned the right way or looking where it ought to look, and it tries to redirect it appropriately.

We believe that authentic character education is precisely about this process—*gradual soul turning.* The goal of moral education for Plato is to bring one's soul—one's reason, spirit, and appetite—into intelligent harmony. These three seats of human motivation—reason's desire to know, to understand and figure things out; the spirit's ambition for achievement and honor; and the appetite's longing for satisfaction—need to be ordered and guided by reason. Without this proper orientation, we allow ourselves to be ruled by our primitive impulses. Character education is about achieving this order in the soul. In other words, it is about acquiring integrity.

The Six *E*s of Soul Turning

There are several dimensions of teaching that prompt this kind of soul turning. The six words—six *E*s—that describe them can help educators remember how to promote moral development within each student, the classroom, and the entire school environment. These six *E*s represent ways we can provide our students with stronger moral bearings.

Example

As teachers, we are always on exhibit, always being studied by our students. They often know our limited wardrobe better than we do: "That's his Tuesday tie." "Mrs. P. is wearing her Friday jumper." They notice when we've gotten a haircut or when we're long over-due for one. But they are perhaps most skilled at discerning who we are. Many may recall an incident similar to this: on parents' night, shortly before a teacher begins her spiel on what the class will study in language arts, a mother pops her head into the room and says, "Excuse me, are you Ms. so-and-so? I don't have a child in your class, but I drive the car pool with several of your students so I have heard a lot about you—I just wanted to put a face to the name." Whether they like it or not, teachers loom large in the imagination, conversations, and memory of their students. Unfortunately, it is not usually because of our knock-'em-dead lesson plans. Nor is it because of our ability to write stellar examination questions or our skill at creating cooperative learning exercises. It's our goofy jokes, our idiosyncrasies, our gesticulations, our fairness or unfairness, our honesty or dishonesty that go home to the dinner table or acquire full dramatic proportions in the car pool. Yes, some students are too quick to judge their teachers' character—and with incomplete data. For the most part, however, they are pretty accurate judges. They draw their conclusions from the way we habitually treat students and colleagues, the way we prepare and lead our classes, the way we deal with disappointment, mistakes, and humiliation. Our sense of humor or lack thereof, our ability to forgive and forget or our tendency to hold a grudge, our patience or shortness of temper do not escape their keen perception. To paraphrase the observation of Emerson's pilgrim about the Tahitian guru, what we are thunders so loudly in their ears that they cannot hear what we say.

Ultimately, it is the *person,* not the teacher, who makes a lasting impression on his or her students. The first-grade teacher who consoled us when we cried after school, the high school teacher who helped us write our college essay ten times over, the coach who believed we could succeed when failure seemed imminent—these are the people who remain large in our minds. A case could be made that the examples provided by parents, teachers, and all the adults who are closest to children are the most powerful moral educators. As Robert Coles summed it up in his book *The Moral Intelligence of Children,* children "witness" our lives:

> We grow morally as a consequence of learning how to be with others, how to behave in this world, a learning prompted by taking to heart what we have seen and heard. The child is a witness; the child is an ever-attentive witness of grown-up morality—or lack thereof; the child looks and looks for cues as to how one ought to behave, and finds them galore as we parents and teachers go about our lives, making choices, addressing people, showing in action our rock-bottom assumptions, desires, and values, and thereby telling these young observers much more than they realize.[1]

As educators we must reflect often on the cues we give our students. To assess how we are doing as exemplars for our students, we might want to raise the following questions, both to ourselves and with our colleagues:

- Do I exhibit good habits as a teacher, administrator, coach, or staff member—habits my students can adopt and put into practice in their own lives?

- Do I strive to live by the school's core virtues or philosophy?
- Do my professional relationships with faculty, parents, and students reflect the virtues I hope to inspire in my students?

Explanation

To enhance our students' understanding of specific virtues and of the moral life in general, we need to offer explanations. We need to explain what good habits are and why they are important—not by stuffing students' heads with rules and regulations but by engaging them in the great moral conversation about the human race. The very existence of this dialogue makes us human. A private school teacher, tired and discouraged by the hostility of her sophomore students, explained the meaning of friendship to them. "Many had never heard that values like compassion and trustworthiness are needed to be a true friend," she told us. She decided to ask her students to read essays on friendship by Cicero and C. S. Lewis. After a series of class discussions, she related, "My students began to understand what it means to be a friend."

Similarly, a guided study of an early passage in George Orwell's chilling novel *1984* powerfully caught the interest and attention of a group of high school seniors. The narrator, Winston Smith, announces to his female compatriot, Julia, "I hate purity, I hate goodness. I don't want any virtue to exist anywhere. I want everyone to be corrupt to the bones." When Julia readily responds, "I'm corrupt to the bones," and their subsequent sexual act is described by Winston as a "political act," the students engaged in a lively discussion. The passage sparked questions and comments ranging from how the fictionalized political system could dehumanize relationships to the problems of sexual misconduct, use and abuse among teenagers today. Several of them spoke of the breakdown of friendship and the dangers of being treated as an object. They talked about what virtue and goodness meant to friendship and sexual intimacy. After class ended, one young woman who had grown pensive and quiet during the discussion stayed behind.

Quietly crying at her desk, she looked up at her teacher and said, "I have been so used by my boyfriend."

This incident illustrates the power of explanation as it emerges from the curriculum. This student was not only awakened to her own problem but to the opportunity to talk about it and seek advice from someone in a position to help.

Children first acquire habits through imitation and practice. To help them mature, then, it is important for teachers to illustrate what virtues look like in action. Age-appropriate definitions, class discussions, film clips, and role plays are all helpful means of explanation. The more contextualized we can make virtue, the better. For example, a fourth-grade class might observe what the virtue of respect looks like on a field trip to the theater, noting everything from the atmosphere on the bus to the applause at the theater to people's behavior at lunch at McDonald's. The more we grow accustomed to using and explaining the language of virtue, the more children will understand what words like *patience, consideration,* and *integrity* mean. Finally, and we discuss this more fully in Chapter Seven, we need to explain to students how to acquire good habits and virtues. If we want to help students develop their own virtues, we should acknowledge and discuss the dedication, loyalty, and sportsmanship of students on field trips, at pep rallies, and at awards ceremonies. In this way, students will come to better understand what it takes to lead their lives well as students, athletes, club members, and friends—not simply talent, guts, and personality but also commitment, hard work, and perseverance.

Ethos, or the Ethical Environment

Classrooms and schools are ethical communities, either good or bad. Teachers play a key part in cultivating and sustaining the ethos of these communities. Does the teacher respect the students? Do the students respect one another? Are classroom rules and teacher expectations fair? Are they justly enforced? Does the teacher play favorites? Are ethical questions such as "What is the right thing to do?" part of the classroom dialogue? As teachers, we have to help our students see that civility, courtesy, and friendship matter. We cannot simply invoke rules to gain commitment from students. We need to guide students to attain their highest ethical potential and to foster relationships based on trust and mutual respect throughout the school community.

Disgusted by the foul language used by their students, members of a New Hampshire senior high school faculty joined forces to stamp out rudeness and obscenities. At an in-service meeting just before the school year started, they discussed ways to promote a more positive climate in their classrooms and throughout the school. "When students arrived on the first day of school," recalled the principal, "I announced that we were all going to work toward using a new kind of language, one free from obscenities and rudeness. We involved the students in changing a crude environment into a better one."

Teachers and administrators can do many things to improve their school's ethos. A first step is to ask ourselves the right questions. What aspects of school appearance can we take better care of (for example, cleaning up graffiti, keeping bulletin boards up to date)? What aspects of student behavior can we be more attentive to (for example, stamping out foul language, addressing the problems of cliques and exclusion on the playground)? What can we do as faculty and staff to build more unity among ourselves and build stronger relationships with students (for example, team-teaching units, peer evaluation, traditions such as student-teacher luncheons or basketball games)? Such questions are important, because there is little doubt that the ethical environment in our classrooms has a steady and strong influence on students' character and their sense of right and wrong.

Experience

Experience is one of our greatest teachers. In the same way that competence in one's field is achieved with time and experience, moral maturity comes with experience. Character, as we have seen, is not developed just by learning about words such as *kindness* and *honesty*. It involves our whole life—what we think, feel, and do, and why. Students need to become moral *actors,* not simply moral talkers. Many children come to school without the discipline of fulfilling chores like doing the dishes or taking out the garbage. Many are immersed in a self-centered, pleasure-dominated world of MTV, video games, promiscuity, drugs, or simply "hanging out." This is certainly not the case for all students; nevertheless, all students do need to involve themselves in more worthwhile activities. We can provide a constructive alternative to passive comfort seeking in our classrooms and schools.

Whether it is by painting the cafeteria together or by planning a clothing drive for a homeless shelter, students need to experience responsibility. Activities like these get students thinking about the needs of others. They remind students that they are needed by people less fortunate than themselves and also by their classmates and teachers, who need their help to plan such activities well. Increasingly, schools are introducing service learning programs at each grade level so that students have the opportunity to initiate and take responsibility for such projects from an early age. The experience of playing games with the elderly in a nursing home or visiting children in a local hospital helps students appreciate how much they have and how much more they can give. But virtues do not take root simply as a result of participating in a service program; an ethic of service and responsibility has to carry over to other parts of students' lives.

Many virtues—perseverance, consideration, responsibility— can be cultivated simply by doing one's work well. Virtues also arise from struggling against negative peer pressure or being willing to learn from one' mistakes, failures, and disappointments. But for such experience to be truly instructive, teachers need to help students make sense of it. Teachers need to invite students to reflect on their afternoon at a children's hospital and to remind them that academic responsibility means researching and presenting a group project effectively or writing a meticulous lab report. Teachers need to prompt students to think about what they can learn from a particularly low test score or from not getting a callback for the school play. In short, for experience to be an effective character educator, it requires guidance. Experience—supported by example, explanation, exhortation, and high expectations—teaches students that their character is not a set of inert traits but a capacity to give of their talent, their time, and their selves in productive and satisfying ways.

Exhortation

Character education, or gradual soul turning, is achieved not only by example and explanation but also by inspiration. Someone once said, "A mediocre teacher tells, a good teacher explains, a superior teacher demonstrates; but the great teacher inspires." Inspiration—moving students to want to become better—is key to moral growth. A child discouraged by academic, athletic, or artistic failure often needs something stronger than sweet reason to ward off self-pity. So do students who attend school passively, flirt with racist ideas, or get denied entrance to a college of their choice. Sincere exhortation is needed.

When a fifth-grade class in upstate New York learned of its low scores on a statewide test, the teacher exhorted her students with pep talks. "I also led them in discussions about the qualities of a good student," she said. "My class felt that a good student achieved good grades. But I helped them to understand that a good student is also someone who makes class contributions, does homework, and assists other students." We should not underestimate the power of inspiration and hope in the face of discouragement or the power of admonishment in the face of intolerable behavior such as cruel teasing and cheating. Students need to know that we care about them and about the kind of people they are becoming.

With heartfelt exhortation, we can both lift them out of the dumps and correct them as needed.

Expectations of Excellence

In addition to what they see, what they hear, and what they are inspired by, students are moved to change by what interests and motivates them. The bad news is that students report that they feel alienated in school, disconnected from their teachers, and often frustrated or unmotivated by their academic work. A February 1998 study by the Public Agenda Foundation revealed that "three-fourths of teens enjoy going to school, but most have serious complaints about the atmosphere and quality of education. Half the students surveyed say their school does not challenge them to do their best; two-thirds feel they're not living up to their potential; and three-fourths believe they would learn more if there were higher standards." In personal interviews, students complain about "how little work they do to earn acceptable grades . . . [and] how boring and meaningless their classes are." One student expressed with frustration, "I think [teachers] don't take us seriously enough. We're really smarter than they think. It's how far they push us. . . . I think a lot of kids—even those getting D's and stuff—can do a lot better."[2]

The good news is that students can do more, and they *want* to be challenged. Socrates refers to the latent "power to learn . . . present in everyone's soul." Our task as teachers is to tap that power and point it in the right direction. We all need motivation and a little coaching in order to achieve. Students need goals, expectations, and standards of excellence worth striving toward. It is a simple truth in the workplace that people usually rise to the level of responsibility they are given. We cannot underestimate this potential in our students. This does not mean that teachers should become unrelenting drill sergeants. We are suggesting instead that we take a closer look at how engaged, focused, and interested our students are in their work. We invite you to consider the following questions:

- What is the level of student attention, discourse, and collaboration in my classroom?
- What are the expectations I hold for my students? How do these expectations correlate with the level of student engagement, interest, and performance in my classroom?
- Am I employing a variety of pedagogical approaches to tap students' "power to learn," to help them connect with the material being taught?
- Do I hold high expectations for myself as a professional educator? Do I seek professional development, collaboration with my colleagues, evaluation, and support?

Reconciling Multiple Viewpoints

It is impossible to become an adult without forming moral views and attitudes. But what teachers do with their personal moral viewpoints is a thorny and controversial issue. On the one hand, teachers can strive to hide their own moral values, either by ignoring moral issues or continually deflecting questions of morals back to students. "Values clarification" advocates urge the latter approach, so that the teacher will remain neutral and will not impose the "cold hand of orthodoxy" on students. On the other hand, some believe that the struggle for students' hearts and minds is so important that emotion-laden—even irrational—propagandizing is perfectly acceptable. Teachers must steer toward a middle ground between these extremes. They need to clearly communicate the centrality of moral questions in their own lives as they help their students grapple with their own moral problems. And when it is appropriate, they should share their own views. The rub, of course, is determining when it is appropriate. There is a solid ground of core moral values in our quite pluralistic nation. Without it, we would not be able to live together in harmony. The overwhelming majority of people want children to be honest, to respect private property, to be fair in their judgments, and to take responsibility for their actions. The same is true concerning specific negative actions, such as physically intimidating people, cheating, and lying. Occasionally, an emotionally charged issue comes up for which there is no consensus, such as abortion. Such issues are few, however, and teachers need to respect community sensibilities and religious beliefs. The point is that students should see their teachers as people who are obviously concerned with the moral realm. Nothing could be more dangerous than to have children taught by moral eunuchs.

Sometimes teachers can misconstrue a particular moral viewpoint as a moral imperative. To be honest in our work, speech, and action is a moral imperative, and we can expect as much from our students. But there are some moral questions we cannot agree on, such as whether killers should be sentenced to death, whether homosexual marriage should be legalized, and whether government should remedy economic injustice by redistributing wealth. Exposing students to different views on such topics is not inappropriate in itself, but it is definitely inappropriate for a teacher to advocate a particular view, passionately or otherwise, on issues for which there is no moral consensus in the community. That said, it is important for teachers to remember that students do need guidance on how to take matters of social, political, and moral importance seriously. They need to be urged not only to study the relevant facts but also to seek advice from credible and trustworthy sources, to talk with their parents and with youth and religious leaders. They need to know that we want them to mature into persons who hold convictions but also to remain open to dialogue, to a more refined understanding of the truth than simple black and white answers. They need to learn that individuals can disagree cordially with others and always treat them with respect, even if they do not share or respect the particular view they hold.

There are core values on which our sense of community rests, and these provide the basis for character education. When teachers advocate their own particular view on a highly charged topic, however, they overstep their bounds. It is neither their right nor their responsibility to present ideas that are offensive to parents. Of course, our schools need teachers who stand for something, teachers who hold views; but teachers cannot become mouthpieces for a political ideology.

The Role of Teacher Education

Students come to schools of education somewhat unanchored with respect to the moral authority they will have as teachers. Recently, after an hour-long lecture on character education and an exploration of the terms *values, morals, ethics,* and *virtue,* fifteen undergraduate education students filed quietly into one of our classrooms for discussion. We anticipated a lively session. Instead we found them hesitant. In fact, they were eager to change the subject. A few stirred, looked around, and then stared at their books. One brave young woman broke the deadly lull: "It's really hard to talk about this, because I know how my parents brought me up and what morals and values they instilled in me. Some of my teachers lived in a way totally opposite from what I believe is right." Two students nodded in agreement. Another student added, "You know, I had an excellent teacher in high school who never told us what he believed; he just challenged our values and played devil's advocate when we began to side with him." "Would you ever have gone to him for advice about something serious?" one of his classmates asked. "No, I guess I wouldn't have, because I had no idea where he stood." And there the discussion ended.

Students are quite astute about their teachers' moral principles or lack thereof. When one of us was asked to give a presentation to an introduction to ethics class arguing that virtue can, in fact, be taught, a college sophomore responded with frustration. "I agree virtue *should* be taught. But I've seen so many teachers who aren't virtuous. *Teachers* should be taught virtue, first."

Some aspiring teachers are uneasy with the moral discomfort and even indifference they perceive among experienced teachers. Part of the reason for the confusion and apprehensiveness among many teachers concerning morals in the classroom is that they have been given no mandate, no guidance or training on morals in their teacher preparation programs. Unfortunately, teacher education has been unusually silent about character education in recent years. Drawing more and more from psychology and sociology, teacher education programs in many colleges and universities have all but dropped the history and philosophy of education. They have tended to ignore the moral dimensions of teaching and learning, treating them as too controversial or borderline religious.

One of the stumbling blocks preventing schools from embracing character education, then, is that few teachers have been prepared for this work. This is ironic, since the majority of teachers enter the profession with the goal of devoting their life to the betterment of the young. To some, betterment means learning the skills of literacy or science or how to be precise at math. Most would-be teachers, however, have the more general goal of helping children become better human beings, better people—what we would call people of character. In a recent study by Alice Lanckton of middle school history and social studies teachers, fully one-third of the thirty respondents thought of character education as their priority in teaching, but not one of them could remember hearing anything in their undergraduate teacher education courses (professional or liberal arts) about moral, character, or value education. Character education, once a mainstay of teacher education, has clearly slipped into the null curriculum at our schools of education.

We too have heard disconcerting testimony from education students, teachers, and researchers about the absence of the moral domain from their training. In his reflective piece "The Interior Life of a Teacher," Robert Starratt captures this indifference to teachers' character within our education programs. On completing a master's in education, a long-time history teacher asks himself, "Am I a better person for my several years of experience at the University? I think my courses and readings have broadened me. But, you know, I was struck that never once was I challenged to be a better person by any of my professors. No one showed the slightest interest in my growth as a person. I could have been a drug pusher, a wife beater. . . . It simply wouldn't have made a difference. . . . The courses simply dealt with prepackaged knowledge that got passed around."[3]

Although there are stirrings within the teacher education community to give character education greater prominence, the great majority of American teachers are very unsure of what they can and should do as character educators. Teachers occasionally ask us, "What *exactly* do you want us to do? I know I'm a role model, but is that enough?" The question is often loaded with their own personal frustration about having to do what is an increasingly difficult job under increasingly difficult circumstances. Having heard that they are now being asked to be "character educators," many feel burdened and believe they are unjustly being asked to take on a task that someone else (parents! religious leaders!) should be doing. Nevertheless, most teachers quickly see that their work, of preparing students for life, is by its very nature moral. Still, the question persists: "What should I do to become a character educator?" We believe there are seven particular competencies teachers need to develop to become character educators:

1. Teachers must be able to model good character and character building themselves. They need not be paragons of virtue, but they must be visibly "at work" on their own character.
2. Teachers must make the development of their students' moral life and character a professional responsibility and a priority.

3. Teachers must be able to engage students in moral discourse about the "oughtness" of life; they must be able to talk to students about what is right and what is wrong in life.
4. Teachers must be able to articulate clearly their own position on a range of ethical issues while not unnecessarily burdening students with their views and opinions.
5. Teachers must be able to help children empathize with the experience of others—in effect, help them to get outside of themselves and into the world of others.
6. Teachers must be able to establish in their classrooms a positive moral ethos, an environment characterized by high ethical standards and respect for all.
7. Teachers must be able to provide activities, in school and in the community, that will give students experience and practice in behaving ethically and altruistically. In effect, they must help their students become moral actors.

These competencies should all be a part of teacher education programs and professional and in-service work.

Building Commitment to Character Education

Commitment is built in to what it means to be a teacher. Most of us did not enter the field for the money or the fringe benefits. Teachers generally don't have a private secretary, let alone a private office. Some teachers share a desk in a classroom and a corner of a table in an overcrowded faculty room. Some schools have the amenities of additional phone lines or individual desks, but many teachers are their own mobile office. The school day affords little opportunity even to excuse oneself to use the bathroom. (To be a teacher, a colleague of ours once quipped, you need to be part camel.) Bells, meetings, phone calls, messages to and from parents, and communications with specialists, counselors, and occasionally parole officers punctuate the day. After school, it's providing extra help, monitoring detention hall, helping with the school newspaper, coaching basketball, or making a trip to the local library to plan for the upcoming unit on the medieval age. Where does a teacher fit in commitment to character education?

There is no easy formula. A teacher, as we have suggested, is both the artist of her own life and a mentor guiding young apprentices. We believe, along with Gilbert Highet, that teaching is an art and not a science. Highet's reflections speak quite eloquently to what we mean by commitment: "Teaching is not like inducing a chemical reaction: it is much more like painting a picture or making a piece of music, or on a lower level like planting a garden or writing a friendly letter. You must throw yourself into it, you must realize that it cannot all be done by formulas, or you will spoil your work, and your pupils, and yourself."[4]

The six *E*s and seven competencies represent a set of ways in which teachers can provide students with some moral bearings. For the most part, though, a commitment to character education means throwing yourself into your teaching and your interactions with students. In schools that have become social services malls, the specialists have taken over. Guidance counselors, death and grieving specialists, and sex educators have taken away from teachers' traditional relationship and work with students. Naturally, there are issues that require specialized professional support for students. However, what we find more and more is that teachers are regarded only as subject matter specialists or information dispensers. The teacher-student relationship is being dehumanized.

What students respond to, however, is not mere subject matter expertise. Philip Tate, a professor of education and a colleague of ours, has done research on excellence in teaching and the characteristics that distinguish teachers as excellent. From a study of over a thousand teachers who have been nominated as "teachers of the year" (representing a range of grade levels and subjects), he offers three main findings. First, an excellent teacher is one who serves as a counselor or advisor to students. Second, an excellent teacher stimulates and motivates. He or she awakens students' interest in learning by encouraging and inspiring them. Third, an excellent teacher is committed and dedicated. Committed teachers "show interest in their students, their school, their teaching, and their field." Each of these traits speaks more about the teacher as a person and about her relationships with her students than about her knowledge base or skills. They indicate teachers who throw themselves into their work with students.

Four Virtues That Promote Commitment

In the following paragraphs we discuss four virtues related to the characteristics Tate has identified. Cultivating these virtues, we believe, can help teachers make the commitment to character education.

Professional Responsibility

What students need from us, first and foremost, is for us to be good teachers. A sixth-grade boy in a small suburban school recently shared his frustrations with us. "Our gym teacher is strictly from Jupiter. Instead of teaching gym, he teaches about life in the army," he explained, rolling his eyes. "He tells us things like, 'if you're bored, you must be a bore. You get out of life what you put into it!' By the time he's finished," he continued, exasperated, "there's only fifteen minutes left to play. . . . It's so frustrating because he does it all the time. Now we call them [his speeches] 'The Keys to Life.'" "Are you bothered by what he's saying?" we asked him. "It's fine," the boy answered, "but don't do it during our time. He lectures us about what we do wrong—such as, if we exclude a student. He talks about how we need to treat students with fairness and respect. Yeah, he's got a point. But do we need to hear it every single class?"

Being committed to character education does not mean becoming a moral missionary, preaching to the young about goodness at every turn. Concern for the moral life of students must be balanced, free of excessive didacticism and tedious moralizing. At a more fundamental level, teachers must show their commitment by regular performance of their professional responsibilities. This is demonstrated by actions such as starting classes on time, being well prepared to teach, correcting papers promptly, being a supportive colleague, and being available to students who are in trouble or in need, whether it be academic or personal. Commitment is demonstrated by the way in which we do our work.

Trust

As public school teachers, staff, and administrators, we have an enormous obligation to preserve the public trust placed in us by parents, students, and community members. There is no question about it—educators bear a special responsibility. Seventh-grade teacher Kim Ruland summed it up in these words:

> At exactly 7:20 A.M., they arrive. When the bell rings, I experience a fleeting moment of panic and at times absolute terror. But as the lockers begin to open and slam shut, as voices shout greetings down the hall, and my door swings open, the panic is gone. It has to be. For the next five and a half hours, there are no coffee breaks with coworkers nor time to read the newspaper. I cannot run out to lunch or make a haircut appointment. My day belongs to one hundred seventh graders. . . . Their minds, bodies, and souls are all in my care, a responsibility for which no one can be entirely prepared.[5]

Students depend on us. They come to school with a myriad of small and large fears. From fear of failure to being bullied, from fear of not being accepted to not living up to mom or dad's expectations, children bear their own anxieties. They need to know that all the adults in the school share the conviction that we can all learn from our mistakes, even our failures. Trust, as many leadership experts contend, is one of the most powerful human motivators. Good teachers trust their students and inspire confidence in them. Trust is essential to effective character education.

Moral Courage

In a community committed to character education, authority is not merely wielded as power but exercised as moral courage. Young people need to see moral courage before they can put it into practice. Children and adolescents look first to adults to see how we live by our convictions, to understand why we tolerate some things and put our foot down on others. They need to lean on the courage of adults until they develop their own. They rely on adults to intervene swiftly and decisively when learning, individual dignity, or physical safety is at stake. One of the things that young children tend to size up in a teacher (or bus driver, librarian, or coach) almost immediately is whether or not they can count on him or her. If a teacher makes light of the hurtful comments one student makes to another in a cooperative learning group or overlooks incidences of cheating and dishonesty, children are left morally abandoned. And they will soon decide to fend for themselves by looking for authority and courage elsewhere.

Moral courage can also be seen as taking the initiative with students, particularly those who are "shut in" or "shut out." Reflecting back on her years in middle school, a college student we know explained, "I think I would have gotten in a lot less trouble if someone had just asked me, 'Why are you so unhappy? Why are you wearing black all the time? Why are you losing so much weight? Why are you letting yourself get C's and D's?' No one really cared. It wasn't until I got to high school that I met some teachers who took a personal interest in me and challenged me to achieve."

Justice

Along with responsibility, trust, and moral courage, we also need to practice the virtue of justice. Children recognize justice (and its counterpart, injustice) from a very young age. They begin the "That's not fair" cry as early as three years of age. Justice is not a matter of treating everybody the same but rather one of giving each student what he or she needs. During a radio program we did recently, one teacher relayed a disconcerting tale about what had happened to a student in her school as a result of their new character education initiative. The school had adopted a number of core values, one of which was the work ethic. After a sixth-grade student had missed several days of school to help her mother with the younger children in the family—a typical practice among newly settled immigrant families—the teacher sent home a notice to her parents indicating that Lorena "had not been living up to the work ethic very well." Flying under the flag of character education, this teacher believed she was fulfilling her obligation and giving an honest report of her student's progress.

What this story poignantly illustrates, besides insensitivity to the needs of an individual student, is how character education can be misunderstood by teachers. Technically, the teacher may have had grounds for such an assertion, because the student's frequent absences had hindered her capacity to excel academically. Obviously, we are not advocating that children miss school frequently to help their parents. We are advocating, however, that teachers make just judgments, taking their students' circumstances into account. A more just solution might have been to write a note suggesting that it was obvious that Lorena had a tremendous work ethic and sense of loyalty to her family, but the school was concerned about the number of days she had missed. This could have been followed by a request to work out some sort of agreement with the family that would facilitate their daughter's keeping up with her schoolwork.

Strategies for Building Commitment

Character education can take root in a school only when the administration, teachers, and staff believe in what they are striving to accomplish. There are several ways to achieve critical mass in terms of ownership.

Bring Everyone Aboard

As educators who are sensitive to the complexity of moral development, we need to remind ourselves that character education does not happen overnight. Nor does it happen under the direction of a few people (that is, in the laboratory of the "character education classroom"). We cannot relegate character education to the guidance counselor or the in-house social skills specialist. Whether we teach math, social studies, or health; whether we coach gymnastics, volunteer on field trips, direct the spring play, or drive the yellow school bus, we are all, like it or not, character educators. Many schools have made a concerted effort to draw their bus drivers into their character education efforts. Teachers, administrators, and bus drivers together discuss with students what a *respectful, safe,* and *friendly* bus ride "looks like and sounds like." Bus drivers are grateful for the support and eager to second the school's character expectations. When playground monitors and cafeteria, custodial, and secretarial staff hold students accountable for "please and thank you's," being courteous, respecting others, cleaning up their own mess, and putting things back where they belong, they too reinforce the school's character education efforts.

Increasingly, community members step in to schools and classrooms to share their professional experience and expertise. These forums are wonderful opportunities for firemen, lawyers, politicians, and environmentalists to share what it takes to succeed—the requisites of character, such as cooperation, loyalty, hard work, concentration, willingness to learn, and integrity. Business leader Sanford McDonnell (author of the Foreword) was instrumental in launching St. Louis's character education initiative: PREP (Personal Responsibility Educational Process). McDonnell, who was concerned that the city was graduating students that were articulate but dishonest, mechanically skilled but self-centered, sees character education as central to the moral life of the business world.

"Feed the Teachers So They Don't Eat the Children"

The sage advice to "feed the teachers so they don't eat the children" is critical to effective character education. The adults in the school need to be able to study, discuss, and reflect on the significance of the school's effort to foster good character in its students. They need time to make sense of and shape the character education philosophy and core virtues of the school. They need to understand the initiative in terms of their own lives and in terms of their work with students. In our experience, educators and school employees need time away to partake of one another's experience and wisdom. They also need substantive food for reflection. That is, they need some grounding. There is a corpus of morally inspiring texts, ancient to contemporary, that can help us answer the following important questions:

- What do we mean by character?
- What does good character look like?
- What is the difference between values and virtues? How do we deal with conflicting values?
- Why is character education important in our daily work and relationships with students?
- Where and how do we integrate it into the curriculum?

There are a variety of ways to foster reflection among faculty and staff. Some schools provide inspirational quotes and incisive readings on character for all school employees. They put the issues of school climate and student character on the faculty agenda for every meeting. Lynn Lisy-Macan, principal of the Brookside Elementary School, in Binghamton, New York, pioneered a monthly "reflection piece" that is published and shared with the entire school staff. The publication invites teachers to write about the best thing they did that month related to character education. The value of this exercise, Lisy-Macan says, is that it "builds educators' sense of accomplishment and self-esteem." But more importantly, she adds, it forces them to deliberate and reflect on their work.

At Pattonville High, in St. Louis, Missouri, during their monthly hour-long staff development block, teachers gather for optional workshops. A reading group that took up William Bennett's *Book of Virtues* last year and began his sequel, *The Moral Compass,* in 1998 has won the faithful attendance of nearly one-third of the faculty. "We don't limit our discussion to school," social studies chair Leonard Sullivan says. "Often we talk about our personal lives and family experiences." After reading Bennett's chapter entitled "Hearth and Home," they discussed how they could help students from broken homes. Another teacher adds, "I was able to use one of the stories to help a student who was having a really difficult time." A third teacher opted to include Aristotle's definition of true friendship in his unit on Greece as a consequence of the reading group. In short, what these teachers contend is that time spent in guided reflection and study has a tremendous payback.

Pursue Professional Development

Perhaps the most desirable and rewarding experience for teachers who wish to deepen their understanding of character education is what we have called a teachers' academy. Such a program has been a major component of our Center for the Advancement of Ethics and Character (CAEC) since 1989. Our academy offers teachers a concentrated intellectual retreat where they are brought together, typically away from their home schools, to read, reflect, write, converse with scholars, and discuss with fellow teachers. The programs are usually one to two weeks in length. Ideally, teachers are in residence. Texts are at the heart of our teachers' academy programs. The content varies widely, however, from Aristotle, Plato, and the Bible to Nadine Gordimer, Gwendolyn Brooks, and Nien Cheng. These texts are set off by clips from contemporary movies, strategic planning sessions for curricular revision, and discussion of schoolwide practices and policies. The academy gives educators an opportunity to study these morally inspiring texts, examine the works' inherent ethical concepts, and interact with scholars and colleagues who are equally devoted to enriching their ethical understanding of themselves and those around them.

Some teachers say the academy was the most academically demanding work in their professional experience. They enjoyed the intellectual stretch and the challenge of tailoring character education to fit their own work with students. As one teacher put it at the end of a week-long program, "I was really mentally tired on Monday morning. Now, I wish that school was starting sooner so I could get started implementing everything I've learned here." The variety of selections and topics for discussion stimulate moral conversation and relate character education to all subjects and grade levels. Our previous academies (in New Hampshire, Massachusetts, and Georgia) proved to be deeply satisfying experiences for teachers, and they have reported that they were able to transfer effectively what they learned to their classroom and school. A New Hampshire academy participant summed it up in these words: "The academy's content will shape and color faculty meetings, school assemblies, publications, interactions with parents, and my personal behavior."

Crafting Our Own Lives

Early in the semester, an education professor began his lecture before a group of aspiring young teachers with Socrates' adage "The unexamined life is not worth living." He then proceeded to discuss the importance of self-knowledge in deciding on a profession, especially teaching. Taking notes, the students seemed interested. But as the professor moved into a story about the famous *David* in Florence, pens stopped and students settled more comfortably in their seats. He spoke of Michelangelo's decade-long search for the perfect stone from which the *David* would emerge. Gradually, his explanation blended into a metaphor for teaching: "We here at the university can help you, but you must do the real work of making yourself a teacher." Referring to late-night conversations he had

had with a college roommate several years ago, he quoted his friend as saying, "I think the purpose of life is to make ourselves as pleasing or as beautiful to God as possible, or in another respect, to make ourselves a work of art—to craft or sculpt our lives." Good teachers, he concluded, are those who work to become their very best—building on strengths, smoothing rough edges, achieving contour, and catching light. When he paused, the lecture room was silent.

Great educators—parents, teachers, coaches—like artists, create beauty through their own life work and offer chisels, paintbrushes, and polish to their students. Character education demands that all the adults in a school take their own character seriously. In this way, they inspire the young artist by being artists themselves. Although this sounds quite lofty, what we are really talking about is correcting quizzes promptly, being vigilant about students teasing one another, and keeping the faculty room a clean and upbeat place to work.

Being a role model is not enough. There is something cardboard about the very concept of being a role model. On one level it is passive—we simply need to model good behavior and hope students get it. There is the danger of relinquishing our responsibility for the moral education of our students by saying, "I'm a role model, isn't that enough?" It also suggests that we may be simply *playing a role*. Our students need to see that their teachers are, in fact, working on themselves, too. What will have a lasting impact on them is not the role we play for them but the person that we *are* for them. As one teacher participating in our academy eloquently put it, "This [character education] is really about us, isn't it . . . about the way we lead our lives."

Chapter Seven

Helping Students
Take Command

Teaching is very here-and-now work. A teacher has to keep her eyes and mind on not only the material being taught but also the twenty-plus personalities in front of her, their knowledge of the subject, their learning skills and weaknesses, and countless other factors. As teachers, we must focus on the immediate: "What can I do to keep this class from sinking into the after-lunch doldrums?" "Why is Paula so distracted today? Is she depressed about something?" "What can I do for Jamil, who is way ahead of the rest and showing signs of boredom?" The here and now demands our attention. It also limits our vision.

At the end of Chapter Six, we referred to Michelangelo's long quest for just the right stone, the stone that contained within it his *David*. When he looked at stones, he saw not only textures, imperfections, and fault lines but also the works of art that would eventually emerge from them. In perhaps less dramatic ways, good teachers are able to lift their mental gaze from the immediate and see the potential of their students. They look past the acne-scarred, annoying know-it-all and see a creative mind capable of great organizational feats. They see beyond a dull boy with no expression to perceive a steady worker and happy family man. They look at a dreamy girl and know there is a creative artist trying to emerge. Although many of us see what we are convinced is the reality, these great teachers see the potential. Instead of merely the here and now, they see the *might be* and the *can be*.

Limited perceptions of youth are nothing new. There is a famous fragment from early Greece, attributed to Socrates, that has a decidedly modern ring to it: "Our youth now love luxury. They have bad manners, contempt for authority, show disrespect for their elders, and love to chatter in place of exercise. They no longer rise when others enter the room. They contradict their parents. They chatter before company. They gobble their food and terrorize their teachers." This censuring spirit is evident in George Chapman's famous line, "Young men think old men are fools, but old men know young men are fools." What is at work here is more than intergenerational tension; there is something deeply embedded in the human psyche that makes the older generation focus a critical eye on the young. Roger Allen has commented on this phenomenon: "In case you're worried about what's going to become of the younger generation, it's going to grow up and start worrying about the younger generation."

"Fixing" Our Kids Versus Getting a Fix on Them

America is a nation eager to experiment. We are fascinated with the new and the untried, ready to blast off in new directions with optimism and little reflection. Many of our recent social experiments, such as dual-earner families, easy divorce, rapid mobility, mass media, and the drug culture, have had deeply troubling effects on young Americans. And it is not simply the children of unsupportive families or broken homes who are affected by our new lifestyles.

Recently we had an encounter with a couple who, when they heard of our interest in character education, immediately turned the conversation to their teenage daughter, Vivian. "We just can't get her attention," they told us. "She always has her eyes on the television set! Or she is on the phone with her friends, who we've never met." They rattled off a long list of complaints about their

Vivian in particular and teenagers in general. Finally, having exhausted their grievances, they cheerily announced that they had cleverly coordinated their work schedules and in ten days were off for their annual winter holiday, this year to Jamaica. When we asked if Vivian would be going, they quickly responded, "Oh, no. She has school." Who was going to take care of her? we wondered. Well, that wasn't quite settled, but they were sure she could stay with a friend. Although these parents are obviously not candidates for any Parent of the Year awards, this incident is emblematic of the way many children are being raised today. As Pogo said some decades ago, "We have met the enemy, and it is us!" Many parents, on perpetual vacation from serious child raising, are seizing on character education as something the school can do, something that will shape up their children.

What is being called the Character Education Movement is seen by some as an organized effort to shape up the young and get them ready for prime time, for their adult responsibilities. There is no shortage of indicators that our children as a group are in trouble—educationally, morally, spiritually, and in many other dimensions of their lives. There is more than a hint of worry about their condition in the responses of parents and educators to character education initiatives. However, a school's character education efforts should be seen as much more than just another reactive effort designed to straighten out our young people. In her recent book *Character Education in America's Blue Ribbon Schools*,[1] Madonna Murphy points out that the majority of blue-ribbon schools she studied allot 50 percent or better of their character education effort to drug education and self-esteem programs. These separate specialized programs designed to "prevent" problems do not necessarily promote strong moral character. Character education is proactive, not reactive. We need to be wary of trusting mere transfer of information on social issues and ills as a character building experience. Presenting the so-called hard facts will not necessarily straighten students out.

M. Scott Peck writes about the need for mature people to continually "redraw their maps" of the things around them. This is often traumatically discovered by a parent who has been dealing with a child on a level that the child has surpassed or by a teacher who failed to notice that a gifted student's work has badly deteriorated. As teachers, we especially need to keep redrawing our conceptual maps. In a society that changes as rapidly as ours does, there is a need to continually update our understanding of key concepts. We suspect that many of us are using outdated maps of childhood and not fully acknowledging the profound differences that have made the experience of childhood and youth quite different from just a generation ago.

The Endangered and Encapsulated Child

Living in smaller and smaller families, often at great distances from other relatives and with parents who are preoccupied by their work or recreation, today's children nevertheless find direction for their lives. They have replaced the earlier authoritative voices of parents, teachers, and clergy with other voices. Some of the nation's cleverest salesmen are quite interested in our children, and they have crafted seductive messages to capture their attention and imagination. No longer needed to help the family earn a living, and with few chores to do other than garbage detail and cleaning their rooms, our children have vast amounts of free time.

All across America, students come home from school in the early afternoon and have nothing much to do, not even homework. Although large numbers of students are deeply involved in their schoolwork or extracurricular activities, even larger numbers are not. They seek stimulation and escape in television shows or computer games or the phone. When this pales, many drift to riskier escapes, such as drugs and promiscuity. Recent studies, for example, have shown that most teenage impregnations occur between the hours of 3:00 and 6:00 P.M., when parents are not at home. Young people have been seduced by empty pleasures and abandoned by those who are supposed to guide them into adulthood. Vices flourish and virtues are stillborn.

Our point is not that children are more wretched than ever before or that they are so steeped in idle pleasures that they are beyond the reach of efforts to develop their character. Rather, our point is that character educators—be they teachers or parents—need to see the targets of their efforts in their true context. The world of today's children is not just a Homer Simpson–plus-MTV world, requiring only a V-chip here and a smoking ban there. Theirs is a world in which they have thin relationships with adults and are largely left on their own to craft their own character. Thus it is important for teachers to have a fresh map of where students are, individually and collectively, to help us locate their potential, their possibilities, and their promise.

Youth and Their Potential

It is easy for educators, in our quest to stretch students intellectually, to lose sight of young people's enormous capacity for altruism and idealism. It is the rare student who does not yearn to be noble, to do heroic things. They are elevated by accounts of heroic accomplishments, particularly those of other young people. They are deeply affected by books such as Helen Keller's *Story of My Life* and *The Outsiders*. They are strongly moved by feats such as the trans-Canada walk by the young Terry Fox, who after losing a leg to cancer hobbled the length of his country to raise funds for cancer research and also to demonstrate what "disabled" individuals are capable of. Fox and the thousands of young people like him give silent testimony to Pearl S. Buck's statement, "The young do not know enough to be prudent, and therefore they attempt the impossible—and achieve it, generation after generation."

Young people all over the world, but particularly in the United States, reacted strongly to the story of the Pakistani boy Iqbal

Masih, who at four years old was sold to a carpet factory owner and spent six years chained to a loom for fourteen hours a day. Masih gained his freedom, and his subsequent efforts contributed greatly to the freeing of over three thousand other children. His harsh life and the fact that he was recently gunned down by Pakistan's carpet Mafia while riding his bike has triggered enormous outrage and efforts by schoolchildren to eliminate child labor.

Even the most sullen, self-occupied adolescents crave a cause to which they can devote themselves. Speaking in 1946 at a Gettysburg College commencement, Dwight D. Eisenhower spoke of the necessity for this youthful idealism: "Fortunately for us and our world, youth is not easily discouraged. Youth, with its clear vista and boundless faith and optimism, is uninhibited by the thousands of considerations that always bedevil man in his progress. The hopes of the world rest on the flexibility, vigor, capacity for new thought, [and] fresh outlook of the young."

This idealism is not dead. Witness the explosion of volunteerism in the 1990s, the throngs of young people participating in walks for hunger, pro-life marches, and AIDS awareness activities. Thus, character education need not take a "shape up or ship out" approach; rather, it should be driven by an elevated vision of what each of our students is capable of becoming. More important, as educators we need to be able to communicate and transfer this vision to them.

The Many Roads and Stages of Character Education

Character formation is an individual process. Some children respond to the call early on and with great intensity. Others succumb to their weaknesses and aggressively resist the efforts of those around them to help them. Some are challenged to shape their character by a life they encounter in a book. Others respond to an athletic coach's proddings. Still others are moved to change by working with the less fortunate. Just as there are no quick fixes, there is no one sure road to acquiring a strong moral character.

The process of character formation varies greatly, too, from age to age and stage to stage. Moral maturation is a gradual, developmental affair. Thus the particulars of what a classroom teacher does with her students will depend very much on what grade level she teaches. The character education challenge for a kindergarten teacher might be to get her new students to stop running around the classroom, whereas a high school science teacher could be trying to get his seniors to stop binge drinking on weekends. Child psychologist and educator David Isaacs[2] points out that specific virtues are best cultivated at particular developmental stages. He stresses, for instance, that children age seven and younger do not have the necessary knowledge or experience to rely on their own judgment or authority; they need to trust and listen to the adults who care for them. Hence, for this age group the virtue of obedience is essential.

Order is another important virtue to instill in the youngster, so that he learns how to take care of his toys and clothes, putting them back where they belong and contributing to the overall care of the home or classroom. Generosity, too, needs to be taught quite explicitly. Although some children appear ready and willing to share their toys, it does not mean they possess the virtue of generosity, Isaacs explains. They simply do not yet appreciate the value of what they possess, and therefore they freely give (and take) at will. These virtues are best fostered at home under the loving authority of parents, but increasingly, child care providers and preschool educators need to help instill these good habits in children.

Isaacs suggests that between the ages of seven and twelve, when children's will begins to assert itself more, virtues such as diligence and courage (fortitude) can strengthen children's character and help them channel their energies and desires properly instead of impulsively. Then, as their reasoning powers mature in adolescence, the virtues of understanding, practical wisdom, and good judgment should be cultivated more deliberately. This developmental scheme offers a helpful framework for implementing character education. Although at all three stages the head, the heart, and the hands should be engaged, it is clear that there are age-appropriate emphases. In the earlier years, greater emphasis should be placed on properly guiding the hand toward good habits and practices, from sharing playthings to hanging up one's coat. Then, in the middle years, the head and the heart become the locus of character education.

Learning to take time out from play to sit down and complete one's homework or to help out with a family chore is not simply a matter of training. It is also a matter of commitment. This is where the head and heart come together. Desire to do the right thing—to be responsible to themselves and others—enables children to respond well to the variety of demands and choices life presents them. Without character, children (as well as adults) may become complainers, seeing themselves as victims of the challenges and suffering that come their way. To develop commitment, children need to be moved by the interest and support of good teachers and engaging material. Or (in the case of doing the laundry, for example), they need to be compelled to help by a feeling of obligation to the family that loves and provides for them.

During adolescence, the head, or reason, must be engaged more fully in the cultivation of virtue. Teenagers need to understand moral principles. They need to learn to give intelligent explanations of their own decisions and to judge the reasonableness of others'. The heart remains an enormous player throughout: moral maturity means that we not only ask what is the right thing to do but also are motivated by the desire to do it. Reasoned reflection, combined with the practice of good habits, pulls the moral life into sharper focus. In his great work *The Analects*, Confucius wrote "learning without reflection leads to perplexity; reflecting without learning leads to perilous circumstances." The more the head, heart, and hands work in sync, the greater the overall integrity of character. This synchronization—this integrity—takes time to cultivate and must be sustained over a lifetime. What do we mean by *integrity*? Our colleague Edwin Delattre has articulated it well:

"Literally, integrity means wholeness—being one person in public and private, living in faithfulness to one set of principles, whether or not anyone is watching. Integrity is to a person what homogenization is to milk—a single consistency throughout."[3]

Psychiatrists continually remind us that people are longing for wholeness, for a moral center that will enable them to make sense of and direct their lives. The great hunger of the twentieth century is the hunger for meaning. Our students are no exception. For students to take their own character development seriously, they must see it as a worthwhile pursuit. We have observed four reasons why young people engage in promiscuity, violence, or drug and alcohol abuse: first, a desire to be accepted, to fit in or be "cool"; second, boredom; third, a lack of compelling interests or responsibilities to pull them elsewhere; and fourth, to escape from pain or meaninglessness in their lives. What, then, can we offer students to combat these four horsemen of self-destruction?

What Students Really Need

No one parent, minister, or teacher can give a child character. There is a great deal adults can do, but in the end each child is responsible for forging his own character. Nevertheless, there are some common elements that all students need in order to become crafters of their own character. What follows is a brief outline of some of these common needs, which must be artfully addressed for each unique child.

An Attentive Ear

One-way communication is the teacher's chief failing. Although educational texts and courses are filled with inquiry strategies, questioning skills, and admonitions to draw children out, the rule in most schools is that teachers talk and students listen (or pretend to listen). We know things. They don't. Time is short, so we talk.

With what seems to us a note of irony, Oliver Wendell Holmes wrote, "It is the province of knowledge to speak, and it is the privilege of wisdom to listen."

Over and over again, children and adolescents report that no one listens to them and no one understands them. They have questions, uncertainties, and huge insecurities, and the adult world all too often turns a deaf ear to them. Listening to your students—and listening well, by making eye contact and giving your full attention—sends a powerful message to them. When students are taken seriously by others, they begin to take themselves seriously. Teachers need to attend to students in many ways. They not only need to listen but also to hear, to keep a keen ear and eye open to catch what is going on in the world of their students. And they need to do more than just passively listen. They need to register the stories students choose to tell because these stories often reveal who they are and what they aspire to become.

One of the positive things that values clarification advocates promoted was the clarifying question: "What do you think your greatest strengths are?" "How would you like to change the world you live in?" "Who do you admire most?" The intent of the clarifying question is to get the student to come to a greater understanding of his own thoughts. It is not a means or a springboard for the teacher to start a sermonette. Rather, it is an invitation for serious reflection and an opportunity for the teacher to discover what is really going on in the lives of her students. Careful listening lets students know that we are taking them seriously. It communicates to them in a way that words cannot that we have true regard for them and that they are worth our time and attention.

Inspiration

Heroism and respect for human potential are constantly under assault in the "Era of Cool." Having been fed a constant diet of scandals, flawed heroes, and human deceit, our media-saturated students are frequently quite suspicious of life. The sour nihilism that pervades popular culture seeps into their life at school. Perhaps what many of our students report reading in their middle school boys' or girls' room, "Life sucks; then you die," sums up the pervasive message. Despite this cynicism, young people hunger for ideals and stars to guide their lives. Although many writers point to the underside of youth—the waste, the myopic self-occupation, and the rest—many others see further into the soul of youth and perceive deeper desires. A famous nineteenth-century American educator, Madeleine Sophie Barat, once wrote, "the young are built for heroism, not pleasure." George Bernard Shaw captured this true longing of youth in *Man and Superman:* "This is the true joy in life, the being used for a purpose recognized by yourself as a mighty one; . . . the being a force of Nature instead of a feverish, selfish little clod of ailments and grievances complaining that the world will not devote itself to making you happy."[4]

The issue, of course, is how to keep students from becoming "feverish, selfish little clods of ailments and grievances" and to tap their latent idealism. The frequent answer is to "motivate" them. But this simply evades the question. Teachers who are able to motivate students, to inspire them to go well beyond what they thought was possible, have two important qualities. First, they are able, in various ways, to get across to the students their very real regard and concern. At some level, the student perceives that the teacher is on his side, rooting for him. Second, as we mentioned in the previous chapter, teachers who inspire students also communicate trust. They give a troubled and troubling student the responsibility to collect the money for the field trip. They give responsibility to the defiant, hostile girl who has been using her popularity to block any real learning in class. These teachers are able to communicate this trust without threats or conditions but rather with confidence that students will do what is expected of them and do it well. Although they have to be ready to tolerate failures and pick up the pieces, they will save many students. These teachers foster true self-respect. As Joan Didion put it, character is "the willingness to accept responsibility for one's own life; [it is] the source from which self-respect springs."

Love

Human beings crave love. Children cannot develop into fully mature persons without it. If love and nurturing are not in their lives, they will seek it out with the intensity with which an animal dying of thirst seeks water. Much of the trouble students get into, from disrupting classrooms to promiscuous sexual behavior, comes down to, as the song goes, "lookin' for love in all the wrong places." A sense of truly being loved is deeply satisfying and enables students to get on with their responsibilities. To paraphrase the child psychologist Urie Bronfenbrenner, every child needs to know that at least one adult is crazy about him.

The love about which we are speaking is not a sentimental or soppy love. Some scholars make a distinction between liking and loving, which differs from everyday usage but is especially important for teachers. To like someone is to be attracted to him, to be pleased by him and to want to be with him. To love someone is to have strong feelings of goodwill for her and to desire what is best for her. In a way, to like someone is an almost involuntary response of the heart. We are attracted to people. We find them pleasing. To love someone, by contrast, is an act of the will, a choice to be lived out in deeds. Many students, due to the scars of their upbringing or their own bad habits, are hard to like. But the teacher committed to character education must not only love the flawed young person, she must keep before her the image of the person that student can become. As Harold Hubert put is, "Children need love especially when they do not deserve it."

One of the teachers we admire most works magic with sixth graders. He is able to elicit extraordinary and creative efforts from his students. His behavior communicates to his students, from the most gifted to the most challenged, "Listen. I want nothing but your very best work. I'm going to make real demands of you. And you can make demands on me. We are in this together." A teacher's love, then, is a love that can make demands on students, that can challenge them, criticize them, and correct them. Experiencing this kind of love, students submit to the pushes and pulls of education and character formation because they know "this teacher loves me; this teacher has my best interests at heart." Headmaster of the Roxbury Latin School, F. Washington Jarvis promises the parents of prospective students, "If you send your son to our school, I can promise you that we will know him and we will love him." Visiting the school, one can feel the students' sense of belonging. Real love, as William A. Ward explains, "is a great transformer, turning ambition into aspiration, selfishness into service, greed into gratitude, getting into giving, and demands into dedication."

A fourth-grade teacher related a story about a nine-year-old student, Tanya, who had already experienced more than her share of emotional trauma. Nevertheless, she explained, she would not "spare" Tanya correction when she needed it:

> My children need to be disciplined—and at times strongly. But a reprimand carries infinitely more weight when students know that it stems from care, not dominion. I remember one of troubled Tanya's troubled days. She had had a tough morning, and as we were entering the lunchroom she hurled an insult at one of the other students. I pulled her aside, drew near her face, and spoke firmly: "Do you understand that I care about each of the students in this classroom as much as I care about you? I don't let them hurt you, and I can't let you hurt them. I care about you and them too much to let you act the way you have acted today."

Structure

Parents and educators can easily agree that they want students who graduate from our schools to be creative, independent, self-directed, and free. The development of these qualities is a high priority for all concerned. However, generations of educators have confused the process for the product. They have cast aside ideas of order, hard work, and self-discipline and designed schools around these more personally expressive ideas. The philosopher Christina Hoff Sommers has recently written about this point[5]: "We are living through a great experiment in 'moral deregulation,' an experiment whose first principle seems to be: 'Conventional morality is oppressive.' What is right is what works for us. We question everything. We casually, even gleefully, throw out old-fashioned customs and practices. Oscar Wilde once said, 'I can resist everything except temptation.'"

To suggest, as we do, that students need structure—not only to learn new concepts but also to acquire the virtues and dispositions of good character—is not to harken back to rigid discipline, to screwed-down desks and quills and inkpots. Throughout this book we have used the metaphor of students as the artists or craftsmen of their own character. The art school, then, may be illuminating on this point. People who present themselves to become artists are received into a guild that is clearly committed to that goal, of transforming nonartists into artists. They study the masters. Art covers the walls and lines the halls. It is in the air. They submit to the guidance and criticisms of the instructors, themselves practicing artists committed to their own improvement. The neophytes learn the basics of their craft. They learn the skills of drafting and perspective. They study the qualities of paints, canvases, and brushes. The school celebrates their growth and achievement. The culture of the art school is designed to give young artists the structure upon which to build their professional careers.

Schools committed to character likewise provide a structure. The content of the curriculum fires the child's moral imagination. The adults in the building, although not all paragons of virtue, commit themselves to developing their own character. The halls, the school grounds, and the classrooms reflect the school's focus on character. Inspiring words are everywhere. Pictures of great men, women, and children surround students. The structure reflects Aristotle's advice that children should be in the presence of excellence every day. Classrooms and schools, then, need to surround students with excellence: excellent music, architecture, stories, and lives. A junior high we have visited near Columbus, Ohio, has a central hallway devoted to pictures and biographies of all the famous men and women who graduated from the school. They call it the Hall of Fame. It clearly communicates to students at the school that they are part of a tradition and that the people in their community and school expect them to do something with their lives. It provokes in them a sense that they are part of a continuum, that they are expected to be excellent and to do something for others.

Friendship

The late Ralph Tyler, one of this century's most influential educators, was fond of asking his fellow educators (often in the heat of discussing this or that curricular reform that promised to excite the minds and hearts of students), "Do you know why the great majority of students come to school every day? Not out of love for learning or to please their parents and teachers. They come to school to see their friends."

Parents are frequently more aware of the importance of friends to students than are teachers. Besides the constant problem of getting them to come inside for dinner or off the phone and back to their homework, there is the pain, rarely seen by teachers, that comes with being excluded from a sleepover or dropped by a friend. "Why doesn't anyone like me?" is a question that can break a parent's heart. Another factor complicates the making and keeping of friends. Thomas Lickona refers to it as the "put-down" culture of many of our schools. For students steeped in the dialogue of *Beavis and Butthead* and Bart Simpson, the cutting comment is king. Slurs and insults reign. Nothing undermines a school environment quite so effectively as this style of interaction, by which the mark of success is to cause another person emotional pain.

The desire for friendship is particularly strong among the current generation of American students. Many of them have moved often in their lives. With few roots, they especially want to be accepted. This desire to be with friends and to be liked as a friend does not mean, however, that children naturally know how to be a friend. True friendship is a virtue; it is a way of being. Students often confuse their desire to belong for friendship.

There is much that teachers and administrators can do to stimulate real friendships. Besides modeling friendship in their own lives and interactions with one another, they can consciously work to create an ethos of friendship. They can directly attack the "put-down" culture through a frontal campaign: "That is not the way we do things at Lincoln Middle School." Many students are among the first to support such a change. In character-building schools, students are in the vanguard of this effort to replace put-downs with courtesy and friendship. Further, teachers can teach about friendship. Literature and history are filled with accounts of friendships. These narratives can not only provide models but also help excite the desire for true friendship. Also, they can provide occasions for clarifying the very real difference between the need for friendship and the hunger to be accepted, between friendship and exploitation.

Wanting to *be* a friend, rather than just *have* friends, is an important first step. But knowing is not the same as doing. Teaching students the skills of friendship and how actually to make or be a friend is of a different order from simply pining after popularity. It is a topic that is of great interest to students, from kindergarten through high school. Learning how to be a good friend is an excellent topic to engage students in the whole idea of crafting a virtue, of making themselves individuals of character.

A Process for Gaining Good Habits and Shedding Vices

One way to define an adult is as someone who takes his own character seriously and is serious about the character of those around him. Again, a character educator is like an art instructor who works on his own art while helping others become artists. The good art teacher does not just point to the great masters or talk theory to his students. He helps them hone their craft. They learn how to stretch canvas on a frame, how to select brushes and clean them when they are dirty, how to mix paints, and so on. The teacher is intent on teaching his students the skills and habits of the true artist. Students in the care of serious artists, students who have been shaped by a community of virtue can attest to its influence. As Anna Juraschek, graduating senior of the Montrose School in Natick, Massachusetts, which has had character development as a central part of its mission from its inception, put it, "At Montrose, we have been encouraged to take risks, to question the moral rightness of issues, to consider morality above our image, to take a stand, and above all, to be truthful."

Peter Greer, of Montclair-Kimberley Academy, in Montclair, New Jersey, challenges his students this way:

> Students, if you are to have a good life, you must attempt to lead a good life. To lead a good life at home, at school, and later on, you must develop character. You cannot buy character; you must work on it every day. You know you are on the right track in developing character when you meet the definition of integrity: that you act the same in public as you do in private. To develop character, you must cultivate your intellect, by reading literature about right actions, and cultivate good habits, by being of service to others and treating others fairly.[6]

Jon Moline, president of Texas Lutheran University and a moral philosophy scholar, reminds us that "as Aristotle taught, people do not naturally or spontaneously grow up to be morally excellent or practically wise. They become so, if at all, only as the result of a lifelong personal and community effort."[7]

Getting students to want to form good character is an important first step, but it is not enough. They need "character know-how." They need to know how to seek advice, how to be helpful to others, how to handle being rebuffed, how to set good goals for themselves. In particular, if our students are truly to become artisans of their own character, they need to know how to craft a virtue and how to eliminate a bad habit or vice.

There is a gnarled old adage: "The road to Hell is paved with good intentions." The road to weak character is similarly paved. Many of us want to acquire particular virtues, such as patience or diligence, but we never quite get there. We know that a particular virtue represents a *good* that we want. We deeply desire it, and we may even occasionally display it. However, it doesn't become *part of us*. Similarly, we have certain vices, such as irritability, doing sloppy work, being tardy, and being overly critical or uncharitable, and although we know these vices weaken us and we desire them to disappear, they clearly *are* part of us. We simply don't know how to go from intention to habit. The steps of the process are murky and illusive:

Step 1: Engage

Before we can actually decide to acquire a virtue or eliminate a vice, our attention has to be focused on it. This can happen in many ways, but often it is the result of encountering someone who displays the virtue or the vice in a high degree (for example, someone who is extraordinarily generous or someone who is particularly miserly). Often a virtue grabs our attention through a story or a biographical account. The first step, typically, is to *engage* the mind and the moral imagination.

Step 2: Personalize

When we recognize in ourselves a lack of virtue or the need to eliminate a vice, we acknowledge a *personal* weakness. From this flows a desire to acquire the virtue or rid ourselves of the vice or bad habit. The abstract virtue or vice becomes personalized. It becomes a personal issue, a personal need.

Step 3: Understand

Having focused on the virtue (or vice) and developed our own hunger to acquire it (or shed it), next we need *understanding*. We need to learn more about the virtue or vice in question. This crucial step is accomplished in many ways: through direct study, through stories, through the personal examples of others, through friendship, and through the explanations that come from discussions and conversations. The formal curriculum of schools can play a crucial role here.

Step 4: Commit

Somewhere in the process, we must make the *commitment* to "go for it." There must be a personal moving of the heart so that we are ready to make the effort to overcome the vice or acquire the virtue. Ideally, when we make this commitment we are aware of the difficulties and ready to accept the challenge. The commitment can be made real in various ways: mentally, to ourselves; in a written statement for ourselves or others; in public, to attract group support. However it is expressed, a formal decision to commit is crucial.

Step 5: Plan

Knowledge and commitment are not enough. We need a reasonable, personal *plan* to build a virtue or put aside a vice. A good plan is one that is realistic and comprehensive, draws on the available supports, and considers the dangers that can possibly derail our efforts. Ideally, the plan should be written out in detail.

Step 6: Act

Acting actually has two aspects. First is putting the plan in action, that is, performing the various elements of the plan on a regular basis. For instance, we might plan to read something every day about the virtue we are trying to acquire. Or we might make a point of recommitting ourselves to the goal each morning. Second is performing the virtue or suppressing the bad habit. Here is where all of the study, planning, and commitment bear fruit. And this is when the virtue becomes an actual habit or the bad habit is finally broken.

Step 7: Monitor

We need to keep checking our progress at following the plan and achieving our goal. Even the best plans need adjustment and modification. Often a parent, teacher, or friend can act as a coach, helping us to *monitor* our progress.

Step 8: Persist

Acquiring a virtue or breaking a bad habit is like setting out on a long march. Here is where one of the most useful human virtues, *persistence*, is necessary to help us craft other virtues and eliminate vices. We need to stay with the plan, to stay on task. Also, since lapses, failures, and backsliding are common, we need to be resilient. We need to be ready to pick ourselves up, smile at our weakness, and set out anew. One of the most important human skills is the ability to form habits and break habits. Thoreau recognized this precious truth when he wrote, "I know of no more encouraging fact than the unquestionable ability of man to elevate his life by conscious endeavor."

Conclusion

Great artists have great visions. Great teachers have visions of their students' potential and are able to inspire and excite them with that vision. Their vision is not limited to academic achievement and material success. Rather, it encompasses students' virtue and character; it is a vision of students living joyful and rich lives, contributing to those around them, and in turn becoming themselves teachers of character.

The message of this book is perhaps best summarized on a small sign in the turn-of-the-century Massie Heritage School, preserved by the community in Savannah, Georgia. The sentence, carved in wood in this old American classroom, captures the seriousness of education for teachers and students alike. It speaks to the truth that students are "works in progress" and to their need to be the crafters of their own characters. It is the essence of character education: "What you are to be you are now becoming."

Appendixes Part One

Good Ideas

The Character Education Manifesto

*Is there no virtue among us? If there be not, we are in
a wretched situation. No theoretical checks, no form of
government, can render us secure. To suppose that any
form of government will secure liberty or happiness
without any virtue in the people is a chimerical idea.*
—JAMES MADISON

*To educate a man in mind and not morals is to educate
a menace to society.*
—THEODORE ROOSEVELT

In his January 23, 1996, State of the Union address, President Clinton echoed the concerns of Madison and Roosevelt with an urgent call: "I challenge all our schools to teach character education, to teach good values and good citizenship."

American schools have had from their inception a moral mandate. Moral authority, once vested firmly in both our schools and our teachers, has receded dramatically over the past few decades. Although many teachers are valiantly working to promote good character in their classrooms, many are receiving mixed and confusing messages. Attempts made to restore values and ethics to the school curriculum through values clarification, situational ethics, and discussion of moral dilemmas have proven both weak and ephemeral, failing to strengthen the character and behavior of our young people. Our schools too often champion rights at the expense of responsibility and self-esteem at the expense of self-discipline.

Distressed by the increasing rates of violence, adolescent suicide, teen pregnancy, and a host of other pathological and social ills assaulting American youth, we propose that schools and teachers reassert their responsibility as educators of character. Schools cannot, however, assume this responsibility alone; families, neighborhoods, and faith communities must share in this task together. We maintain that authentic educational reform in this nation begins with our response to the call for character. True character education is the hinge upon which academic excellence, personal achievement, and true citizenship depend. It calls forth the very best from our students, faculty, staff, and parents.

We, the undersigned, believe the following guiding principles ought to be at the heart of this educational reform:

1. Education in its fullest sense is inescapably a moral enterprise—a continuous and conscious effort to guide students to know and pursue what is good and what is worthwhile.
2. We strongly affirm parents as the primary moral educators of their children and believe schools should build a partnership with the home. Consequently, all schools have the obligation to foster in their students personal and civic virtues such as integrity, courage, responsibility, diligence, service, and respect for the dignity of all persons.
3. Character education is about developing virtues—good habits and dispositions that lead students to responsible and mature adulthood. Virtue ought to be our foremost concern in educating for character. Character education is not about acquiring the right views—currently accepted attitudes about ecology, prayer in school, gender, school uniforms, politics, or ideologically charged issues.

4. The teacher and the school principal are central to this enterprise and must be educated, selected, and encouraged with this mission in mind. In truth, all of the adults in the school must embody and reflect the moral authority that has been invested in them by the parents and the community.

5. Character education is not a single course, a quick-fix program, or a slogan posted on the wall; it is an integral part of school life. The school must become a community of virtue in which responsibility, hard work, honesty, and kindness are modeled, taught, expected, celebrated, and continually practiced. From the classroom to the playground, from the cafeteria to the faculty room, the formation of good character must be the central concern.

6. The human community has a reservoir of moral wisdom, much of which exists in our great stories, works of art, literature, history, and biographies. Teachers and students must together draw from this reservoir, both within and beyond the academic curriculum.

7. Finally, young people need to realize that forging their own character is an essential and demanding life task. And the sum of their school experiences—successes and failures, both academic and athletic, both intellectual and social—provides much of the raw material for this personal undertaking.

Character education is not merely an educational trend or the schools' latest fad; it is a fundamental dimension of good teaching, an abiding respect for the intellect and spirit of the individual. We need to reengage the hearts, minds, and hands of our children in forming their own characters, helping them "to know the good, love the good, and do the good." That done, we will truly be a nation of character, securing "liberty and justice for all."

A Seven-Point Program

Steven S. Tigner,
Boston University and the University of Toledo

The following reflections fall into three parts. The first part proposes a classically based cluster of seven points on which a program of character education in the schools might profitably focus. The second part indicates in outline some of the ways in which each of these points can be addressed within the context of school life. The third part reviews the outcomes toward which such a program of character education would work.

I

1. The most fundamental trait of persons of good character is that they take people seriously *as persons.* "Golden Rule" expressions of the insight embodied in this trait are as close to being culturally universal as any proverbial wisdom. In the West its most influential expression has been the Biblical dictate to "love your neighbor as yourself" (Lev 19:18,34) as that came to be interpreted in the second "Great Commandment" (Mt 22:36–40) or "Royal Law" (Jas 2:8) and taught in the parable of the Good Samaritan

Reprinted from the *Journal of Education,* 1993, *174*(2), pp. 14–22. Used with permission.

(Lk 10:25–37). This, then, is the first and primary element on which a program of character education in the schools might profitably focus: *taking people seriously as persons.*

2. What it means to take others seriously as persons commonly dawns over our moral horizons initially in relations of friendship. Friends are the people whom we first learn to take seriously *for their own sakes.* Friendly relations constitute a kind of moral paradigm for social relations in general. "Friends don't let friends drive drunk." Friends *care* for each other. Developing and broadening the scope of this mutual concern into a sense of community is a second element on which a program of character education in the schools ought to focus.

3. To understand what it is to take other people seriously as persons one must also know what it is to take *oneself* seriously as a person. This involves more than self-knowledge of one's own traits and abilities. It involves knowing what it is to take responsibility and to be responsible. If nothing is ever my fault, if I always have an excuse, if the buck never stops here, then I am not really a *person.* Similarly, if I never see others as blameworthy, if I always excuse their behavior, if I never hold them accountable, I am not treating them as persons, but as victims or pawns. A school concerned with character development will help students develop senses of responsibility for what they think, say, and do. It will help develop their *autonomy.*

The autonomous person is literally "self-governed," and as the first three elements of our cluster center on developing the notion of personhood, so the final four elements focus on the cardinal virtues of self-government.

4. Courage is an *executive* virtue of self-government, a settled disposition to take stands that are neither too bold nor too timid, to feel confidence or fear at levels that are genuinely appropriate in circumstances of challenge or threat. As an executive virtue, a

virtue of carrying out directives but not deciding what those directives are, it can of course be allied with any mission. There can be a courageous enemy in any war. Courage, like the other moral virtues, requires wisdom to set it on the right course.

5. Temperance (or "moderation" or "self-mastery")—English doesn't have a really adequate equivalent for the Greek *sôphrosúnê*, which is what we actually need here—is a *legislative* virtue of self-government, a settled disposition to take pleasure in good and beautiful things and to enjoy those activities which enhance the quality of intellect, of action, and of creative expression in oneself and in others. As a legislative virtue it bids us to enjoy life, but to do so within those limits that can be sensibly sustained. Wisdom must join with temperance here in illuminating a course of life which will steer it safely between its chief despoilers: debauchery and depression.

6. Justice as a *judicial* virtue points to the cluster of dispositions that need to be exercised by people when they take on roles as apportioners, arbiters, and rectifiers. Its aim is fairness in distribution, in conciliation, and in correction. This moral virtue, too, must rely on the relevantly informed directives of wisdom. Indeed it may actually be better to think of it primarily as practical wisdom applied to cases of apportionment, arbitration, and rectification.

7. Wisdom is the autonomous person's department of intelligence, involved in all decisions of the executive, legislative, and judicial branches of internal government. Aristotle's division of this department into theoretical, practical, and productive sections continues to be useful. Theoretical wisdom, *sophia,* is concerned with *understanding;* practical wisdom, *phronesis,* with how to do things; and productive wisdom, *techne,* with how to *make* things. From the Latin equivalents of the Greek words we get our English *science, prudence,* and *art,* though these English words include only a portion of what the Greek notions encompass. A good school education is

concerned with cultivating wisdom in all three varieties. Each variety has a role to play in character education in addition to the roles it plays in other aspects of the curriculum.

II

1. Teachers and other school personnel best promote dispositions in students to *take people seriously as persons* by taking students themselves seriously as persons. Indeed, there is no other way to do it. It must be made clear to students that *who they are*—the *persons* that they are (and *are becoming*)—really matters.

The problem in getting this notion across lies not so much in its intrinsic difficulty as in certain competing notions that tend to crowd it out. There are currently three main ones to worry about. The most ancient and persistent of these is a preoccupation with one's status or reputation or "image." In 399 B.C., Socrates chided his Athenian jurors on this score with the rhetorical question, "Are you not ashamed of your eagerness to possess as much wealth, reputation, and honors as possible, while you do not care for nor give thought to wisdom or truth, or the best possible state of your soul?" (*Apology*, 29de.) Much the same challenge might be brought today against those persons who appear to be more concerned with the quality of their résumés than with the quality of their lives.

To be concerned with the state of one's soul, as Socrates put it, is to care about the kind of person one is. And, if Socrates was right, this really ought to occupy first place among our concerns about ourselves. More important than *what we have* is *who we are*. "I go around doing nothing but persuading both young and old among you not to care for your body or your wealth in preference to or as strongly as for the best possible state of your soul," he says (*Apology*, 30ab).

Socrates came up with a wonderful slogan that gives this common concern with reputation just the right turn inward. I have seen it posted on school walls in Maine and New Jersey. It comes from Xenophon's *Memorabilia: Be the kind of person that you want people to think you are.*—Socrates

A second notion competing with *seriousness about persons* is the self-esteem movement's advocacy of willful blindness to people's shortcomings in inducing them to feel good about themselves. I am not being serious about persons if I don't distinguish their finer efforts from their failures. Encouragement that doesn't discriminate between excellent and shoddy performance signals the positively harmful message that the quality of one's effort doesn't matter. To deprive students of feeling *bad* about doing less than their best is to deprive them of one of their chief incentives to grow, improve and mature. Much to their detriment, it positively invites them down the easy slide to mediocrity.

The third misguided notion competing with seriousness about persons is more subtle, partly because it is cloaked in "common sense" utilitarianism (or "welfarism," as it is sometimes more aptly called) that reduces rational decision-making to cost/benefit analysis. When I regard other people primarily as potential beneficiaries of my actions, I am reckoning them as animate *objects* within the sphere of my own universe of experience rather than as fellow *agents* in a universe of autonomous beings. Such benevolence is implicitly patronizing and violates the condition of respect for others that is embedded in the morally fundamental injunction to take people seriously as persons. Another sign that I have seen posted on school walls provides an apt corrective to the blindness of welfarism. This one is Kant's second formula of the categorical imperative: *So act as to treat humanity, whether in your own person or in that of another, always as an end and never as a means merely.*

2. In relations of friendship we characteristically acquire our first taste of salutary *community* outside the structure of families, and friends are typically the persons whom it is most natural for us

to begin taking seriously *for their own sakes.* No school-age child is too young to want to *have* friends or hence to have a cultivatable interest in what it takes to be a friend.

It has been a significant achievement of persistent media attention that virtually every high school student in America today at least recognizes the slogan, "Friends don't let friends drive drunk." That is of course an important specific lesson, but it can also provide a pedagogically valuable hook on which to begin hanging more general insights into the nature and value of real friendship, and of community in general. None of this is automatic, however. It needs explicit discussion and examination to be driven home. That is one reason why, as Socrates famously noted, "It is the greatest good . . . to discuss virtue every day" *(Apology,* 38a).

The literature of friendship is as rich and varied as works in any other area at the same reading level, and friendship provides an excellent theme around which to promote moral reflection and growth throughout the school years. School should be a friendly place, a place where friendships are not only formed, and grow, and flourish, but where they are also seriously talked about.

Aristotle proposes an illuminating analysis of "friendship," as it is usually translated—though the *philia* he is discussing actually extends over a wider variety of social relations. We associate with some people because we *admire* them, he says; others because we need to for practical reasons, and still others because they're *fun* to be with. These nonexclusive categories of association are usually referred to as friendships of *virtue,* of *utility,* and of *pleasure,* respectively. It is not uncommon for our associations with people whom we *admire* to be both *useful* and *pleasant* as well, however, and when this occurs we have the makings of a "perfect" or complete friendship.

There, in a nutshell, is the beginning of a classical understanding of social relationships. Some high school students I know do in fact penetrate the challenging prose of Aristotle's discussion of *philia* in Books 8 and 9 of the *Nicomachean Ethics.* Others are more easily hooked on Cicero's classic essay, *On Friendship*. Current anthologies of the literature of friendship published by W. W. Norton and by the Oxford University Press include excerpts from both Aristotle and Cicero.

3. The democratic political ideal of self-government is paralleled on the individual level in the ideal of autonomous persons, people who assume responsibility for themselves. The path toward effective self-government on either the political or the individual level is notoriously tortuous. It cannot simply be thrust upon people, either collectively as societies or individually as persons. The wisdom-loving parts of societies or of individuals too easily fall prey to the power-loving, profit-loving, and pleasure-loving parts. Hubristic, plutocratic, and apolaustic elements are always among us socially, and within us individually. Plato's great insight in the *Republic* was that it is possible for these to be brought into harmonious community.

Wisdom rules in well-ordered societies and souls not by force but by persuasion. Government by persuasion depends upon a populace enabled and ready to listen, that is, a populace that is "disciplined" in the strict sense, one with practical experience of the power of choruses and teams, for example. In Socrates' Athens, education sensibly began with music and sport (among the other things included in *mousikê* and *gymnastikê*).

No popular school of thought ever focused more intensely on self-government of the soul, on assuming responsibility for oneself, than did Stoicism. Epictetus' *Handbook* remains popular among the "great books" not just because it is so short, but because it has great appeal to the adolescent mind eager to join William Ernest Henley in declaring, "I am the master of my fate;/ I am the captain of my soul" ("Invictus," 1888).

One has to work one's way up to become captain, of course. It takes years. But eventually becoming captain of one's soul means accepting the fact that "the buck stops here." Soul-captains do not whine, complain, fuss, gripe, grumble, pester, or invent excuses. We help students become responsible by giving them responsibilities—homework, among other things—and then holding them accountable. And the more that students can become engaged in serious, explicit thinking and writing about what it is to take responsibility for themselves, the better.

4. Courage is not the absence of trepidation, but of harboring it only to an appropriate extent. "I will have no man in my boat who is not afraid of a whale," sensibly warns Starbuck, chief mate on the *Pequod* (Herman Melville, *Moby Dick*, Ch. 26). During the course of a good school education, both timidity and bravado should characteristically give way to straightforward confidence in taking a stand within one's limits, in proceeding prudently with one's work in the world, and of fearing only genuinely fearful things.

Schools should carry in their basic design and governance the kinds of community support and pedagogical practices that foster in students an expectation of success and, consequently, an increasingly settled disposition to face challenges with confidence and hope. Strictly speaking, this amounts to *encouraging* students, both steeling them against irrational fears (e.g., math anxiety, fear of speaking in public) and cautioning them against imprudent adventurism (e.g., drug abuse and other forms of recklessness).

5. The Greek *sôphrosúnê* (translated variously as "temperance," "moderation," "self-control," or "self-mastery") literally means "soundness of mind." The negative or repressive connotations of these English renderings are entirely inappropriate. Persons with *sôphrosúnê* "know themselves"; they know their capacities and their limitations from having developed and tested them. They are ideal self-legislators.

The salutary results of repeated self-testing and self-development, both of which fall under the notion of *practice,* are nowhere more obvious than in athletics and music. It is no accident that conventional Greek education began with *gymnastikê* and *mousikê,* as noted above. Disciplined effort and practice pay off in increased competence and self-mastery, opening new avenues of self-expression, enjoyment and service.

The athlete and the musician come to have "soundness of mind" with respect to their own varieties of sport or music. There is no spontaneous transfer of lessons learned in these domains to other areas of life, however. Each lesson must be mastered on its own ground with the same patience and practice that one devotes to running sprints or playing scales.

6. "That's not fair!" is commonly among the earliest moral utterances of children. The fairness of parents, teachers and other persons in authority continues to rank very high among the criteria by which younger people sit in judgment over older ones. Justice is a pervasive moral concern of human beings generally. Literature at every reading level and the human record in all ages abound with examples of justice championed and justice denied.

Student concerns with justice provide splendid opportunities for cultivating their serious reflection on matters fundamental to good character. "Being fair is treating everybody the same," can be seen even by young children to be true in some sense but inadequate in others. Occasions for discussing such issues crop up repeatedly in school life.

Literature, current events, and much that goes on in school life provide excellent invitations to principled thinking, to taking people seriously as persons, to weighing merits, claims, interests, needs, and abilities, to recognizing the importance of impartiality and of getting the facts right.

Explicit attention to justice in the school community means fostering respect for persons, recognizing merit, levying sanctions consistently, responding to needs and answering to interests in principled ways, and discouraging prejudicial tendencies to regard, refer to, or act toward other people in ways that gloss over their identity as individuals.

7. Wisdom is clearly a major key to the right conduct of one's life. A good school education ought to be concerned with cultivating wisdom and each of its theoretical, practical and productive varieties, and each sort has a role to play in character education in addition to the roles it plays in other aspects of the curriculum.

Among Aristotle's more famous openers is the beginning of what we know as the Metaphysics: *All men by nature desire to know.* Human beings naturally want to grow in understanding; they want to know what to do and how to behave while doing it; and they want to know how to produce things and effects in the world. The practical wisdom that guides conduct is of course most central to character education.

John Stuart Mill eloquently observed: ". . . any mind to which the fountains of knowledge have been opened, and which has been taught, in any tolerable degree, to exercise its faculties—finds sources of inexhaustible interest in all that surrounds it: in the objects of nature, the achievements of art, the imaginations of poetry, the incidents of history, the ways of mankind, past and present, and their prospects in the future" *(Utilitarianism,* Ch. 2). A good school education ought to be enjoyed not because it has been made amusing, but because it has opened the fountains of knowledge—theoretical, practical, and productive—and exercised one's faculties in engaging ways.

Many academic disciplines aim at understanding human conduct in theoretical ways. A great deal of what students encounter in their studies in history and literature and in the natural and social sciences bears directly on their appreciation of the fascinating complexities of the world and in the patterns of human conduct that those complexities render either wise or foolish. The main caution here is to avoid the reductionisms that sometimes contaminate works of the more narrow enthusiasts to be found in most disciplines.

Today's most popular academic courses in ethics are increasingly issue-oriented rather than theoretical. There are a few theoretical challenges—the challenge of Gyges' Ring in Plato's *Republic* and the challenge of "relativism," for example—that really cry out for attention in any character education curriculum, however.

Practical Wisdom is informed intelligence operating in the sphere of human action. It is built on personal experience in growing up, working with and listening to other people, and it is well advised to draw heavily upon the accumulated wisdom of humankind. This wisdom finds expression in sayings, lessons, fables, stories, novels, plays, poems, proverbs, parables, precedents, principles, and other such reflections on human experience across cultures and down through the generations. William J. Bennett's recent anthology, *The Book of Virtues,* is the best currently available one-volume collection of such materials.

The cultivation of our creative capacities—the development and exercise of our crafting abilities—has long been recognized as a major function of education. Not only do such operations increase our facility to be productive in the world in the more obvious ways, but they serve our theoretical and practical ends as well.

As Plato saw, the quickest and most natural route into the realm of theoretical thinking lies in mathematics. And as Maria Montessori saw, the most effective entries that young children have into mathematics are in manipulative exercises that engage multiple sensory channels with both contemplative and calculative mental operations—solving puzzles with variously shaped blocks, for example. This kind of play develops both crafting and cognitive abilities in tandem.

The exercise of our artistic and technical talents is not only among the personally most satisfying activities in which we engage, but it also plays a major role in our service to others, of course. Thus does productive wisdom join with theoretical and practical wisdom in advancing further aspects of character education.

III

Were all seven of these points conscientiously attended to in character education, by the time students graduated from school they might characteristically and generally be expected to act, speak, and think in ways that are (1) respectful, (2) friendly, (3) responsible, (4) confident, (5) temperate, (6) fair, and (7) informed. These traits may manifest themselves in an indefinitely large number of ways, but here are some of them.

1. They will be civil in their relations to other persons, taking them seriously, and neither truckling to them nor patronizing them.

2. They will show goodwill and compassion in their relations with others, having friends by being friends. They will have discovered the practical limits of intimacy and of reserve, and will know the value of shared experience, both in the sharing of their own experience and in being receptive to other people's accounts. They will not betray confidences or participate in mischievous gossip. They will be sensitive to others' needs and quick to offer assistance when they are in a position to be helpful.

3. They will be responsible students and members of the community, doing assigned tasks diligently and on time, being faithful in attending rehearsals and practice sessions, volunteering to do things that are worthwhile even when they don't look like fun, and budgeting their time, effort, and money in prudent ways.

4. They will be confident in exercising the powers of thought, action, and speech which they actually possess, but concomitantly prudent in gauging their limitations. They won't be afraid to decline invitations to join in acts of vandalism or otherwise hurtful behavior, or to call attention to the stupidity of racist or sexist stories and jokes.

5. They will have known joy in the exercise of hard-won competence and gained sufficient particular knowledge of their own appetitive and aspiring natures, their passions and propensities, interests and inclinations, to become intelligent managers of their time and judicious cultivators of their talents. Relaxation and amusement will each have a place in their lives, but neither will eat up all of their leisure time. They will know enough of their own make-up to deal prudently with both temptations and challenges.

6. They will be principled in their behavior, aspiring not to do, say, or judge anything that they would not endorse others doing, saying, or judging in the same way in relevantly like circumstances. They will see the value in cultivating personal speech and behavior patterns that can be consistently maintained both in public or in private without prejudice or embarrassment. They will be open, fair, and trustworthy.

7. They will be reflective about their own experience, knowledgeable about the workings of the world around them, and able to act, speak, and think in productive and imaginative ways.

Many fine educators whom I know are already thoroughly committed to helping students develop in these ways. But no one I know supposes that we are yet doing enough.*

---

*I am grateful to Robert Flynn and Tonya Geckle for helpful criticisms of an earlier draft of this article.

An Overview of the Virtues

James B. Stenson

As children grow from infancy to adulthood, they need to acquire certain character strengths: sound judgment, a sense of responsibility, personal courage, and self-mastery. These habits of mind and will and heart have traditionally been called the *virtues*: prudence, justice, fortitude, and temperance. Children internalize these lifelong habits in three ways, and in this order:

1. *By example:* children learn from what they witness in the lives of parents and other adults whom they respect (and thus unconsciously imitate).
2. *Through directed practice:* children learn from what they are repeatedly led to do or are made to do by parents and other respected adults.
3. *From words:* children learn from what they hear from parents and other respected adults as explanations for what they witness and are led to do.

We can define the virtues—the lifelong habits—we need to cultivate in our own lives and in the lives of our children in the following ways:

Sound Judgment (Prudence)

- Respect for learning and intellectual accomplishment—
"culture."
- Understanding of human nature and life experience: motivations, values, and priorities in life.
- Habit of considering the past *causes* and future *implications* of present events and circumstances.
- Ability to recognize the good, the true, and the beautiful and to discern these from the evil, the false, and the sordid.
- Powers of moral and intellectual discernment—ability to distinguish (partial list)

> sacrifice (purposeful effort) from drudgery (pointless effort)
> responsible spirit of service from immature egoism
> true friends from acquaintances and accomplices
> heroes from celebrities
> rule of law from personal rules
> an office (such as the presidency) itself from the person in office
> conscience from feelings
> reasoned opinions from feelings
> love from eroticism
> noble and beautiful from sordid and squalid
> healthy skepticism and shrewdness from cynicism
> proven facts and certain knowledge from hypotheses and assumptions
> humor and wit from mean-spirited ridicule
> healthy self-respect from hubristic pride
> integrity from pragmatism
> self-mastery, or "class," from self-indulgence
> calculated risk taking from impulsiveness
> courtesy and good manners from boorishness
> honorable competition from ruthless ambition
> team collaboration from selfish individualism

Responsibility (Justice)

- Acknowledging and respecting the rights of others—the basis for our duties and obligations.
- Habit of doing our duties, whether we feel like it or not (includes the notion of professionalism: ability to perform at our best no matter how we feel).
- Respect for rightful authority. (Authority means, among other things, the right to be obeyed.)
- Living with the consequences of our decisions and mistakes, including neglect.
- Refusal to see oneself as a *victim.*
- Habit of honoring our promises and commitments even when this involves sacrifice.
- Habit of minding our own business, staying out of matters that do not concern us.
- Refraining from gossip, detraction, and rash judgment; giving people the benefit of the doubt and respecting others' right to presumption of innocence.

Personal Courage (Fortitude)

- Acquired ability to overcome or endure difficulties, including pain, inconvenience, disappointment, setbacks, worry, tedium.
- Habit of overcoming anxiety through purposeful, honorable *action.*
- Attitude of seeing *escape* as something unworthy, even dishonorable.
- Realization that "anticipation" is usually worse than "reality." Projected problems are generally lighter and easier than we expect them to be.
- Confidence in problem-solving abilities, built through lifetime practice in solving problems.
- Determination to overcome personal shortcomings. If we are shy, we learn to be friendly and a "good listener." If we are

impulsive, we practice restraint and reflect on consequences. If we are lazy, we strive toward purposeful action. If we do not understand something, we make an effort to study it.

Self-Mastery (Temperance)

- Acquired ability to say "no" to ourselves and our lower inclinations.
- Habit of *waiting* for rewards—and *earning* them.
- Enjoying pleasures and goods in moderation, such as food, drink, entertainment, even work.
- Lifelong habit of saying (and meaning), "Please," "Thank you," "I'm sorry," and "I give you my word."
- Habit of living courtesy and using good manners toward everyone, without exception, and doing this even in the face of rudeness or provocation.
- In a word, "class": self-restraint, etiquette, healthy self-respect, active concern for the dignity and needs of all around us, and active spirit of service.

Some "Life Lessons" Young People Need to Learn

- A shortcut to personal happiness: forget about your ego and give yourself generously to serving the needs of those around you, starting with your family.
- Love is not just sweet sentiments. It is really the willingness and ability to undergo sacrificial difficulties for the sake of the welfare and happiness of others. In a sense, love is sacrifice.
- Hard work without some ideal is just drudgery; hard work with some ideal becomes noble, adventurous sacrifice.
- Popularity is not so important as respect. If you strive too hard to have people like you, they probably won't. But if you strive to win their respect, then they will both like and respect you. (All respect comes from some perception of strength.)
- If you have self-respect, you will win the respect of others.

- Nobody respects a liar, a gossip, a cynic, or a whiner. If you act like one, people may temporarily find you amusing, but they will mistrust you and hold you without honor.
- Never make promises lightly, and when you make them, you must keep you word.
- If you read a lot, and discerningly, people come to value your judgment.
- Sometimes it requires more wisdom to take good advice than to give it.
- Character is what you have left over if you ever go broke.
- The real riches in life are family, friends, health, and a good conscience. Everything else is gravy.

The Montclair Kimberly Academy Declaration

Dr. Peter Greer, Headmaster

MKA has committed itself to enhancing the moral life of its students and adults. To accomplish this, there is agreement with the following precepts:

In order for faculty to engage students in frequent, explicit, and useful moral conversations, the faculty must themselves participate in studying, writing, reading, and talking about ethics.

In order for the program of ethics and formation of character to be successful, faculty should integrate the readings and activities into what is already being taught in all subject areas.

In order for students to understand the *public issues* that swirl around them and to cope with the moral thickets in which they find and will find themselves, they must first understand *private decency:* courage, self-mastery, justice, wisdom, responsibility, respect, friendship, and integrity.

In order for MKA to be successful, our faculty welcomes parents, "the first teachers," to participate in studies that address the moral life at home and at school.

In order for faculty, students, and parents to make sense of ideas and to use effectively the resources available in the area of ethics and the formation of character, there is confidence in a general framework that provides us with a common literacy: that to have a good life, one must lead a good life. To lead a good life, one must be able to govern (control) oneself. To govern oneself, one must (1) cultivate the intellect (theoretical wisdom) by reading about how to lead a good life and to establish good habits, and (2) cultivate good habits (practical and productive wisdom) by engaging in activities that assist in the development of character—enduring marks.

The Boston University Educators Affirmation

Steven S. Tigner

Each spring, juniors in the Boston University School of Education participate in a Junior Pinning Ceremony, during which they recite the Educator's Affirmation. With this oath, students affirm their commitment and dedication to the life of an educator.

I DEDICATE myself to the life of an educator, to laying the living foundations upon which successor generations must continue to build their lives.

I DEDICATE myself to the advancement of learning, for I know that without it our successors will lack both the vision and the power to build well.

I DEDICATE myself to the cultivation of character, for I know that humanity cannot flourish without courage, compassion, honesty, and trust.

I COMMIT myself to the advancement of my own learning and to the cultivation of my own character, for I know that I must bear witness in my own life to the ideals that I have dedicated myself to promote in others.

In the presence of this gathering, I so dedicate and commit myself.

Appendix F

Character Quotes

Children

What we remember from childhood we remember forever.
—CYNTHIA OZICK

Raise your children so that others will love them.
—BILLBOARD IN MINNEAPOLIS

A child is a person who is going to carry on what you have started. He is going to sit where you are sitting, and when you are gone, attend to those things which you think are important. You may adopt all the policies you please, but how they are carried out depends on him. He will assume control of your cities, states, and nations. He is going to move in and take over your churches, schools, universities, corporations. The fate of humanity is in his hands.
—ABRAHAM LINCOLN

A hundred years from now it will not matter what my bank account was, the sort of house I lived in, or the kind of clothes I wore—but the world may be different because I was important in the life of a child.
—YMCA POSTER

Long before a child went to school, from seventeenth-century
to early twentieth-century America, he learned simple verities.
And he learned them first, not from teachers of philosophy
or ministers of the Gospel, but literally at his mother's knee
through such collections as Mother Goose. In Mother Goose
we find moral lessons that were thought to be far too important
to await the public schools at age six. "If wishes were horses,
beggars would ride." This is Mother Goose's reminder to forget
about the pleasure principle. Remember the reality principle,
the child was told. Don't be misled by the attraction of wishful
thinking.
—JOHN R. SILBER, CHANCELLOR OF BOSTON UNIVERSITY

We've got to work to save our children and do it with full respect
for the fact that if we do not, no one else is going to do it.
—DOROTHY HEIGHT

The young do not know enough to be prudent, and therefore
they attempt the impossible—and achieve it, generation after
generation.
—PEARL S. BUCK

Teachers

I touch the future. I teach.
—CHRISTA MCAULIFFE

In a completely rational society the best of us would aspire to
be teachers and the rest of us would have to settle for something
less, because passing civilization along from one generation to
the next ought to be the highest honor and the highest responsibility anyone could have.
—LEE IACOCCA

In your classroom—right now—you may have the next leader for
the world.
—Lillian Katz

If you have some respect for people as they are, you can be
more effective in helping them to become better than they are.
—John W. Gardner

What you are thunders so loudly that I cannot hear what you say
to the contrary.
—Ralph Waldo Emerson

All that is necessary for evil to triumph is for good people to do
nothing.
—Edmund Burke

I hope God will guide our feet as parents—and guide America's
feet—to reclaim our nation's soul, and to give back to all of our
children their sense of security and their ability to dream about
and work toward a future that is hopeful—and attainable.
—Marion Wright Edelman

Democracy and Freedom

America is great because she is good, but if America ever ceases
to be good, America will cease to be great.
—Alexis de Tocqueville, 1835

Without a moral and spiritual awakening there is no hope for us.
—Dwight D. Eisenhower

I thank God that I have lived to see my country independent and
free. She may enjoy her independence and freedom if she will. It
depends on her virtue.
—Samuel Adams

Only a virtuous people are capable of freedom. As nations become corrupt and vicious, they have more need of a master. . . . Nothing is of more importance for the public weal, than to form and train up youth in wisdom and virtue.
—BENJAMIN FRANKLIN

Where, after all, do universal rights begin? In small places, close to home—so close and so small they cannot be seen on any maps of the world. Yet they are the world of the individual persons; the neighborhoods; the school or college; the factory, farm or office. Such are the places where every man, woman and child seeks equal justice, equal opportunity, equal dignity without discrimination. Unless their rights have meaning there, they have little meaning anywhere. Without concerned citizen action to uphold them close to home, we shall look in vain for progress in the larger world.
—ELEANOR ROOSEVELT

To secure the blessings of liberty, we must secure the blessings of learning.
—MARY FUTRELL

The Need for Moral/Character Education

Moral education is not a new idea. It is, in fact, as old as education itself. Down through history, in countries all over the world, education has had two great goals: to help young people become smart and to help them become good.
—THOMAS LICKONA

While there is much public concern with educational matters such as pupil reading scores, the fact is that the available data disclosed that youth character disorders—as measured by matters such as increased suicide, homicide, and drug use among youth of all races and classes—has become a more profound problem than the decline in formal learning.

—PROF. JAMES S. COLEMAN

Men possess a moral nature; but if they are well fed, warmly clad, and comfortably lodged without at the same time being instructed, they become like unto beasts.

—CONFUCIUS

The continuing sharp decline among college students in their commitment to the traditional moral values of society . . . is, in my opinion, the predictable result of the prevailing philosophy of higher education. It is a philosophy which denies any institutional obligation to provide an understanding of our moral heritage, and which proudly protects those who reject that heritage.

—DR. JOHN A. HOWARD

Our astounding crime rate is largely due to lack of ethics, which, in turn, is due to lack of ethical instruction in the schools and other opinion-forming institutions.

—DRS. GEORGE C. S. BENSON AND THOMAS S. ENGEMAN,
    FROM AMORAL AMERICA, 1975

Any system of education that is without values is a contradiction in terms. A system that seeks bad values is bad. A system that denies the existence of values denies the possibility of education. Relativism, scientism, skepticism, and anti-intellectualism, the Four Horsemen of the philosophical Apocalypse, have produced that chaos in education which will end in the disintegration of the West.

—ROBERT M. HUTCHINS

Most of the psychology on this . . . value-free, value-neutral model of science . . . is certainly not false but merely trivial. . . . This model which developed from the study of objects and things has been illegitimately used for the study of human beings. It is a terrible technique. It has not worked.
—DR. ABRAHAM MASLOW

Education makes a greater difference between man and man than nature has made between man and brute. The virtues and powers to which men may be trained, by early education and constant discipline, are truly sublime and astonishing.
—JOHN ADAMS

In addition to the fact that Johnny still can't read, we are now faced with the more serious problem that he can't tell right from wrong.
—WILLIAM KILPATRICK

It is not the brains that matter most, but that which guides them— the character, the heart, generous qualities, progressive ideas.
—FYODOR MIKHAYLOVICH DOSTOYEVSKY

Character and Respect for Self and Others

No man is free who is not master of himself.
—EPICTETUS

There is no truth more thoroughly established than that there exists in the course of Nature, an indissoluble union between virtue and happiness.
—GEORGE WASHINGTON

That you may retain your self-respect, it is better to displease the people by doing what you know is right, than to temporarily please them by doing what you know is wrong.
—WILLIAM J. H. BOETCKER

In my day, we didn't have self-esteem, we had self-respect, and no more of it than we had earned.
—JANE HADDAM

Character is the foundation stone upon which one must build to win respect. Just as no worthy building can be erected on a weak foundation, so no lasting reputation worthy of respect can be built on a weak character.
—R. C. SAMSEL

To laugh often and much; to win the respect of intelligent people and the affection of children; to earn the appreciation of honest critics and endure the betrayal of false friends; to appreciate beauty; to find the best in others; to leave the world a bit better, whether by a healthy child, a garden patch, or a redeemed social condition; to know even one life has breathed easier because you have lived. This is to have succeeded.
—RALPH WALDO EMERSON

If you want to know how to live your life, think about what you want people to say about you after you die, and live backward.
—UNKNOWN

The best portion of a good person's life is the little nameless, unremembered acts of kindness and love.
—WILLIAM WORDSWORTH

All virtue is summed up in dealing justly.
—ARISTOTLE

What you do not want done to yourself, do not do to others.
—CONFUCIUS

When evil men burn and bomb, good men must build and bind. When evil men shout ugly words of hatred, good men must commit themselves to the glories of love.
—MARTIN LUTHER KING JR.

When you cease to make a contribution, you begin to die.
—ELEANOR ROOSEVELT

Great necessities call out for great virtues.
—ABIGAIL ADAMS

When we do the best that we can, we never know what miracle is wrought in our life, or in the life of another.
—HELEN KELLER

I sometimes think that the lives of many burdens are not really to be pitied, for at least they live deeply and from their sorrows spring up flowers, but an empty life is really dreadful.
—ELEANOR ROOSEVELT

You don't get to choose how you're going to die. Or when. You can only decide how you're going to live.
—JOAN BAEZ

Caring can be learned by all human beings, can be worked into the design of every life, meeting an individual need as well as a pervasive need in society.
—MARY CATHERINE BATESON

Character and Integrity

Once you tell one lie, you need to create a whole bodyguard of lies to protect it.
—WINSTON CHURCHILL

There is a big difference between what we have a right to do and what is right to do.
—JUSTICE POTTER STUART

No man can always be right. So the struggle is to do one's best; to keep the brain and conscience clear; never to be swayed by unworthy motives or inconsequential reasons, but to strive to unearth the basic factors involved and then do one's duty.
—DWIGHT D. EISENHOWER

What is right is right even if no one is doing it. What is wrong is wrong even if everyone is doing it.
—UNKNOWN

Character and Work

You may be disappointed if you fail, but you are doomed if you don't try.
—BEVERLY SILLS

Be of good cheer. Do not think of today's failures, but of the success that may come tomorrow. You have set yourselves a difficult task, but you will succeed if you persevere, and you will find a joy in overcoming obstacles. Remember, no effort that we make to attain something beautiful is ever lost.
—HELEN KELLER

It takes as much courage to have tried and failed as it does to have tried and succeeded.
—ANNE MORROW LINDBERGH

Work is such a beautiful and helpful thing and independence so delightful that I wonder there are any lazy people in the world.
—LOUISA MAY ALCOTT

A bad workman always blames his tools.
—PROVERB

Action Strategies

One Hundred Ways to Bring Character Education to Life

Building a Community of Virtue

1. Develop a school code of ethics. Distribute it to every member of the school community. Refer to it often. Display it prominently. Make sure all school policy reflects it.
2. Institute a student-to-student tutoring program.
3. Promote schoolwide or intraclass service clubs to serve the school, class, or external community.
4. Encourage students to identify a charity or in-school need, collect donations, and help administer the distribution of funds.
5. Ensure that the schools' recognition systems cover both character and academics.
6. Recognize a variety of achievements, such as surpassing past personal achievements or meeting a predetermined goal.
7. Consistently prohibit gossip and, when appropriate, discuss its damaging consequences.
8. Enforce a zero-tolerance policy on swearing. Prohibit vulgar and obscene language in the classroom and on school property.
9. Use morning announcements, school and classroom bulletin boards, and the school newsletter to highlight the various accomplishments—particularly character-oriented ones—of students and faculty members.

10. When conflicts arise around the school or class, teach about discretion, tact, and privacy—and about discreetly informing appropriate adults of the conflict.

11. Have students take turns caring for class pets and taking them home over weekends and holidays. Discuss and demonstrate the responsibility required to care for living creatures.

12. Invite student volunteers to clean up their community. With parental support, encourage students to build a community playground, pick up litter, rake leaves, plant trees, paint a mural, remove graffiti, or clean up a local park or beach.

13. Find out the significance behind your school's traditions and emphasize those that build school unity.

14. Display the school flag. Learn the school song. If you don't have either, have a contest!

15. Have ceremonies to mark the beginning and end of the school year and for teachers and staff members who are leaving.

16. Examine school assemblies. Do a minority of students control the majority of assemblies? How could more students be involved? Are the chants at pep assemblies appropriate? Do they build school spirit without demeaning other schools?

17. Ensure students behave responsibly and respectfully when watching athletic competitions.

18. In physical education and sports programs, place a premium on good sportsmanship. Participation in sports should provide good habits for the life beyond sports.

19. Hang pictures of heroes and heroines in classrooms and halls. Include appropriate explanatory text.

20. Make the school a welcoming place. Can people walking through the school halls get a good idea of what is happening in classrooms? Is the principal frequently visible to students? Are there clear welcome signs prominently placed near the school's main door?

21. Start a school scrapbook with photos, news stories, and memorabilia reflecting the school's history and accomplishments.

Involve school members in contributing to and maintaining the collection. Show it off to visitors and new families.

22. Publicly recognize the work of the "unsung heroes" who keep the school running: the custodians, repairmen, secretaries, cafeteria workers, and volunteers.

23. Develop a system of welcoming and orienting new students to the school.

24. Prohibit the display of any gang symbols or paraphernalia on school property. Remove graffiti immediately—including in student bathrooms.

25. Let students take some responsibility for the maintenance and beautification of the school. Classes could "adopt a hallway," shelve misplaced books, plant flowers, and so on. Post signs identifying the caretakers.

Mining the Curriculum

26. Have students do a major paper on a living public figure ("My Personal Hero"), focusing on the moral achievements and virtues of the individual. First, do the groundwork of helping them understand what constitutes a particularly noble life.

27. In history and literature classes, regularly weave in a discussion of motivations, actions, and consequences.

28. Insist that quality matters. Homework should be handed in on time, neat and complete. Details do count.

29. Include the study of "local heroes" in social studies classes.

30. Help students form friendships. When forming cooperative learning groups, keep in mind both the academic and emotional needs of the students. These groups can be an opportunity to group students who might not otherwise interact with one another.

31. Ensure that students have a firm understanding of what constitutes plagiarism and of the school's firm policy against it. But more importantly, help them to understand why it is wrong.

32. Celebrate the birthdays of heroes and heroines with discussions of their accomplishments.

33. Choose the finest children's and adult literature to read with your students—literature rich with meaning and imagery. Don't waste time with mediocre or unmemorable texts.

34. Don't underestimate the power of stories to build a child's moral imagination. Read aloud to students daily.

35. Conduct literature discussions—even in the youngest grades. Ask questions that encourage reflection. Don't immediately jump to "the moral of the story" while ignoring the richness, beauty, or complexity of the text. General questions could include: What did this book make you think about or feel? Tell me about [a character's name]—what kind of person was he? Why do you think the author wrote this book—what did she want to say to the reader? Don't leave a story, however, without having students grapple with its moral message.

36. Build empathy in literature and social studies classes by teaching children to put themselves in the shoes of the people they are reading about or studying.

37. Read and discuss biographies from all subject areas. Help students identify the person's core or defining characteristics.

38. While studying about great men and women, do not consistently avoid the subject of personal weakness—especially in the upper grades. A study of a person's "whole" character can provide a powerful lesson in discernment and compassion. Consider a thoughtful discussion of the following question: Can a person be "great" (and good) and still have some character flaws?

39. Teach students to write thoughtful letters: thank-you notes, letters to public officials, letters to the editor, and so on.

40. Assign homework that stimulates and challenges students. Engaging and demanding assignments will give rise to self-discipline and perseverance.

41. Set up a buddy reading system between an older and younger class. Carefully teach the older students techniques that will

help make their teaching experience successful. Impress upon them the responsibility and patience required when helping those who are both younger and less skilled in a subject than they are.

42. Have students memorize poetry and important prose selections, such as the preamble to the Declaration of Independence or the Gettysburg Address. In the process, make sure they understand the ideas that make these works worthy of committing to memory.

43. In science, address with each unit (when appropriate) the ethical considerations of that field of study. Students need to see that morality and ethics are not confined to the humanities.

44. In math classes, specifically address the habits—such as courage, perseverance, and hard work—required to be a successful math student. Class rules and homework policies should reflect and support these habits.

45. In social studies, examine—and reexamine yearly, if the curriculum affords the chance—the responsibilities of the citizen. What can students do right now to build the habits of responsible citizenship?

Involving Teachers, Administrators, and Staff

46. Choose a personal motto or mission statement.

47. Tell your students who your heroes are and why you chose them.

48. Lead by example. Pick up the piece of paper in the hall. Leave the classroom clean for the next teacher. Say thank you.

49. Employ the language of virtue in conversations with colleagues: *responsibility, commitment, perseverance, courage,* and so on.

50. Make your classroom expectations clear and hold students accountable.

51. Admit mistakes and seek to make amends. Expect and encourage students to do likewise.

52. Follow through. Do what you say you will do. For example, administer tests when they are scheduled; don't cancel at the last minute after students have prepared.

53. If you engage in community or church service, let your students know in an appropriate, low-key manner.

54. Illustrate integrity: let students see that you yourself meet the expectations of hard work, responsibility, gratitude, and perseverance that you place upon them.

55. Give students sufficient and timely feedback when you evaluate their work. This demonstrates to students that their work matters and that teachers take an interest in their improvement and success.

56. Teach justice and compassion by helping students separate the doer from the deed.

57. Stand up for the underdog or the student who is being treated poorly by classmates. But use discretion: sometimes use an immediate response; sometimes use a private small-group meeting—perhaps the person in question ought not be present.

58. Use constructive criticism (individually and collectively), tempered by compassion. Use class discussions as opportunities to teach students to do the same when responding to one another.

59. Include in faculty and staff meetings and workshops discussions of the school's moral climate. How can the ethos of the school be improved?

60. Begin a bulletin board where teachers and administrators can share their own "One Hundred Ways . . ."

Involving Parents

61. Create a written code of behavior for the classroom and the school. Ask parents to read and sign the code, as a pledge of mutual support.

62. Consider having a parent representative present while developing such school codes.

63. Make the effort to notify parents of student misbehavior, via notes, phone calls, and personal visits.

64. "Catch students being good" and write or call parents to report it.

65. Communicate with parents about appropriate ways they can help students with their schoolwork.

66. Send a letter home to parents before the school year starts, introducing yourself, your classroom, your enthusiasm, and your expectations, particularly your hope that they will help you help their child.

67. Involve as many parents as possible in the PTO.

68. Frequently share the school's vision and high ideals for its students with parents.

69. Open a dialogue with parents. They can be a teacher's greatest ally in helping students succeed. They can provide pertinent, invaluable information about their children's academic and social background, interests, talents, difficulties, and so on.

70. In the school newsletter, inform parents of upcoming events, units of study, and opportunities to participate in school and after-school activities.

71. Develop a list of suggested readings and resources in character education and share it with parents.

72. When appropriate, provide literacy classes or tutors for parents.

73. Provide parents with access to the school library. Provide a suggested reading list of books with solid moral content that make good read-alouds.

74. Structure opportunities for parents to meaningfully participate in classrooms, beyond providing refreshments and chaperoning field trips. For example: reading with students, presenting a lesson in an area of expertise, tutoring, sharing family heirlooms, helping organize class plays or projects.

75. Send out monthly newsletters to parents that include details on your character education efforts.

76. Include anecdotes of commendable student performance in the school newsletter.

77. Include a "parents' corner" in the newsletter, where parents can share parenting tips, book titles, homework helps, and so on.

78. When your school welcomes a new student, welcome the student's family as well.

79. What can your school do to encourage greater attendance at parent-teacher conferences? Examine the times they are held and how they are advertised. What is being done to reach out to the parents who never come?

80. During parent-teacher conferences, ask parents, "What are your questions or concerns?" Then listen carefully to their answers.

Involving Students

81. Begin a service program in which students "adopt-an-elder" from the community. Arrange opportunities for students to visit, write letters to, read to, or run errands for their adoptee.

82. Structure opportunities for students to perform community service.

83. Prohibit students from being unkind or using others as scapegoats in the classroom.

84. Make it clear to students that they have a moral responsibility to work hard in school.

85. Impress upon students that being a good student means far more than academic success.

86. After students have developed an understanding of honesty and academic integrity, consider instituting an honor system for test taking and homework assignments.

87. Provide opportunities for students to both prepare for competition and engage in cooperation.

88. Help students acquire the power of discernment, including the ability to judge the truth, worth, and biases of what is presented on TV, the radio, and the Internet.

89. Invite graduates of the high school to return and talk about their experience in the next stage of life. Ask them to discuss what habits or virtues could make the transition to work or college successful and what bad habits or vices cause problems.

90. Have students identify a substantive quote or anecdote from which they can begin to develop a personal motto.

91. Overtly teach courtesy.

92. Make every effort to instill a work ethic in students. Frequently explain their responsibility to try their best. Create minimum standards for the quality of work you will accept—then don't accept work that falls short.

93. During election years, encourage students to research candidates' positions, listen to debates, participate in voter registration drives, and if eligible, vote.

94. Use the language of virtue with students: *responsibility, respect, integrity, diligence,* and so on, and teach them to use this language.

95. In large middle and high schools, assess what is being done to keep students from "falling through the cracks." Every student needs at least one teacher or counselor to take specific interest in them.

96. In middle and high schools, consider instituting (or strengthening) an advising program. Advisors should do more than provide job and college information—they should take an interest in the intellectual and character development of their advisees.

97. Hold students accountable to a strict attendance and tardiness policy.

98. Through stories, discussion, and examples, teach students about true friendship. Help them recognize the characteristics of true friends and the potentially destructive power of false friendships.

99. "Doing the right thing" is not always an easy choice—especially in the face of peer pressure. Help students, both individually and as a class, to see the long-term consequences of their actions. They may need the support of a responsible adult both before and after choices are made.

100. Remind students—and yourself—that character building is not an easy or a one-time project. Fashioning our character is the work of a lifetime.

This list was created and updated by the staff of the Center for the Advancement of Ethics and Character (CAEC) at Boston University, with input from numerous teachers and administrators. If you would like more information about the center's membership program or the Character Education Network, please call the CAEC at (617) 353-3262 or write to Center for the Advancement of Ethics and Character, 605 Commonwealth Ave., Boston, MA 02215.

Pitfalls to Avoid in Character Education

1. Do not keep parents in the dark—they are your number-one allies. The same is true for community leaders (clergy, civic groups, PTO). Hold public meetings on your program, and give everyone an opportunity to hear about it and share in it.
2. Do not keep the district office, the superintendent, or the board of education in the dark either. In fact, every character education program should have a clear mandate from the school authorities.
3. The program should not "belong" to a few enthusiasts or zealots. A successful program will need the commitment of the entire school community, from the school principal to the bus drivers.
4. Do not rely on posters, slogans, and other quick and glitzy character education gimmicks alone. Good character education is the quiet, steady, patient development of good habits (virtues) and the pursuit of learning that engages and stimulates character development.
5. Do not count on extrinsic rewards to cultivate virtues. Although virtuous behavior needs to be acknowledged, it needn't always be rewarded. Character education is about inspiring students to do the good; interesting them in worthwhile pursuits, both academic and extracurricular; and helping them to internalize good habits.

6. Avoid the "Do as I say, not as I do" mentality. Individual actions speak louder than words; it's our deeds that really give witness to what's most worthwhile. These are what compose our most powerful lessons in character. Remember, seeing is believing. Character education has to be on the forefront of our personal agenda if it is to have any influence on our students.

7. Do not reduce literature study to the search for a moral lesson. Great stories, including those that make up our historic tradition, are rich in artistic, literary, and philosophical value. Let students discover and enjoy the narrative first, and speak to the elements that make it great. Then help them plumb the work for its moral meaning. In the end, the stories will be much more memorable.

8. Do not reduce character education to "acquiring the right views." Also do not be deceived into thinking character education is simply about debating moral dilemmas—particularly on the most controversial topics. Solving moral dilemmas and debating an array of value positions will not build virtue or intellectual integrity, for that matter. Students must be encouraged to be intellectually honest, to ground their discussion by gathering facts, to respect the religious significance attached to certain moral issues, and to remain humble before what they have yet to learn.

9. Do not be deceived into believing that a "character education course" at your school will relieve you of your responsibility of educating for character in other areas, whether you teach math, English, science, art, or French. Learning and teaching are moral in nature. The expectations you hold, the encouragement you provide, and the sustained intellectual and personal challenge your students experience in your classroom have much more staying power than a mini-sermon on hard work.

10. Do not neglect the million and one opportunities to celebrate, model, communicate, and teach virtue in the hallways, in the cafeteria, on the playing fields, and in the faculty room.

11. Character education is not something that we "do to" students. It is not about imposing or instilling values or giving character. It is about helping children accept as their personal project the development of their own character.

Ten Commandments for Parents

Someone has recently quipped that if the Lord waited to the 1990s to deliver to Moses the Ten Commandments, He would have couched them in the spirit of the age and called them the Ten Suggestions. In summarizing our advice to parents, we are harkening back to the language of an earlier era.

The First Commandment: Thou Shalt Put Parenting First

American parents for some time have been on vacation from their children. The results are in and they don't look good. Raising good children, children of character, demands time and attention. Educators have recently discovered that the key to good teaching is time-on-task, the ability to keep the student engaged in learning. Good parents make their children their first work.

The Second Commandment: Thou Shalt Be a Good Example

Face it! Deal with it! It's part of the job. No one likes having continuously to be a "good example," but it just comes with the territory. In fact, you can't avoid being an example—for good or ill. Modern psychologists have discovered what people knew centuries ago, that humans learn primarily from the example of those around them. They learn not only how to walk and talk but also their moral values that way.

The Third Commandment: Thou Shalt Not Carry This Burden Alone

All the people around our children are potential models for good or ill. Although parents are the strongest examples, others influence their moral values and attitudes, too. Brothers and sisters, neighbors, their children, relatives, bus drivers, and especially teachers all influence them. We must be alert to the type of example these people are providing our children and, where we can, arrange the worlds of our children so they are exposed to the best and are safe from the worst.

The Fourth Commandment:
Thou Shalt Be Deeply Involved in Thy Child's School Life

Parents are the child's primary character educators, but teachers and the schools are also major players. It is important to know what is going on in your child's school life, from the curriculum to the playground, from the classrooms to the bathrooms. Teachers, in particular, need to know of your interest, and they need to feel your support for their work as character educators.

The Fifth Commandment:
Thou Shalt Monitor What Enters Thy Child's Heart and Mind

Good character means developing a sense of what is right and wrong, what is a good person and a weak person. Besides the real people and real events in a child's life that shape character, there are books, television, music, and films that are constantly delivering moral messages to our young. Parents must control the flow of ideas that wash over their child. They must be their own V-chip.

The Sixth Commandment: Thou Shalt Stick to the Basics

Children are not born with good characters and a fully developed set of moral values. They need a long process of learning. Don't start out expecting heroic values or a highly developed moral sense. Teach basic habits of honesty, concern for others, and responsibility. As they grow, focus on persistence, prudence, and justice. Help them build their characters on the firm foundation of basic habits or virtues.

The Seventh Commandment: Thou Shalt Punish with a Loving Heart

Children need limits. They need to know what they can do and what they cannot do. They need rules and procedures. And they will, alas, overrun these limits and break these rules. Reasonable punishment is an aspect of human learning, particularly of forming good character. But children must understand what punishment is for and know that its source is parental love.

The Eighth Commandment: Thou Shalt Use Moral Language

Events should not simply be called "appropriate" or "inappropriate." Behavior that is hurtful to others ought to be labeled as "wrong" or "bad." Human actions that contribute to the well-being of family members and others or to the advancement of the common good should be clearly labeled as "good" and "right." Children cannot develop a moral compass unless the people around them use such language.

The Ninth Commandment:
Thou Shalt Not Reduce Character Education to Words Alone

A child should learn early that good character is much more than words—and that "talking the talk" is one thing but "walking the walk" is what counts. Parents should help children by promoting moral action through self-discipline, good work habits, and kind and considerate behavior toward others and through community service. Children must know that the bottom line in character development is behavior—*their* behavior.

The Tenth Commandment:
Thou Shalt Make Good Character a High Priority in Your Home

Parents and children have many pressures on them. They have many demands on their time and many distractions in their lives.

The modern world is constantly screaming for our attention, time, and energies. Our children must know that our first concern for them is that they use their formative years to make themselves strong individuals, that they make themselves people of good character.

Curriculum

Exemplary Moral Education Curricula

The Core Virtues Program

Developed by Mary Beth Klee of the Crossroads Academy, in Lyme, New Hampshire, Core Virtues is a K–6 character education program designed to complement the E. D. Hirsch Core Knowledge Sequence. (The Core Virtues program can be used independently of the Core Knowledge Sequence, however.) The program teaches virtue through daily reading, writing, discussion, and morning meetings. The list of core virtues includes respect, diligence, gratitude, and courage; they are taught over a three-year cycle. Core Virtues is organized around a monthly virtue with seasonal relevance. It includes age-appropriate definitions of the virtues, guidelines for morning meetings, and a wide selection of engaging literature.

For more information on Core Virtues, please contact Crossroads Academy, 95 Dartmouth College Highway, Lyme, NH 03768; phone: (603) 795-3111; online: www.crossroadsacademy.org

The Learning for Life Program

Learning for Life is a K–12 character education program carefully developed and researched by an affiliate of the Boy Scouts of America. The program has curricular lessons based on moral values such as respect and responsibility and certain skills such as "meeting deadlines," for each of the various grade levels. The lessons are short and easily woven into the school's curriculum. The training required is minimal but effective. A recent study by an independent research firm showed dramatic growth in understanding of the curriculum's core values, as well as marked improvement in student behavior. Positive change was particularly evident among urban students. Learning for Life is an excellent supplement to any school's character education program.

For more information on Learning for Life, please contact Learning for Life, 1325 West Walnut Hill Lane, P.O. Box 152079, Irving, TX 75015-2079.

The Giraffe Project

The Giraffe Heroes Program™ is a story-based curriculum that teaches courageous compassion and fosters the leader in every child. Divided into K–2, 3–5, and 6–9 editions, the program begins by telling students the stories of brave, caring "Giraffes," people from age 8 to 108 who have stuck their necks out for the common good. Giraffes are of every color and creed, working on hundreds of issues. Students then look in their schools, families, neighborhoods, and communities to find more real heroes, whose stories they bring back to their classmates. In the final phase of the program, the students go into action themselves, creating and carrying out a service project they design to address a public problem that concerns them. "The Seven Neckbones"© process guides them from choosing their project to successfully completing it. Students in the program have done research, written letters, made presentations, spoken in public, solved problems, negotiated, worked with media, and dealt with conflicts. The Giraffe Heroes Program can be integrated into social studies and language arts and is widely used by guidance counselors. Giraffe programs meet schools' needs for community service, character education, and service learning and can be used in conjunction with other curricula.

Trainings are available. A new program for high schoolers and young adults will be available in January 1999.

For more information on the Giraffe Heroes Program, please contact the Giraffe Project, P.O. Box 759, Langley, WA 98260; phone: (360) 221-7989; fax: (360) 221-7817; Web: www.giraffe.org/giraffe; e-mail: office@giraffe.org

The Loving Well Project

Developed at Boston University with a grant from the Department of Health and Human Services, "The Art of Loving Well: A Character Education Curriculum for Today's Teenagers" offers an ingenious approach to integrating "relationship education" into the curriculum. Loving Well teaches that "it is the quality of our relationships that determines the quality of our lives." The program's brochure captures its purpose succinctly: "Experience may sometimes be the best teacher, but in the areas of love and sexuality, experience can be painful if not dangerous. The Loving Well Project helps adolescents learn responsible sexual and social values through good literature, which reveals the complexity of life and love relationships. Healthy friendships, romances, and families require sensitivity and insight into ourselves and others. The curriculum includes activities that enable students to learn vicariously from their readings and from conversations with teachers, parents, and friends.

For more information on The Art of Loving Well, please contact the Loving Well Project, School of Education, Boston University, 605 Commonwealth Avenue, Boston, MA 02215; phone: (617) 353-4088; fax: (617) 353-2909.

Sample Mini-Unit: "Jonah and the Whale"

Grade Level: Kindergarten/First/Second
Related Virtues: Responsibility, Persistence

Note: There are several good picture-book retellings of the biblical story of Jonah. Among the best are those by Allison Reed and Kurt Baumann. The following questions and activities are general enough to suit any complete retelling of the Jonah story.

Warm-Up

1. Read and reread the following poem with students. Engage them in a choral reading activity with the poem.

> **Good-Bye, Six—Hello, Seven**
> I'm getting a higher bunk bed.
> And I'm getting a bigger bike.
> And I'm getting to cross Connecticut Avenue
> all by myself, if I like.
> And I'm getting to help do the dishes.
> And I'm getting to weed the yard.
> And I'm getting to think that seven
> could be hard.
>
> (from *If I Were in Charge of the
> World and Other Worries,* Judith
> Viorst, Atheneum, 1993)

Use this poem to talk about what it means to grow older. For example, first-grade teachers could use the poem to discuss the differences between kindergarten and first grade. What have they learned that they didn't know in kindergarten? What new responsibilities do they have? The class together could write a new poem: "Good-Bye, Kindergarten—Hello, First Grade."

2. The biblical story of Jonah describes a young prophet who tries to run away from a difficult responsibility—a man who wants the enjoyable parts of being a prophet without the more challenging responsibilities that come with the calling. As you read (and reread) this story with the children, ask them to listen for answers to these questions: (1) What good decisions does Jonah make? (2) What mistakes does he make? (3) Why did he run away?

Talk Time: Key Questions

1. What did this story make you think about? Tell me about Jonah.

2. In the beginning, why was Jonah afraid to do what God asked him to do?

3. Was running away a good decision? Why or why not? What could Jonah have done besides run away?

4. What do you think Jonah was thinking about during the storm? How was he feeling? What was he thinking about when he was inside the whale?

5. What can we learn from this story? What did Jonah learn?

6. Do we ever act like Jonah by trying to avoid doing something we're supposed to do? Does running away make things better?

7. Why did God send Jonah to Ninevah, and what could have happened if Jonah hadn't gone? (Point out that as a prophet, it was Jonah's job—his responsibility—to warn people when they were wicked. This job wasn't always easy, but it was very important.) What specific responsibilities do students and teachers have (to

themselves and to each other)? Brainstorm a list of these responsibilities, pausing to discuss why each is important.

Extra! Extra!

1. Using the ideas generated from the list of responsibilities
from Question Seven, create a class motto. As a class, design and
post the motto, memorize it, and recite it often.

2. Have students respond in art and words to the title, "What
Jonah Learned in the Belly of the Whale."

Sample Mini-Unit: *Sadako and the Thousand Paper Cranes*

Grade Level: Third/Fourth
Related Virtues: Diligence, Sacrifice, Hope, Courage
Deborah Farmer, CAEC

Warm-Up

Though *Sadako,* by Eleanor Coerr, is a short and simple read, students need to be prepared for the themes and history it contains. Students need some background on both the culture of Japan and the dropping of the bomb on Hiroshima. This could be taught in several ways. Below is one possible scenario:

Pull down a world map and have the students locate Japan. What do they notice? How big is it? How far away from the United States? Does anybody know anything about Japan? Bring in pictures of Japan and its people—women in traditional kimonos, Buddhist temples, tatami floors, big cities, rice fields, etc. Have the students look at the pictures carefully and tell you what they notice. Help the students understand a few of the basics of Japanese culture.

Explain that many years ago, the United States and Japan were fighting against each other in World War II. The war was almost over—Germany had surrendered—but the Japanese government wouldn't give up. U.S. President Harry Truman wanted to end the war before more American soldiers died. He made the difficult (and controversial) decision to drop an atomic bomb—the first nuclear weapon—on the Japanese city of Hiroshima.

Talk Time: Key Questions

Prologue to Chapter 3

1. The prologue tells us that Sadako is considered a heroine in Japan. As students read each chapter, they should record what they learn about Sadako. Tell the students that we want to learn as much as we can about her so that we can begin to answer the question, "Why is Sadako a heroine?" Give students time each day to discuss their observations.

2. In Chapter 2, Sadako visits Peace Park on Peace day. Read the following sentence: "If any of the bomb victims came near Sadako, she turned away quickly." Why did she do this?

Chapter 4 to Chapter 6

1. How does Sadako's family respond to the news that Sadako has leukemia? How do you think their lives will change?

2. What is the "story of the cranes"? Do you think folding cranes will help Sadako? Why or why not?

3. Discuss Chizuko. Chizuko is a loyal friend in Chapter 5. If you had a friend who was sick or whose life had changed, what could you do to help them?

4. Discuss Kenji. Why is his outlook on life so different from Sadako's?

5. How is Sadako changing?

Chapters 8 and 9

1. Sadako isn't the only brave character in the book. Who else shows courage? Read the students the following passage from Chapter 8:

Mrs. Sasaki spent more and more time at the hospital. Every afternoon Sadako listened for the familiar *slap-slap* of her plastic slippers in the hall. All visitors had to put on yellow slippers at the door, but Mrs. Sasaki's made a special sound. Sadako's heart ached to see her mother's face so lined with worry.

The leaves on the maples tree were turning rust and gold when the family came for one last visit. Eiji handed Sadako a big box wrapped in gold paper and tied with a red ribbon. Slowly Sadako opened it. Inside was something her mother had always wanted for her—a silk kimono with cherry blossoms on it. Sadako felt hot tears blur her eyes.

"Why did you do it?" she asked, touching the soft cloth. "I'll never be able to wear it and silk costs so much money."

"Sadako chan," her father said gently, "your mother stayed up late last night to finish sewing it. Try it on for her."

With great effort Sadako lifted herself out of bed. Mrs. Sasaki helped her put on the kimono and tie the sash. Sadako was glad her swollen legs didn't show. Unsteadily she limped across the room and sat in her chair by the window. Everyone agreed that she was like a princess in the kimono.

Why did Mrs. Sasaki sacrifice to make this kimono for her daughter?
2. Sadako died before she could make one thousand cranes. Were the cranes a waste of time . . . or were they important? [After some discussion of Question 3, the teacher may want to point to this passage in Chapter 8: "She never complained about the shots and almost constant pain. A bigger pain was growing deep inside of her. It was the fear of dying. She had to fight it as well as the disease. The golden crane helped. It reminded Sadako that there was always hope."]
3. Why do you think the author wrote this book?

Extra! Extra!

1. Creative Writing: Haiku is a type of Japanese poem that Sadako would have been familiar with. Haiku is made up of three non-rhyming lines. The first line contains a total of five syllables, the second line contains seven syllables, and the third line has five syllables. The goal of a haiku is to create a picture in the mind of the reader. For example:

> The first golden crane
> Comforted weak Sadako
> Creased with hope and love

Once introduced to this form, students should write poems based on *Sadako and the Thousand Paper Cranes*. They should try to capture an image, character, or important theme. Additionally, the class could write a group haiku about Sadako's diligence and keep it posted on the bulletin board.

2. Teach the students how to make paper cranes for the purpose of demonstrating the physical diligence required for the weakened Sadako to complete 644 cranes. Give them an opportunity to write and talk about the experience. If the students want to turn this activity into a service project, the Japanese government in Hiroshima hangs thousands of cranes yearly in memory of those who died in the blast. Children from across the world send in strung cranes to be displayed.

Sample Mini-Unit: *The Little Prince*

Grade Levels: Sixth, Seventh, Eighth
Related Virtues: Truth, Responsibility, Wisdom, Empathy
Deborah Farmer, CAEC

The Little Prince, by Antoine de Saint-Exupéry, invites readers to investigate "Truth" as something more than simple "Honesty." The Little Prince is a character given to thoughtful reflection—he is interested in "matters of consequence." However, he quickly discovers that everyone has his or her own idea of what is important in life—and he finds that many of these people are leading sad and trivial lives. After many travels and experiences, the Prince is handed a beautiful truth that cuts through the confusing voices and gives him a new way of seeing:

> And now here is my secret, a very simple secret: It is only with the heart that one can see rightly; what is essential is invisible to the eye.

Warm-Up

1. Before teachers introduce *The Little Prince,* they should bring in a quote that is personally meaningful—one that has taught them something or caused them to think differently. As students study

The Little Prince, they will be asked to respond to quotes from the text, explaining:

1. What the quote means
2. How it applies to them or to a real-life situation

Teachers should use their quote to model this type of response.

    2. Give each student the book and five to ten Post-it Notes. Ask students to use these notes to mark sentences or passages that they find interesting, thoughtful, or meaningful. The following quotes from Chapters 8 and 9 could be identified as examples:

- "The fact is that I did not know how to understand anything. I ought to have judged by deeds and not by words."
- "Well, I must endure the presence of two or three caterpillars if I wish to become acquainted with butterflies."

    During the class discussions, or at other points during the week, encourage students to share and discuss their choices with their classmates.

Talk Time: Key Questions

Lesson 1

By this class, students should have completed Chapters 1–9.
    1. Ask for students' responses to the book thus far.
    2. Ask students to respond to the following excerpt from Chapter 7:

> I know a planet where there is a certain red-faced gentleman. He has never smelled a flower. He has never looked at a star. He has never loved anyone. He has never done anything in his life but add up figures. And all day he says over and over, just like you: "I am busy with matters of consequence!"

What does this mean? What is a "matter of consequence"?

3. We can learn a lot about the characters in the book—and people in general—by figuring out what is important to them. (Look to the text for evidence.)

- What is important to the prince?
- What is important to the flower?
- What is important to the narrator?

4. What if someone were to "read" your life? What would stand out as being important to you?

Assignment for Week 2

Read Chapters 10–15. Break students into five groups and assign one chapter to each group; each chapter contains a visit to a different planet. For the next lesson, they should prepare a presentation about their chapter that answers the questions: What is important to the man the Little Prince meets in your chapter? Is he happy—why or why not? Encourage creativity (news report, interview, skit, game show, poem, etc.)

Lesson 2

Student presentations! Conclude the presentations by returning to what the Prince believes to be important, highlighting the following passage from Chapter 14:

> "That man [the lamplighter]," said the little prince to himself as he continued farther on his journey, "that man would be scorned by all the others: by the king, by the conceited man, by the tippler, by the businessman. Nevertheless, he is the only one of them all who does not seem to me ridiculous. Perhaps that is because he is thinking of something else besides himself."

Lesson 3

The students should have finished the book. The discussion will focus on Chapter 21.

  1. Tell me about the Prince and the Fox. What happened? What was the fox's secret?

> And now here is my secret, a very simple secret: It is only with the heart that one can see rightly; what is essential is invisible to the eye.

Write this quote on the board or overhead and let students reflect for a moment on what this might mean. Invite them to share their thoughts.

  2. A few pages later, in Chapter 24, the Prince comments, "The stars are beautiful, because of a flower that cannot be seen." The narrator continues:

> When I was a little boy I lived in an old house, and legend told us that a treasure was buried there. To be sure, no one had ever known how to find it; perhaps no one had ever even looked for it. But it cast an enchantment over that house. My home was hiding a secret in the depths of its heart. . . .
>
> "Yes," I said to the little prince. "The house, the stars, the desert—what gives them their beauty is something that is invisible."

Do you think the same thing is true of people?

  3. Is beauty on the outside or the inside? What can we see? (appearance, clothing, skin color, toys, jewelry, the cars driven) What can't we see? (love, dreams and hopes, friendship, kindness, loyalty, hurt)

Extra! Extra!

1. Hand each student a paper with the heading:

"It is only with the heart that one can see rightly;
what is essential is invisible to the eye."

Beautiful Truths About _____.

Have them fill in their name in the blank. Students should silently pass the papers around the room. On each paper they should record something they admire or respect about that person. Students should refrain from commenting on the *visible,* i.e., physical appearance.

2. Have the students search the book and their notes and markings to identify their favorite passage or quote—one that taught them a truth. Have them write a letter to a friend or loved one relating the passage and describing what it means and what they learned. This activity allows students to "reflect thoughtfully"—a hallmark of a morally matured person. Allow sufficient time for students to revise their letters and share them with the class.

Notes

Chapter One

1. Frankl, V. E. *Man's Search for Meaning.* New York: Washington Square Press, 1984, p. 135. (Originally published 1959.)
2. "Saving Grace." *People,* Aug. 28, 1995, pp. 40–41.
3. We have used David Ross's translation of Aristotle's *Nicomachean Ethics* (New York: Oxford University Press, 1925) for all our Aristotle references.
4. Glendon, M. A. "Forgotten Questions." In D. Blankenhorn and M. A. Glendon (eds.), *Seedbeds of Virtue: Sources of Character, Competence, and Citizenship.* Lanham, Md.: Madison Books, 1995, p. 2.
5. See *Specimens of the Table Talk of Samuel Taylor Coleridge.* Jotted down after evenings with Coleridge, these records of his conversations were published one year after his death by his nephew, Henry Nelson Coleridge. Woodring, C. (ed.). *The Collected Works of Samuel Taylor Coleridge: Table Talk.* Vol. 14. Princeton, N.J.: Princeton University Press, 1990. (Original edition 1836.)
6. "Emerging Trends." Princeton Religious Research Center, Dec. 1993.
7. Tigner, S. "Character Education: Outline of a Seven-Point Program." *Journal of Education, 1993, 175*(2), p. 15.

Chapter Two

1. Kreeft, P. *Back to Virtue.* Fort Collins. Ind.: Ignatius Press, 1992, p. 26.
2. Jarvis, F. W. "Beyond Ethics." *Journal of Education, 1993, 175*(2), p. 61.
3. See Egan, J. "The Thin Red Line." *New York Times Magazine,* Jul. 27, 1997, p. 20.
4. Sommers, C. H. "Are We Living in a Moral Stone Age?" *Imprimis, 27*(3), p. 4.
5. Lewis, C. S. *The Abolition of Man: How Education Develops Man's Sense of Morality.* New York: Macmillan, 1947, pp. 95–121.
6. Oldenquist, A. "'Indoctrination' and Societal Suicide." *Public Interest,* Spring 1981, *63,* p. 81.

Chapter Three

1. Gonzalez, D. "New Life, Far from the Bright Lights." *New York Times,* Jan. 25, 1998, Sect. 15, p. 28.
2. Grant, G. *The World We Created at Hamilton High.* Cambridge, Mass.: Harvard University Press, 1988, p. 195.
3. Jarvis, F. W., from his headmaster's address to the student body at the opening of fall term, 1996.

Chapter Four

1. Lockerbie, D. B. "The Wisdom Behind the Craft: Teaching Who We Are." *Character,* 1997, 5(4), p. 1.
2. Sleeper, J. "Two Worlds Collide on the Levin Death." *Boston Globe,* June 11, 1997.
3. Patterson, K. *A Sense of Wonder: On Reading and Writing Books for Children.* New York: Plume, 1995, p. 69.
4. Sertillanges, A. D. *The Intellectual Life.* Westminster, Md.: Newman Press, 1948, p. 76.
5. Kilpatrick, W. *Books That Build Character.* New York: Touchstone Books, 1994, p. 23.
6. Rosenblatt, L. *The Reader, the Text, the Poem.* Carbondale: Southern Illinois University Press, 1978, p. 44.
7. Lopez, B. *Crow and Weasel.* New York: HarperCollins, 1990, p. 60.
8. Coerr, E. *Sadako and the Thousand Paper Cranes.* New York: Bantam, 1977.
9. Greer, P. "Respect: Making It Stick." *Character,* 1997, 6(1), pp. 1, 4.

Chapter Six

1. Coles, R. *The Moral Intelligence of Children: How to Raise a Moral Child.* New York: Plume, 1997, p. 5.
2. Public Agenda Foundation. "Getting By: What American Teenagers Really Think About Their Schools." Poll, released on Website, Feb. 11, 1998.
3. Starratt, R. "The Interior Life of a Teacher." *California Journal of Teacher Education,* Spring 1982, pp. 31–39.
4. Highet, G. *The Art of Teaching.* New York: Knopf, 1950, p. viii.
5. Ruland, K. "Life's Lessons Are Part of the Curriculum." *Boston Globe,* Jan. 31, 1998, p. F1.

Chapter Seven

1. Murphy, M. *Character Education in America's Blue Ribbon Schools: Best Practices for Meeting the Challenge.* Lancaster, Pa.: Techtonic, 1998.

2. Isaacs, D. *Character Building: A Guide for Parents and Teachers.* Dublin, Ireland: Four Courts Press, 1976.
3. Delattre, E. J. "Teaching Integrity: The Boundaries of Moral Education." *Education Week,* Sept. 5, 1990.
4. Shaw, G. B. *Bernard Shaw: Collected Plays with their Prefaces.* Vol. II. New York: Dodd, Mead, 1971.
5. Sommers, C. H. "Are We Living in a Moral Stone Age?" *Imprimis,* 1998, *27*(3), p. 3.
6. Greer, P. "Respect: Making It Stick." *Character,* 1997, *6*(1), p. 1.
7. Moline, J. N. "Classical Ideas About Moral Education." *Character,* 1981, *2*(8), p. 8.

Index